Philosophy of Meaning

Volume II

Translated from French by DeepL, reviewed by the author

Cover image:
Walker Evans (American, 1903-1975)
Highway Corner, Reedsville, West Virginia, 1935
Gelatin silver print
25.4 x 20.6 cm
Getty Museum Collection
Digital image courtesy of Getty's Open Content Program
Public Domain

Philosophy of Meaning

Volume II

To live without philosophizing is properly to have one's eyes closed and never attempt to open them.

René Descartes, *Principles of Philosophy*, letter-preface, 1644

Life without music is simply a mistake, a tiresome task, an exile.

Friedrich Nietzsche, *Letter to Peter Gast*, 15 January

BOOK II

THE MUSIC OF BEING

Introduction

In Book I, devoted to knowledge, we sought to grasp and define what it means to think. To address this question, we took as our starting point the most elementary and immediate conception of the world: that of monism. The fundamental idea of monisms (materialist, idealist, psychologist, etc.) was that our interactions with the world could be expressed in a monolithic and unified way within a coherent overall system. Monism assumed that formal systems, by virtue of their internal logic, were self-sufficient and needed no external confirmation. Paradoxically, despite the fundamental idea of the agnosticism of monistic systems with regard to the idea of truth, we have seen that all monistic systems of thought actually presupposed a normativity that could not be entirely reduced to the system itself. Both materialists and formalists, even if they assumed that matter (or mathematical formalism) could constitute a sufficient matrix of explanation for the world, were in reality always more or less led to assume or accept the idea of an internal coherence of the system, an idea which already referred to the criterion of normativity and which therefore referred back to the question of truth. The reason why monists were so reluctant to accept the idea of truth, however, was that this very idea denied the possibility of a monistic system: to claim to validate or invalidate a system was in reality to place oneself in the position of an observer, i.e. to place oneself outside the system.

The proof of the incompleteness of formal systems having been established as early as the 1930s, one might have expected the epistemological consequences of such a proof to eventually permeate scientific circles. However, the aspiration to unify science and knowledge was so strong in the first half of the twentieth century that the fundamental difficulties highlighted by the incompleteness theorems (which merely formalised within mathematics an idea that had already been discussed within philosophy, particularly critical philosophy) were circumvented or ignored. In contrast to the monistic conception of the world, however, we now have to accept the fundamentally dual structure of the world: mathematics and mathematicians, matter and rule, subject and object, signifier and signified, speaker and interlocutor, cause and effect, consciousness and time, consciousness and space, man and language, man and systems. This duality, as we have seen, is the fundamental condition of dynamism and the active root of all layered systemic constructions. The question of truth is thus intimately linked to the problem of duality, i.e. to the possibility we have of extracting ourselves from things in order to try to say them.

In my introduction to Book I, I said that music had been for me a key to the general problem of truth (it was, moreover, approximately the thousandth time I listened to the Eagles' *Hotel California* that the idea for this book came to me). In the light of developments in our critique of knowledge, this statement now seems even more paradoxical than it did in our opening remarks. Indeed, how can music, which is the non-figurative art par excellence, and undoubtedly the one least directly linked to the problem of signification, and therefore of truth, constitute a key to the question of truth? In music, the question of the structure of truth, envisaged in a dual form, does not manifest itself explicitly. As a result, it is legitimately difficult to identify, at first glance, what it is about music that might open up the problem of correspondence — that of truth as an 'agreement' between a discourse and its object. And with good reason: unlike propositional language, music does not relate to any pre-existing external object. It corresponds to nothing, it imitates nothing. And yet, in music as in language or mathematics, there is an external reference criterion, which is not directly the true, but what we call "the beautiful" (an idea that we will attempt to define in this book). Adopting a method similar to that of the first book, we will first try to understand what music could mean from a materialist and monist point of view, and then attempt to progress in our thinking on the basis of the contradictions we will have identified following our analysis of these theories.

MUSIC FROM A MATERIALIST POINT OF VIEW

WHAT IS AESTHETICS FROM THE MONIST POINT OF VIEW?

1.

In the materialist perspective — and according to its epistemological extensions which lead it towards reductionism and psychologism — music and art in general cannot be apprehended other than within a system with a single level of meaning. The listener, the spectator or the reader are no longer seen as autonomous subjects capable of appreciating and evaluating the work itself. As mere links in a system determined by material laws, they are deprived of their ability to judge and feel. The faculty of aesthetic perception is thus subsumed under a higher unifying principle: matter itself. It is no longer the individual or subjectivity that decides, but the underlying physical organisation: the atom, the protein, the neuron, and more broadly the entire neuronal system. From then on, the human subject becomes the plaything of material processes that determine his reactions even before he is aware of them, as if matter, operating "behind his back", imposed its choices and aesthetic experience on him, thus reducing all artistic creation and reception to impersonal, blind mechanisms. All materialist musical theory is thus based on strong deterministic presuppositions, which reduce man (his emotions, feelings and judgements) to a natural (and material) chain of command. Music and art in general are thus seen as highly elaborate systems of expectations and rewards, systems in which man, like the docile, well-trained dog waiting for his sugar, anxiously hopes for the happy resolution of the tension in which the work (poetic, literary, figurative) or, in our case, the musical phrase, has placed him. This materialist theorisation of art and music in particular found a fairly complete formulation in a dialogue between the neuroscientist Jean-Pierre Changeux and the musicians Pierre Boulez and Philippe Manoury, a review of which appeared in 2014 under the title *Les neurones enchantés, Le cerveau et la musique*[1] (*The Enchanted Neurons, The Brain and Music*). At the start of the dialogue, Jean-Pierre Changeux points out that neuroscience research into reward systems has highlighted not only the phenomenon of the reward itself, but also that of the anticipation of the reward. According to Changeux, anticipation plays a fundamental role in cognitive and behavioural mechanisms, influencing motivation and learning processes well before the actual satisfaction of a need or desire. Changeux states: "Because of the existence of coherence between the parts and the whole in a work of art, the initiation of the composition by a fragment, for example a melodic fragment, such as the beginning of a sentence, creates an expectation that the composition or the meaning of the sentence will be completed. If this does not happen, he notes, or if it is not appropriate — it is said to be incongruous — a particular wave appears on the electroencephalogram (EEG): the N400 wave[2]." So, according to Changeux, there is indeed a "physiology of reward expectation, which the artist knows how to play on to 'manipulate'

---

[1] Op. cit., published by Odile Jacob, Paris
[2] Op. cit., pp. 14 ff. (French Edition)

the emotions of the listener". The theoretical framework is thus established: man, like a training horse, is manipulated by the artist, whose sole aim is to reward or surprise his (potential) audience. The work of art is therefore understood from the outset in its systemic dimension, the system in question, for Changeux, being a game of creation, of prolongation or resolution of a tension with which the artist would come to terms (note in passing that Jean-Pierre Changeux evokes, without really raising the point, the existence of a coherence between the parts and the whole in the work of art, an existence which precisely provokes the listener's expectation and which falls well within the criterion of legality, which we have seen cannot be reduced to the matter or the signal from which it derives). For Jean-Pierre Changeux, the musical work and its harmonic structure are in fact a reflection of the deep, innate dispositions of the brain. For example, Changeux explains, "consonant intervals produce neural activity, trains of electrical nerve impulses of more robust amplitudes than dissonant intervals[3]". Based on these practical and legal predispositions, the music-lover's brain attempts to identify the forms and rules of the work, in the same way as a well-trained machine might. This ability to detect rules (themes, repetition of forms, etc.) in a work is, Changeux asserts, the result of what is known as reinforcement learning. These reinforcement learning models were developed by computer scientists Richard S. Sutton and Andrew

---

[3] Ibid., p. 67

G. Barto[4], who have made a major contribution to work on automatic machine learning. Jean-Pierre Changeux, with the help of Stanislas Dehaene, had himself tried to build a formal organism (a computer programme) that would succeed in a task such as "sorting Wisconsin cards", where the subject selected a winning card according to a rule that he discovered while playing. According to Changeux, the mechanism proposed for this choice was that the possible actions were coded by spontaneous states of activity of groups of neurons that varied from one moment to the next; these are 'pre-representations' anticipating the actions to come. In *Les neurones enchantés*, Jean-Pierre Changeux precisely compares these reinforcement learning programmes (which proceed by inductive trial and error) to the dispositions of a music lover who discovers or listens again to a work. As in the machine learning programme, "the right choice leads to a positive reward, the stabilisation of the anticipation that produced it and the elimination of other[5]." In reality, according to Changeux, the "musical programme" is like one of those children's books whose heroes we are, where each proposition (each musical phrase) brings with it its share of possibilities (and impossibilities) that the artist resolves after a short while, thus satisfying the

---

[4] Richard S. Sutton is a pioneer in reinforcement learning. He is known for his seminal work in the field, including the TD (Temporal Difference) algorithm and his contributions to reinforcement learning theory. Sutton is also the principal author of the book *Reinforcement Learning: An Introduction*, co-authored with Andrew G. Barto, which is considered an essential reference in the field.

[5] Ibid., p. 141

curiosity of the listener who, having projected himself in different possible directions, feverishly awaits the end of the suspense in which the mischievous composer has placed him.

In his exchange with Changeux, Pierre Boulez, although sometimes adopting different positions from those of his interlocutor, lends credence in his own way to the idea that a musical work is based on the anticipation of the listener's expectations. He asserts, for example, that within a musical work, "expectation must be deceived". He adds: "when we expect something, we are reassured when it happens. Then the unexpected happens, and we are not disappointed, but surprised, because it forces us to go further". For Pierre Boulez, the composer must go beyond the listener's expectations, pushing them to "go further". However, even if he qualifies Jean-Pierre Changeux's statement (particularly with regard to the idea of systematically satisfying the listener's expectations), Pierre Boulez accepts his problematic: music is understood as a game of satisfying, postponing or disappointing an expectation created by the composer. However, as soon as the musical work is understood as an organised set of signals for which the brain would have fun decoding the rules of coherence[6] without object, in the manner of a trained machine, the composer remains, as it were, at *ground zero* of meaning. According to this (very restrictive) conception of art, every work "is thus a

---

[6] However, Jean-Pierre Changeux never formalised any concrete problem of the rule and the norm (in the sense of *what is the norm?* and how can we understand it).

matter of coding and needs a decoder[7]", the decoder being our own brain which, not rising to the level of meaning, is regarded as a machine trained to feel satisfaction, frustration or disappointment.

---

[7] Ibid., p. 71

IS MUSIC THE RESULT OF A DARWINIAN EVOLUTIONARY PROCESS?

2.

EVOLUTION IN MUSIC — If we accept the monistic hypothesis, then we have to consider the idea that music is the result of material and mechanical evolution. In other words, we need to look at music not in its meaningful dimension, but rather as a set of signals and *stimuli* that lead to preconditioned reactions in the listener. In *Les neurones enchantés*, Jean-Pierre Changeux places himself squarely within the perspective of this historical process of music: "music", he asserts, "is one of the most eminent forms of culture, or rather of cultures, which have been considerably transformed in just a few centuries, particularly in the West[8]." By emphasising this perspective (to which we shall return later from the point of view of the meaning of music), Jean-Pierre Changeux is seeking to establish a form of parallelism between the history of music and the history of the physical constitution of the human brain. This parallelism, which is only hinted at the beginning of the book, is dealt with quite directly in a later chapter entitled *Mental Darwinism and Musical Invention*, in which Jean-Pierre Changeux suggests that the process of musical creation could come under the heading of epigenetics, that is to say a process of natural selection which, although mechanical in nature, would escape the classic criteria of heredity (epigenetics is a selection process which takes into account the role of behaviour

---

[8] Ibid., p. 17

and the environment on the physical transformations of the brain). He states, for example, that "in the case of the evolution of species, changes take place at the level of the genome; in the case of the mental evolution we are interested in, they take place at the level of neurons and synaptic contacts in the same individual. In the first case, they are genetic; in the second, they have been described as epigenetic[9]. In short, explains Jean-Pierre Changeux, creativity is a selection mechanism that is similar to a selective process at the level of mental connections. Jean-Pierre Changeux also notes that during postnatal development, a Darwinian evolution takes place at the level of connections between nerve cells, with phases of exuberance where variability is at a maximum, followed by phases of selection, stabilisation and selective elimination of connections. This is what Changeux calls "mental Darwinism". Now, he suggests, it is precisely a Darwinian evolution of mental representations that could be taking place in the composer's head. In short, the composer, like the very young child, would be the playground for a vast process of neuronal selection that would take place, so to speak, without his knowledge, in his brain. According to Changeux, creativity is therefore a fundamentally historical process in two respects: on the one hand, it is dependent on the great history of culture in general and that of music in particular, and on the other, it is linked to the little history of the creator, to the cultural heritage of which he is the product and which takes concrete form in the epigenetic process that leads him to express his own creativity. In short, the creative process is part of a great

---

[9] Ibid., p. 127

historical movement of which the composer is only one of the many physical links. In this approach, it is of course the sensitive and material element of explanation that is favoured. This is why Jean-Pierre Changeux repeatedly stresses the physical and formal dimension of music (waves, frequencies, the numerical relationships between notes). In a sense, music is limited to its material expression and the interplay of chain reactions that it provokes. However, Jean-Pierre Changeux's approach — like all monistic discourses in general — lacks an essential link in the chain of thought, a link which, in our view, constitutes the blind spot in Changeux's philosophical thinking. If we accept that music is the result of a double selective process and that it is based, among other things, on a neuronal selection mechanism, then we need to ask ourselves, firstly, what the criteria are that guide this selectivity and, secondly, whether these criteria are the result of an arbitrary contingency or whether they are part of an underlying normativity. However, when these questions are put to neuroscientists or philosophers of consciousness (we are thinking, for example, of the American philosopher of the mind Daniel Dennett[10], who is quoted extensively by French neuroscientists), the answer given generally calls on environmental and social justifications that actually support the fundamental presupposition of Darwinism, which is that of the survival of the species.

For Daniel Dennett, morality, for example, is described as an extension of the survival instinct of the evolved group. For Dennett, the valorisation of so-called

---

[10] See, for example, Daniel Dennett, *Freedom Evolves*

'virtuous' behaviour is linked to the well-perceived interests of the group which, as a group, seeks a form of internal stability against external aggression (a moral conception that brings him closer to the classical utilitarian conception). The neo-Darwinists therefore believe that it is always the superstructure of 'nature' that acts through human beings and human groups, and not human beings themselves. However, we have shown that even this hypothesis implies an external norm, one that the environment imposes on beings trying to adapt to it. For a group to recognise its own interest, it must necessarily perceive a relationship of interest with something external to it. So, far from being strictly monistic, this concept is in fact based on a dual structure, involving interaction between an internal principle (the group, the individual) and an external normative framework (the environment). In the case of music, the Darwinist hypothesis appears even more fragile than in the case of morality. It is in fact difficult to identify an indisputable link between musical creation and the survival of the group, and even more difficult to conceive of an aesthetic theory based on purely functional criteria, stemming from a hidden logic of domination and conservation. Of course, we do not deny the historical links between music and tribalism. For a long time, music was part of a collective, even warlike, logic, marked by the use of percussion, repetitive rhythmic motifs and incantatory structures. However, this origin is not enough to exhaust the meaning of the music, nor to explain its subsequent developments and the diversity of its forms. Just as the subjective origin of knowledge cannot disqualify its most objective manifestations — notably in scientific formalism — the tribal roots of music do not allow us to grasp its essence or limit its scope to a simple adaptive function.

In a book entitled *La distinction*[11], published in 1979, Pierre Bourdieu attempted to reduce music to its social (not to say tribal) functions. At the beginning of the book, Bourdieu set out to destroy Kant's aesthetic philosophy. For Bourdieu, aesthetic judgement did not exist as such. In fact, it was immediately reduced to a codified social judgement. Kant's philosophy, Bourdieu explained, had the effect of separating people into two classes: those with the ability to judge (the bourgeois, or even the upper middle classes) and those without (the proletarians). For Bourdieu, the education of the more privileged classes provided them with all the codes they needed to decipher and understand works of art, the appreciation of which was supposedly reserved for an elite. In Bourdieu's view, the supposed ability of the elite to make aesthetic judgements was in fact the result of the heritage of 'socio-cultural content' that the school and university system valued, transmitted and reproduced. In *Reproduction in Education, Society and Culture* (1970), this idea of the transmission of socially determined content is theorised under the concept of "symbolic violence". Bourdieu's theory of groups (or classes) is in fact derived from Darwinist monist theory: individuals are not free to make their own choices (aesthetic or musical), they are merely the playthings of mechanisms that go beyond them, but whose normative criteria have yet to be defined (the problem of normativity was

---

[11] Pierre Bourdieu, *La distinction, critique sociale du jugement*, 1979 (*Distinction: A Social Critique of the Judgement of Taste*)

more generally the great unthought of philosophy in the 1960s and 1970s[12]). Bourdieu explained, for example, that the working classes preferred Strauss's *The Blue Danube* to Bach's *Well-Tempered Clavier*, which was the preserve of the bourgeoisie and those with higher education, It did not propose an interpretation grid that could explain the individual trajectories that shaped the group statistics (why would a working-class person prefer the *Well-Tempered Clavier* to the *Blue Danube*, for example) or, for that matter, the collective preferences for a particular work by the same artist (why, for example, would a working-class person prefer Strauss's *Blue Danube* to *Simplicius,* by the same author, or why would a middle-class person prefer the *Well-Tempered Clavier* to Bach's *Brandenburg Concertos*?). While Bourdieu's approach is certainly not to be dismissed out of hand (it is hard to dispute that music is a social phenomenon, and that as such it can give rise to the behaviour of classes or social groups, and that class behaviour can very well be the 'emergent properties' of constituted social groups), it failed to explain the phenomena of individual and collective preferences, in short, it did not deal with the problem of taste (the term taste being used here not in the 'bourgeois' sense of 'good taste', but in the sense of individual or collective preference).

In Murray Gell-Mann (an American physicist whom we mentioned earlier in Book I and who is best known for his work on the theory of quarks and for his

---

[12] See Geoffroy de Clisson, *Les Anti-humanistes ou l'avènement des Contre-Lumières*, L'Harmattan, 2021 [The Anti-Humanists or the Rise of the Counter-Enlightenment]

contributions and discoveries concerning the classification of elementary particles and their interactions, for which he was awarded the Nobel Prize in Physics in 1963), we find certain observations typical of monist theories, which, while not entirely devoid of truth (our remark is equally valid for Bourdieu), are nonetheless laughable given their reductive nature: "Likewise" writes Gell-Mann, for example, drawing a parallel between positive reviews and the success of a work or an artist, "the tastes (conscious or unconscious) of the human subject might change under the influence of prices or comments. The program, the computer, the human subject and the marketplace or critic would then constitute a complex adaptive system, with humans being in the loop. In fact, such a system may serve as a kind of crude caricature of how the creative process of real artists sometimes functions[13]." In short, for Gell-Mann, the definition of taste was the result of a complex systemic process with several inputs "with humans in the loop". As the role of humans was not really defined, we understand that, from Gell-Mann's perspective, man (the consumer) had only a fairly anecdotal role in defining his own aesthetic inclinations. But in Gell-Mann, as in Bourdieu, there is no trace of an aesthetic theory, or even the outline of an acceptable explanation of individual preferences. In short, everything that does not correspond to the calibre of the sieve (which was itself deduced from an 'intuitive' analysis that was undoubtedly rather sketchy) is entirely neglected. For Gell-Mann, individual tastes

---

[13] Murray Gell-Mann, *The Quark and the Jaguar*, Adventures in the Simple and the Complex, W.H. Freeman and Company, New York, 1994, 2002, p. 300

could at best be deduced linearly, as in an immense multiple-entry table which, if sufficiently precise, would provide the sociologist or scientist with almost infallible information on the preferences of given social groups or sub-groups. Not only would this multiple-entry table be able to explain our tastes, but it would also provide (the consequence is implacably logical) an approximation "of the way in which sometimes operates in the creative process of real artists". After all, can we really prove Pierre Bourdieu and Murray Gell-Mann wrong? Doesn't the summary description they give of the mechanisms by which taste and preferences are formed, as well as those that govern the process of artistic creation, ultimately correspond to what art has generally become: a huge segmented market that identifies needs and preferences as much as it creates them, a systemic and segmenting advertising machine?

It would be illusory to deny that art in general, and music in particular, occupy a central place in contemporary economic dynamics. Having become consumer products in their own right, they are fully integrated into what is now known as the music industry. In this context, musical works — whether in terms of their genre, themes or arrangements — are largely determined by the expectations of the target audience. In a curious twist of fate, the music industry applies with quasi-mechanical rigour a principle that Bourdieu highlighted: no longer the artist and his audience, but each audience and its artist. This logic reveals the extent to which cultural production revolves around the social structure of taste, sometimes more systematically than Bourdieu himself would have anticipated. Is this (admittedly somewhat depressing) approach enough to define what music is? Fortunately not. By limiting themselves to a purely structural, even superstructural, approach, monist analyses — whether rooted in Marxist historical materialism (as with Bourdieu) or in scientific materialism (as with Gell-Mann) — overlook a fundamental element: aesthetic experience. Yet to ignore the existence of this experience is also to obscure the question of its causes, which cannot be entirely reduced to a mechanistic or utilitarian explanation. As we have pointed out, placing aesthetic experience within a Darwinian logic of survival is problematic, to say the least, unless we radically redefine its framework. By reducing music to a simple product of social or biological determinisms, these approaches ignore the very thing that gives it its irreducibility and meaning. Such a reduction leaves open the question of the origin and scope of the musical experience, which cannot be fully understood without questioning the mechanisms underlying its perception and intelligibility.

The issue of the meaning and intelligibility of music is nevertheless addressed, albeit implicitly, by Jean-Pierre Changeux, when he highlights the genetic predisposetion of the brain to perceive and interpret sounds. He points out that from the twenty-fourth week of pregnancy, the foetus is capable of distinguishing sounds and melodies and reacting to rhythmic variations, while the newborn can detect a false note in a musical sequence. This reflection also extends to the selective processes of the brain, in particular the epigenetic mechanisms which, in the learning of music (as in the learning of language), strengthen certain synaptic connections while leaving others inactive, the latter remaining, so to speak, 'dead letters'. In our opinion, however, Changeux's reflections are lacking in two respects. Firstly, as we have already mentioned, Jean-Pierre Changeux approaches the problem of aesthetic judgement in terms of punishment and reward (which constitutes 'level 0' of signification: I react to *stimuli* according to the effect they have on my body, against the backdrop of the idea that I have to ensure my body's survival, and therefore obtain this much-needed sugar) instead of approaching the problem in terms of pleasure and displeasure (which would here be *level 1* of signification, the notion of pleasure and displeasure opening up to a wider problem of the consciousness of pleasure and therefore of these non-immediately physical criteria). Secondly, Jean-Pierre Changeux neglects, in our opinion, the normative criterion of the selectivity of neuronal pathways. It is certainly accepted that a signifying reality must correspond to a physical reality, but this does not answer an essential question: what is the objective cause of this physical reality? More precisely, in the case of music, what are the criteria that govern neuronal selectivity and the associated synaptic connections? Changeux would no doubt reply that these criteria are environmental and social: music lovers grow up in a given cultural context, are exposed from birth to melodies, learn to recognise and appreciate them and gradually integrate the scales and harmonies specific to their musical culture. In other words, his brain adapts to a pre-existing system of aesthetic values, shaped by his environment. However, such an answer would only displace the problem rather than solve it. Asserting that music is a cultural phenomenon does nothing to explain the criteria of cultural selection itself. What determines the valorisation and transmission of certain sound structures, while others disappear? This question remains unanswered as long as musical tastes and preferences are regarded as mere cultural constructs specific to each group, without their genesis or the principles that guide their selection being really elucidated. Here we come up against the recurring problem of monistic systems, where justification by self-reference leads to insoluble contradictions. In this case, the real question we could ask Changeux and the monist theorists of music is: where does the first melodic line come from and why has our brain identified it as such?

3.

MUSIC AND CHANCE — Returning to the epistemological foundations of Darwinism, we are confronted with the question of chance, or more precisely with the problem of the organisation of matter out of chaos. The big question that Darwinism and neo-Darwinism raise (a question that none of the materialist theories ever really answers directly) is: how and under what conditions can we move from inorganisation to organisation and from organisation to organism? In short, how can we evolve? We know that Darwinists confine themselves to material considerations, which are the methodological presuppositions of their doctrine: it is matter that organises itself by some pre-existing legal process, this organisation (which is, even in Darwinism, a form of miracle, a game with no players, described, The American philosopher Thomas Nagel, without adopting the materialist presuppositions of Darwinism[14], speaks of a "fertilised universe"), or else it is not contained within it and "emerges" as an *ex post* property.

In this materialist perspective, defended by Darwinists and neo-Darwinists (and in particular by Jean-Pierre Changeux in *Les neurones enchantés*), music is seen as the product of the evolution of matter. This matter, through a fortuitous chain of favourable events, manages to organise itself and finds in music a natural extension of this organisation, in the same way that language could be seen as an external manifestation of the structuring of being. If we remain within this evolutionary perspective, we can well describe the emergence of music by making it one of the forms of expression of the sentient organism, in other words, a form of language. In fact, we are not far from adhering to this point of view. Indeed, the idea of music as a fundamental expression of being (Darwinists would undoubtedly speak of sentient organisms, — we can agree on this point) seems to us to correspond to one of the primary dimensions of music, as we shall see

---

[14] Thomas Nagel is an American philosopher born in 1937, known for his work in philosophy of mind, epistemology and ethics. He is a critic of materialist reductionism, notably in his famous article *What is it Like to Be a Bat?* (1974), in which he argues that subjective consciousness cannot be explained solely by physical processes. An advocate of moral and epistemological realism, he challenged the strictly naturalistic approach to the world. His book *Mind and Cosmos: Why the Materialist Neo-Darwinian Conception of Nature Is Almost Certainly False* (2012) extends this critique by suggesting that the universe could contain teleological principles irreducible to mere chance and natural selection.

later. We also subscribe to the idea that music is a form of organisation, a *logos* that stems from our ability to formalise things, to express the world. This *logos*, this logic that determines us as sentient beings, is also what determines music as an expression of being (it is the principle of legislated and legislating reason that we set out in Book I). To ask what *logos*, language or logic are, is always to ask how we apprehend, perceive and express the world.

However, if we suggest, as the neo-Darwinists do, that music is a kind of organised language, we cannot, as they do, dispense with the definition of language and its meaning. By staying at the level of the material, the neo-Darwinists suggested or tried to establish that language is contingent, relative to a certain form of organisation of being in relation to the world. But is this organisation of being in relation to the world really 'relative'? And if so, to what? No matter how we (tirelessly) turn the question, we always arrive at the logical impasse of monism. Against this view, we emphasised in Book I that we are organised in relation to a reality that is external to us, and that we are trying to decode in a *non-contingent* way. If our decoding were contingent (relative, without rules, etc.), we could not have a common world, we could not have a consistent reality, or else (more likely) our decoding would be false and ineffective: it would not allow us to survive in the world that gave rise to us. We know that this is not the case: the organism is always constituted in relation to a reality to which it adapts (this is one of the manifestations of *radical* dualism — pragmatically deduced dualism). It is not "contingent"; on the contrary, it maintains a relation of effectivity with reality (it is this relation of effectivity which, in Darwinism, is the objective factor in the evolution of species). The term relativity is therefore not synonymous here with relativism (as it was with Einstein, albeit in a very different sense!). We organise ourselves (we become organisms) *in relation to* our pre-existing environment. This does not mean that our organisation is devoid of structure or left to chance. On the contrary, it is based on ordered principles, even if these cannot be reduced to a single or absolute framework. The idea of relativity here refers to the mode of *relationship*, not the mode of contingency or anomie. There is indeed a *rule* of adaptation, just as there is a *rule* within any formalism. It is the *nature* of this rule that needs to be qualified, and this is what is lacking in Darwinist epistemology.

If, to return to our reflections on music, we recognise that it is subject to a certain formalism — in the sense that it too obeys rules, notably those of harmony — it would be wrong, however, to conceive of this formalism as purely contingent. It is true that several types of harmony are conceivable, just as the same theoretical framework can give rise to different sets of axioms leading to distinct systems. For example, the tonal system, based on major and minor diatonic scales and a hierarchy of chords, which has structured Western music since the seventeenth century, cannot be considered an absolute system (from which, for example, we could deduce all other systems). Rather, it is part of a plurality of harmonic and rhythmic systems, none of which can claim intrinsic superiority over the others. The modal system, for example, which dates back to medieval and Renaissance music (a system we sometimes find in modern jazz or popular music), is based on interval patterns that are distinct from those of the tonal system (fewer tonal hierarchies, more static chords). The atonal system, popularised in the early twentieth century by artists such as Arnold Schoenberg (notably through dodecaphony), is characterised by the absence of a central tonic note in the melody, the use of series of twelve tones (in dodecaphony) and complex, dissonant chords. We can also mention the quartal and quintal systems (chords built solely on intervals of fourths and fifths), the system of functional harmony (in which each chord has a specific function, the movements being analysed in terms of the progression of harmonic functions), the microtonal system (in which the intervals are smaller than the traditional semitone: quarter-tone, eighth-tone...) and of course non-Western scale systems (Arabic music, for example, which uses maqâms, scales with micro-intervals; Indian music, which uses râgas, specific and codified melodic frameworks; or Balinese Gamelan music, which uses particular pentatonic scales — slendro and pelog). Yet the coexistence of these harmonies is not a sign of "relativism" (if we define relativism as a matter of points of view, i.e. a weapon for disqualifying the idea of truth, even "relative" truth). On the contrary, these harmonic systems do obey predefined rules (the harmonic rules), in the same way that mathematical systems are based on sets of axioms that give rise to other rules. It is precisely these rules that define the harmonic system in question. We could also argue that there could be an infinite number of systems with different rules. However, in all harmonic systems, there are harmonic axioms (it is precisely these axioms that define the harmony and construct the formal system).

The composition of a melody presupposes, first and foremost, the choice of a harmonic system and is not, for this reason alone, the result of complete chance (a harmonic system is chosen from an infinite number of possible harmonic systems, but this infinite number of harmonic systems is more constrained and less open than the infinite number of possible successions of notes that would be played outside a given harmonic system). Moreover, even within a given harmonic system, music obeys a certain number of tacit rules (rules for the composition of the musical phrase, rhythmic and thematic rules, etc.), which themselves depend on the composer's intention. It is always the composer who makes an intentional choice from a set of constrained possibilities — when he or she does not decide to break these constraints by introducing an accident into the melody, changing the rhythm, the structure or the scale. In other words, the development of musical discourse escapes chance in two ways: firstly, precisely insofar as it is constituted as a structured *logos* (which obeys rules that it creates for itself), and secondly insofar as it responds to a conscious intention on the part of the composer (the composer does not blindly type out combinations, like a scientist making hypotheses; he has a clear idea of what he is looking for). When Bellini composed *Norma*, for example, he did not make an arbitrary choice from an infinite number of possible melodies. Instead, he embarked on a narrative that implied a choice of harmony, tonality and style, while at the same time being guided by internal rules that became clearer as the narrative progressed. In this respect, the composer is free — in intentionally deciding on his harmonic and narrative choices — and constrained insofar as an internal logic (that of the work's narrative) imposes itself on him. In a sense, the composer seeks rather than composes. Keith Richards, famous guitarist with the Rolling Stones, said that he could repeat a melodic line for several hours before finding the "right" sequence, i.e. the right *riff*. The melodic line, the theme and the rhythm reveal themselves to the musician according to their own logic. The work is conceived as an encounter that is both the fruit of the productive imagination that suggests the forms, and of the artist's retroactively

(Ctrl + Click on the image for online version)

 critical awareness that catches them on the fly. The moment the artist encounters his melodic line (his theme, his rhythm), he *knows* he has found his *truth*. This discovery owes everything to chance and at the same time owes nothing to chance. This brings us back to the problem of intentionality

that we touched on many times in Book I, a problem that presupposes consideration of the idea of an ontological separation between man and his (cultural, artistic) products, which materialism rejects on principle. However, once we take note of this rejection, it becomes impossible to describe the problem of signification without falling into contradictions and inconsistencies (after all, what can a statement mean outside any signifying system?).

Is there such a thing as musical truth?

> What is true is what we believe; when we no longer believe in anything, nothing! What remains is sensation, but sensation analysed is diamond dust!
>
> Remy de Gourmont, *Sixtine, Roman de la vie cérébrale*, 1890

Legislation at work: Is music formalism?

4.

MUSIC AS THE STRUCTURE OF THE NUMERAL ESSENCE OF THE WORLD — We have seen that the problem of musical composition, if we attempt to develop it from a materialist and Darwinian perspective, comes up against two main obstacles: the problem of the rule on the one hand, i.e. the organisation of music in a normed system (which cannot be reduced to pure matter, consequently), and the problem of signification on the other, which we have linked to the theme of creativity. We now turn to the proposition that music develops with reference to a normed system, that is, that it is, according to the theory we developed in Book I, the product of a certain form of truth.

The musical work, conceived not as a random manifestation (as might be the sound of the wind, for example, playing notes through the crack of a window) but as a voluntary and meaningful act, always develops from an idea, the abstract (or concrete) representation of a melody. It presents signifying regularities that end up drawing a system of rules (harmonic and legal to begin with) and as such express a certain form of legality. But doesn't disharmonic or atonal music, which we mentioned in the previous chapter, run counter to this legalistic vision of music? First of all, music is said to be disharmonic when it does not respect the traditional rules of harmony. Disharmony can take the form of the use of unstable, dissonant or unresolved chords, chord progressions that do not follow classical harmonic relationships (with no clear functional logic) or a sound balance disturbed by sharp contrasts or discordant combinations of sounds. A disharmonic work may be tonal, but it plays on the extreme tension or lack of resolution of the chords (certain passages in Stravinsky's *Rite of Spring*, for example, are disharmonic but remain partly "tonal"). Music is atonal when it is not based on any specific tonality, i.e. there is no central tone towards which the notes and chords gravitate. Atonal music is marked by the absence of hierarchy between notes (no dominant or tonic), by a dissolution of functional harmonic cadences (no classical tension or resolution) or by an exploration of new structural logics, such as dodecaphonic series (Schoenberg, Webern, Berg). Atonal music may be highly organised and structurally coherent, but it avoids any reference to a traditional tonal system (Schoenberg's *Pierrot Lunaire* is an atonal work that does not follow any conventional tonal system). Can we really say, however, that atonal and disharmonic music escape all normative criteria?

On closer examination, Arnold Schoenberg's *Pierrot Lunaire* and Pierre Boulez's *Le Marteau sans Maître*, although not part of the conceptual framework of traditional harmonic music, are not purely arbitrary. Each of these works is based on its own structures of legality, whether it be the serial principle in Schoenberg's work or the rigorously organised formal

CHICAGO SYMPHONY ORCHESTRA

presents

(Ctrl + Click on the image for online version)

models and permutations in Boulez's. In this way, their musical coherence is no longer based on the concept of the harmonic. In this way, their musical coherence no longer resides in classical functional harmony, but in the internal systems of relationships and constraints that give these works their logic and intelligibility. In *Pierrot Lunaire*, Schoenberg does not rely on any dominant tonality but organises his musical discourse through recurring motifs and melodic cells, developed and transformed throughout the work. Although these motifs are not linked to any tonal system, they nevertheless establish an internal coherence, guaranteeing the unity of the musical discourse. Similarly, Boulez's *Le Marteau sans Maître* is based on an integral serialism, in which each sound parameter — pitches, durations, dynamics, timbres — is subject to a rigorous organisation based on predetermined series. Here again, the absence of classical harmonic markers is not equivalent to an absence of structure (on the contrary, the structure remains present and establishes a form of immanent legality). These works illustrate the idea that even outside the tonal framework, music retains its principles of internal organisation, which ensure its intelligibility and coherence. With *Le Marteau sans Maître*, Pierre Boulez, while also claiming intertextuality with René Char's poems (of the same title), places himself squarely within the problematic of meaning and correspondence (the apparent anarchy of the subject does not imply the anarchy of its expressive support).

But what about anarchic or random works? Do they have an internal coherence, a meaningful intentionality? In John Cage's *4'33,* the performer does not play a note for four minutes and thirty-three seconds, leaving silence and ambient noise to fill the sound space. John Cage, influenced by Zen Buddhist culture, encourages the audience to practise attentive listening, becoming aware of each sound, regardless of its source or nature. Cage pioneered the use of indeterminacy and chance in music. *4'33* is one of the most representative examples of this approach, each performance of the work being, by definition, unique (since the ambient sounds are, of course, never the same). With *4'33*, Cage challenges the boundaries of what we call "music" and encourages the audience to consider all sounds, even the most ordinary, as potentially musical. In short, Cage is here at the limit of the criterion of musical intentionality. The ambient hubbub certainly does not fall within this intentional criterion (like the wind that whistles as it rushes through a window opening), but it is nevertheless intended by the "composer" who designates it as "worthy of interest". The listener (who, in this case, is also an actor in the piece, undoubtedly participating in the hubbub with his own commentary on the work) chooses to accept or refuse the

(Ctrl + Click on the image for online version)

composer's proposal. If he accepts the proposal, it is because he too finds it worthy of *interest*. He thus chooses to give it a meaning, a significance, entering at the same time into the dialectic of intentionality. In this acceptance, there is also assent to an implicit rule, that of the absence of musical rules, which is based (all the same) on a tacit contract between the composer and the listener. Now, as soon as the listener accepts this tacit contract, he agrees to enter a signifying and regulated world in which the absence of rules is in fact defined in relation to pre-existing rules (those, for example, which consist of having the orchestra play rather than the audience).

In our world of meaning, the absence of normativity is a fantasy, and randomness is always defined in relation to regularity. This relationship explains the difficulties inherent in the intentional production of a truly random series. In fact, so-called random numbers can only be generated from physical phenomena that are intrinsically unpredictable — although we would still have to specify what 'intrinsically random' means in a deterministic world. Processes such as Brownian motion, thermal noise, electrical circuit fluctuations or radioactive decay are often used to provide a source of randomness. In the absence of these physical phenomena, any attempt to create randomness results in pseudo-random sequences, which are merely mathematical simulations of the properties of randomness. So, the universe of meaning, which is also the universe of intentionality, is in essence inseparable from a form of organisation. In the case of Cage's work, if the content of the work is random (although regularities could undoubtedly be identified from one 'performance' to another), this is not the case with the work itself, which is clearly the product of an artistic or intellectual intention. In a sense, *4'33* is reminiscent of the empty picture frames we sometimes find in front of a tourist monument or a landscape. The interest of the work lies not so much in its content per se (the landscape or the hubbub are not the main object of our attention here) as in the artist's intention, which invites us to take a fresh look at an element that he has not directly shaped. In this sense, the artist is not just creating a work of art; he is inviting us to adopt a posture of active observation, making us attentive spectators of the world. In other words, the meaning of the work is layered, with the artist's intention taking precedence over the content of the work itself.

If we set aside atonal or disharmonic works, which we regard as borderline cases of musical theory (and which nonetheless fall within the criterion of legality, as we have attempted to demonstrate), we note that most musical works develop from a system of harmonic, tonal and rhythmic rules, and as such express a certain form of legality. Jean-Pierre Changeux, for example, rightly points out that "octave, fifth and fourth intervals are expressed in terms of simple numerical ratios, 2/1, 3/2 and 4/3[15]." He adds, however, that "if intervals are perceived as consonant or dissonant, it is always in relation to a given grammar and not in itself[16]", an idea with which we agree. Consonance and dissonance are not absolute (what is dissonant in a given harmonic system may turn out to be consonant in another system and vice versa), they are relative to a given harmonic system which precisely defines what is dissonant and what is not — although a difference would undoubtedly have to be established, if we accept the idea that our ability to detect false notes is 'innate', between what seems naturally dissonant to us, but which we are prepared to accept as such in a given harmonic system, and what seems dissonant within a system that has defined dissonance as such. On this subject, Jean-Pierre

---

[15] Pierre Boulez, Jean-Pierre Changeux, Philippe Manoury, *Les neurones enchantés, Le cerveau et la musique* (*Enchanted Neurons The Brain and Music*) p. 21

[16] Ibid., p. 21

Changeux himself notes the "performance of the baby who shows predispositions to recognise the right fifth or to prefer the major scale[17]", he also notes that "genetic predispositions can be found to recognise a 'false note' in a melody and to perceive the temporal — rhythmic — characteristics of music[18]".

So how can we reconcile what seems to be a genetic predisposition for one system over another (for a particular type of harmony) with the relative (not absolute) nature of systems? It seems to us that these predispositions, far from constituting a form of absoluteness, actually correspond to habits and criteria inherited from our sensitive constitution. In other words, it is undoubtedly easier for us humans to perceive sounds with vibratory frequencies between 20 Hz and 20,000 Hz than sounds outside this range (infrasound or ultrasound), just as we have innate preferences for the major scale (preferences which, moreover, change with age, the minor mode typically being that of nostalgia or melancholy). The way in which we perceive music is therefore undeniably linked to our sensitive predispositions and our habits of perception, just as our way of conceiving space and time is linked to the formal configuration of our sensibility and the experience of our senses. However, this sensitive predisposition, like our habits of perception, does not disqualify our relationship to sound and melody. Here again, relativity does not mean relativism. On the contrary, the criterion of relativity indicates that "the whole system holds together", i.e.

---

[17] Ibid., p. 70
[18] Ibid., p. 213

that it can be expressed, translated and modified by successive logical transformations (as geometries can between themselves). In fact, once we have accepted a harmony, once we have become accustomed to relationships that seem regular or logical, any deviation from these relationships will be perceived as "outside the rule" (this deviation from the rule may very well have its own meaning in the context of the work). What we perceive as a deviation from the rule can thus be explained objectively: dissonance is perceived as a break in the frequency of accepted relationships. If we are subjectively 'conditioned' or initially programmed to favour certain ratios (judged to be consonant) over others (judged to be dissonant), we are nonetheless capable of objectifying the logical reasons for the preferred harmonies (through numerical wave ratios). The problem of the dissonance of the seventh harmonic of the natural scale, for example (the diatonic scale, also called the Pythagorean scale, based on the frequency relationships of the natural harmonics, perceived by our sensitive system as slightly out of tune — too low — in relation to the minor seventh of the equal tempered chord), while it may at first seem to support a subjectivist approach to sound perception, in reality finds a rigorous explanation in the numerical relationships underlying acoustics[19].

---

[19] A harmonic is an additional sound component that accompanies a main sound wave, called the fundamental. When a sound is produced, such as that of a musical instrument or the human voice, it generally contains not only the main fundamental frequency, but also a series of higher

frequencies, which are integer multiples of the fundamental frequency.

Each harmonic has a frequency that is an integer multiple of the fundamental frequency. For example, if the fundamental frequency is 100 Hz, the harmonics will be 200 Hz (2nd harmonic), 300 Hz (3rd harmonic), 400 Hz (4th harmonic), etc.

Harmonics have an amplitude (intensity) that decreases as their order number increases. This means that higher harmonics are generally less audible than lower harmonics.

Harmonics are essential for determining the tonal quality of a sound, often referred to as timbre or tone colour. This is what makes it possible to distinguish the same note played on different instruments or sung by different voices. They help to enrich the sound by giving it its unique and identifiable characteristic. They play a crucial role in the recognition and differentiation of musical instruments and voices. When a guitar string, for example, is played, it vibrates not only at its fundamental frequency but also at several of its harmonics. It is these harmonics that give each stringed instrument its distinctive timbre.

The perceptible shift at the seventh harmonic in the series of natural harmonics is linked to the way in which the harmonic frequencies interact with our auditory perception and with the tuning standards used in music.

In equal tempered tuning* (the most common tuning system in Western music), the intervals between the notes of the scale are divided equally. This means that each semitone is adjusted to be equidistant on a logarithmic scale. However, natural harmonics do not exactly follow this equal distribution of intervals (they are integer multiples of the fundamental frequency of a sound).

The harmonic seventh is particularly problematic because its interval from the root (about a minor seventh) does not correspond exactly to the interval used in equal tempered tuning. In equal tempered tuning, a minor seventh is slightly wider than that produced by the harmonic seventh. This creates a perceptible dissonance when the harmonic seventh is played or heard in the context of a tempered scale. Our auditory perception is sensitive to small differences in frequency and interval, especially in the context of music where we are used to precise tuning. The dissonance caused by the harmonic seventh can be perceived as an auditory shift or discordance, because it does not correspond perfectly to the interval expected in the equal tempered tuning.

The lower harmonics (1 to 6) are generally well integrated into the harmonic and melodic structure of the music. They correspond relatively well to the intervals of equal-tempered tuning and do not cause perceptible dissonance. After the seventh harmonic, the higher harmonics (8 and above) are less perceptible to most people and are often weaker in amplitude. They therefore have less effect on harmonic perception than the lower harmonics.

*The natural scale, based on the tuning of intervals according to simple frequency ratios (such as 2:1 for the octave, 3:2 for the fifth, etc.), produces very pure sounds. However, these exact intervals lead to problems: musical "commas".

The sum of the natural fifths (for example, by superimposing successive pure fifths) does not return exactly to the octave, due to what is known as the "Pythagorean coma". This means that the harmonic cycles gradually go out of tune. The natural scale works well in a single key or a small number of closely related keys. If you change key, some notes become false to the ear, which limits modulation and harmonic freedom. The tempered scale (and more precisely equal temperament, the standard in modern music) divides the octave into 12 equal intervals in terms of frequency (each semitone corresponds to a constant frequency ratio of $2^{1/12}$).

Once again, the subjective origin of all perception is not a definitive argument in favour of relativism. Subjectivity, as we have already seen in the problem of knowledge, can in fact serve very well as the basis for the expression of an objective reality. The quotation (falsely) attributed to Leibniz to the effect that music is an "exercise in arithmetic", with the performer unaware that he is handling numbers[20] is a good illustration of this idea: music, the most subjective of the arts, is in fact built entirely on objective relationships. There are many parallels between objective (scientific) knowledge and music: like the scientist, the musician seeks parsimony: the melodic line is the synthetic ("elegant" as mathematicians would say) expression of a general idea[21]. Like the scientist, the musician achieves a form

---

All fifths, fourths, thirds, etc., are slightly adjusted (detuned from the simple ratios) to allow even distribution. This allows musicians to change key without some notes sounding out of tune. On keyboard instruments (such as the piano or organ), tempered tuning allows you to play in all keys without having to constantly retune the instrument.

[20] Quoted by Philippe Manoury, Ibid., p. 22

[21] The singer Prince is quoted as saying: "Creativity is more than just being different. Anybody can plan weird; that's easy. What's hard is to be as simple as Bach. Making the simple, awesomely simple, that's creativity." (Creativity isn't just about being different. Anyone can come up with something weird; that's easy. What's difficult is to be as simple as Bach. Doing the simple, the beautifully simple, that's creativity).

In a documentary released in 2021 entitled *Get Back*, we witness an interesting debate between Paul McCartney and George Harrison on the process of creating music. During the recording sessions for *Let it Be*, Paul McCartney criticised

of union between the subjectivity of perception and the objectivity of relationships; like the scientist, the musician claims the universality of his discourse (Jean-Pierre Changeux notes on this subject the "universality of *Homo sapiens* song, whatever the culture or language[22]"). While there are many parallels between the scientist, the researcher and the musician, we still need to understand and identify what differentiates scientific research from musical composition. While it is true that a musical work is an immanent manifestation of a form of legality, it cannot be reduced to this manifestation. When we listen to a brilliant piece of music, we are not likely to be ecstatic in the same way as when we follow the development of a matrix calculation or a beautiful integral. If melody is formalism, it is not reducible to that formalism. It is not just a matter of the legality from which it springs.

George Harrison for wanting to add musical motifs before having a clear melodic guideline. McCartney says that you must "always start with the idea". Naturally, we don't intend to settle the debate between these two geniuses here (after all, a clear melodic idea may well emerge from motifs that at first seem incoherent). It is simply interesting to note, for our purposes, this search for clarity and melodic simplicity (the search for the melodic "line" or "theme"). Cf. *The Beatles: Get Back*, 2021, Peter Jackson, a three-part series based on over 60 hours of previously unseen footage and 150 hours of audio shot and recorded during the Beatles' rehearsal and recording sessions between 2 and 31 January 1969.
[22] Ibid., p. 211

5.

> style is a good tool to tell what you have to say but when you no longer have anything to say, style is a limp cock before the wondrous cunt of the universe.
>
> Charles Bukowski, Letter to Douglas Blazek, 1965

IN SEARCH OF FORM — We have just emphasised the formal nature of musical works. This formal character is found in particular in the harmonic foundations of music (which can be modelled in numerical relationships), in rhythm and in the composition of a work as a whole (in the arrangement of phrases or parts between them). The form of the work, however, is not limited to the production of numerical relationships. We must not confuse here two different semantic meanings of the concept of form: on the one hand, form as the foundation of formalism (i.e. in short, as the *logos* of the relationships that govern formal systems); on the other, form as a motif of reality (a motif perceived in sensitive intuition and formalised by the productive imagination, which does not come under systemic formalism). To these two meanings of the term 'form' we could add a third, referring to the mode of expression as opposed to the *substance*. To put it schematically, we could say that "mechanical" form, insofar as it relates to the logical relationships that govern a given system, belongs to the field of analytical judgements (in the sense, for example, of affirming that a given judgement is formally correct), whereas form as "motive" relates to an intuitive and synthetic activity of the mind. If we have attempted to establish the fact that music is subject to a certain formalism (in the first sense, that of formal relationships), we must also point out that its relationship to truth does not stop at this first formalism. Music, in other words, is not just an arithmetical exercise, it is also and above all a search for form (motif). In this respect, it is striking to see the experiences described by artists, almost all of whom emphasise research rather than composition or creation (like Keith Richards, who could spend several hours finding the right *riff*). Musical composition is akin to problem-solving: the musician, like a scientist, *knows* he has found the right phrase, the right note or the right melodic line. The form is "self-evident". This, of course, brings us back to the remarks we made in Book I about the great scientific discoveries (see Book I, § 38 — *Eureka!*): the truth appears to the mind of the musician as it does to that of the scientist: suddenly, like an illumination. In many cases, great musical works are the result of a dream or a sudden epiphany rather than the fruit of long, painstaking reflection. Beethoven, for example, is said to have had the intuition for the *Ode to Joy* (the Ninth Symphony) while out walking; Paul McCartney revealed that he had heard the music for *Yesterday* in a dream; *Clair de Lune (Moonlight)* came to Claude Debussy almost entirely at once, inspired by the light of the Moon; the theme of *Purple Haze* was revealed to Jimi Hendrix during a dream in which he was walking under the sea; the acoustic sequence of *Stairway to Heaven* was inspired to Jimmy Page almost entirely during a single improvisation session (the examples could be multiplied ad infinitum). In the vast majority of cases, moreover, the artists were convinced from the outset that they had *found* a form of truth (without adequacy). In a documentary about the making of *Dark Side of the Moon*, Roger Waters was asked by a journalist if he had any regrets about the album's composition, and he replied (with his usual modesty): "I would have liked, like everyone else, to buy the album in a record shop, go home, put it on my turntable and discover, without ever having listened to it before, the *Dark Side of the Moon* album". His hunch was probably right: the album went on to sell almost fifty million copies and is still one of the five best-selling albums of all time. In our view, this conviction of having *found* something is linked to formal research (the search for the motif, the melodic line), an activity that is a manifestation of our abstract ability to represent forms through the imagination. As in the case of scientific 'discoveries', artistic 'discoveries' do not usually take place in contexts conducive to concentration or formal reflection. The encounter with form does not seem to be the result of an activity of reason, but rather of a combined activity of imagination and understanding, which gives the artist the impression that the form is revealed to him "from outside" ("*there is someone in my head, but it's not me*[23]..."). This

---

[23] Lyrics from the song Brain Damage, on Pink Floyd's album *Dark Side of the Moon*:
The lunatic is in my head
The lunatic is in my head
You raise the blade
You make the change
You rearrange me 'til I'm sane
You lock the door
And throw away the key
There's someone in my head, but it's not me

undoubtedly explains why some of the great musical works were also the result of altered states of conscious-ness (there's no need to recall the widespread use of psychotropic drugs, particularly LSD, in the 1960s and 1970s). In the search for (and discovery of) formal motifs, it is as if form preceded discovery. This idea of the pre-existence of form is widespread among sculptors. Michelangelo, for example, believed that sculpture pre-existed the block of marble and that his role was to liberate it by giving it form. Auguste Rodin also believed that the sculptor should reveal the inner truth of the material and not impose an external form. Brancusi, finally, believed that the ideal form was present in the raw material. His minimalist approach aimed to reveal this essential form. Most composers share this idea that melody *is in the air*, like a form contained in a block of marble that needs to be grasped and revealed. Michael Jackson is quoted as saying of the creative process, "*Don't write the music, let the music write itself*[24]." In this experience of composition, there is precisely the idea that music is not composed, but that it is revealed, that it imposes its own logic, a logic itself linked to a pre-existing form whose groove the musician digs. In a way, the musician is the relay of a melody that precedes him and that he has the task of expressing and transmitting, like Guillaume Apollinaire's TSF antenna[25]). The artist, the composer, thus places himself at the service of a form whose validity he cannot verify other than by the feeling of having 'found' it. In our view, this is indirectly

---

[24] "Don't write music, let the music write itself".
[25] "I think I'm picking up waves from another world," says the Earthman in distress!

one of the key ideas developed by Roland Barthes in *Le degré zéro de l'écriture* (*Writing Degree Zero*). For Roland Barthes, writing should not seek excellence of expression (formal excellence in the sense of respect for formalism), nor redundant 'brilliance' (the idea of a form that would in a sense sublimate the content through an emphatic mode of expression that Roland Barthes rightly describes as over-added and redundant). On the contrary, the style must come close to neutrality, placing itself entirely at the service of the artistic motif (here we leave Barthes' strict point). In short, there must be an identity between style and form (style is not added to the artistic form, it is not an ornament, it is subject to the form, an integral part of it). At the beginning of *Degré zéro de l'écriture*, Roland Barthes cites as an example the (famous) first sentences *of* Camus's *L'Etranger (The Stranger)*: "Today my mother died. Or maybe yesterday, I don't know. I got a telegram from the asylum: 'Mother dead. Funeral tomorrow. Kind regards.' It doesn't mean a thing. Maybe it was yesterday." Here, the completely neutral style contrasts with the tragic importance of the news. We could argue against Roland Barthes that, in this particular case, the style is at odds with what is being expressed. The disagreement, the shift in style, might seem to create precisely one 'stylistic effect'. In our opinion, however, this is not the case. Admittedly, the first two sentences are surprising and may seem shocking to a sensitive reader. However, a careful reading of the passage reveals the source of the hero's confusion. He does not know the precise moment of his mother's death: he has received a telegram from the asylum. We deduce from these few sentences that the telegram is undated (or that it does not specify the date of the hero's mother's death). The hero himself underlines the absurdity of the situation ("it doesn't mean a thing"). If the news of the death of the hero's mother is expressed without any particular emotion, it does not seem to us to be an exaggeration of the hero's coldness (or an effect of the author's complacency). In other words, the expression of the form is in keeping with the form (incidentally, we do not wish to enter into the traditional distinction between content and form here, as this distinction does not seem relevant to us insofar as it has created, in our opinion, an artificial separation between two elements that are merged in the concept of form that we are defending here: for us, artistic form is the formal motif, a motif that subsumes the traditional categories of form — as "style" — and content — as the object of the narrative). The hero is cold (he is the stranger, in other words, like a stranger, he watches his life unfold before him like a film), his language is factual: there is no disharmony or trickery in the expression of form.

In a sense, Francis Ponge's *Le parti pris des choses* (*The Voice of Things*) follows the same logic. For Francis Ponge, it's a question of getting as close as possible to things (the forms we give them) but also of studying what things provoke in us. Of course, Francis Ponge's literary and poetic aim with *Le parti pris des choses* is not to achieve a chimerical neutrality of expression. There is indeed a *bias* in Ponge's work. But this bias is not precisely that of the poet's *ego*, which, through excessive metaphors or an over-exaltation of things, would seek to pre-empt his work. Ponge rejects lyrical and sentimental poetry, adopting an almost phenomenological approach to everyday objects (the association between Francis Ponge and the philosophy of Maurice Merleau-Ponty has often been established). In this way, he seeks a truth that is not that of "style" or poetic emotion, but that of the accuracy of an expression that resonates with our deep and direct perception of things.

It is in this resonance between my experience of the thing and its formal expression (musical in a sense) that the *moment* of artistic form is found: the truth of the phrase, the melody, the poem, the character is reached when it "rings true". The work, freed of the *ego*, is then invested with the *ego* (the ego at the service of the thing and not at the service of itself). What matters, then, is not so much the neutrality of the writing as its strict descriptive correspondence with the perceived form (the formal real, the signified). So it is not so much a question of getting rid of the *ego* at all costs, as Roland Barthes wished, but on the contrary of achieving, through a kind of stripping away of the *ego*, a state of correspondence with the intrinsic truth of the (artistic) form, a state that allows the faithful expression of the form. We can thus conceive of deliberately emphatic forms of ex-pression, or comic and incongruous shifts (which might take the form, for example, of an apparent discrepancy between the mode of expression and the content) without the idea of the neutrality of the formal expression being altered (neutrality being associated with the idea of a muted *ego* rather than with the idea of a flatness of expression). It is only necessary, in this perspective, to abandon the false problematic of form and content in favour of that of formal research, a research that includes the *ideal* form as a motif and its expression as the 'form of the form' (formal expression of the *ideal* motif). In other words, in the artistic enterprise of stripping away the ego, form and substance come together at the same time and are inseparable from each other: form (the "style") is never "added on" to substance, it *is* sub-stance. There can of course be unfortunate misunderstandings. For example, the formal expression of an artistic motif may be missed by its performer (like the bad actor in *Writing Derge Zero*, who plays a "sad" scene with an ostensibly sad tone). In this case, however, it is the artist's intention that is betrayed. If, on the other hand, the content is mediocre, it will never be saved by the form[26]

---

[26] In this case, the artistic object "sounds wrong". Its formal expression (its mode of expression, the way in which the motif is expressed through literary style, for example, or through a musical stylistic effect) will also inevitably sound false. The falseness is not just in the discrepancy between what we think is a bit of an abuse of the term "content and form", it is already in the motif, the type. So, for example, a character in a novel whose author would like us to feel a little too strongly that he is 'false' will sound false in his falseness (just as a character who is described with all the attributes of sincerity will sound false for the same reasons). In music, a motif or rhythmic sequence that has been seen over and over again will sound false insofar as it expresses nothing more than a repetition, which no doubt reflects a form of narcissism (or laziness) on the part of the author or composer who wants to do things "in the manner of" and would actually like to be "in the place of...". The very idea of 'style' induces falsity. Style" as we understand it when we say, for example, "he has style" is, often, a borrowing, in the same way that a "false" or "sincere" character might appear to be taken from a catalogue of characters for writers. In art as

(the form — what we call 'style' — is in our opinion created by the content, it is an emergent property of it if you like...). Thus, formal research is never, and must never be, a search for "style", but always a search for form as a primitive motif, i.e. as an intuition of form (an intuition of "formal motif" and not of "style", which is also commonly called "form", albeit in a very different sense from that which we use when we speak of artistic "form").

Thus, Pierre Boulez is right to note that the activity of listening to music is linked to our ability to identify forms: "we identify a form, most often after repeated listening, but sometimes from the first time we listen[27]". However, it should be noted that our activity of perceiving shapes is linked to the artistic activity of producing shapes. We only perceive forms because the composer has been willing to produce, create or recognise them. This brings to mind Nietzsche's famous aphorism from *The Gay Science*[28]:

YOU HAVE TO LEARN TO LOVE. — This is what happens to us in music: first we have to learn to hear a theme or a motif in general, we have to perceive it, distinguish it, isolate it and limit it to a life of its own; then it takes effort and good will to put up with it, despite its strangeness, to exercise patience with regard to its appearance and expression, charity for its strangeness: — finally there comes the moment when we

---

elsewhere, it seems to us that we must always return, to paraphrase Gödel, "to the fountain of intuition", that is to say, question our relationship to lived experience (and not just to lived experience as it has already been expressed and synthesised by this or that person).

[27] Op. cit., p. 105
[28] Op. cit., § 334

have become accustomed to it, when we expect it, when we feel that we would miss it if it were missing; and now it continues to exert its constraint and its charm and does not cease until we have become its humble and delighted lovers, who want nothing better in the world than this motive and this motive again. —

Here, love (or musical emotion) is aroused by the identification and repetition of a motif that we have learned to perceive, isolate and circumscribe (it should be emphasised here that form is first conceived in the mode of delimitation). This motif or theme is precisely what we call "form", and this form is itself linked to an intention, that of the artist, who fades into the background — without disappearing — to *match* what he is expressing.

6.

MUSIC AS THE RENEWAL AND SURPASSING OF FORM — While musical composition is, in our opinion, undeniably linked to the activity of searching for forms, it would nevertheless be paradoxical to make it a purely deductive activity. The composer is not the exact equal of the mathematician: his activity does not consist in solving formal problems or developing theories from given axioms. Whereas the mathematician starts from sensitive intuition (as we tried to establish in Book I) to arrive at a coherent formal system that enables him, on the basis of a predefined logical *corpus*, to theorise reality (to apprehend it in a systemic and logical way), the composer is not immediately subject to a restrictive logical framework (he is free, for example, to change his "axioms" in the middle of a work, and is not accountable to either coherence or reality). On the other hand, his field of possibilities is not limited to observable reality: on the contrary, he has almost total freedom of formal creation. This is why artistic works, although subject to a certain formalism (an internal logic), are not subject, like scientific propositions, to the criteria of verification or refutation. You can't *prove* that a work is true or false. Unlike the mathematical proposition, the artistic proposition, and in particular the musical proposition, is in direct contact with form; it does not posit form as a hypothesis to be confirmed (as Einstein, for example, had to posit the intuitive hypothesis of the deformation of space-time in his theory of relativity); it is *already* form, a proposition without correspondence that it is up to us to judge as such (we will come back to this). Consequently, as a search for forms, the activity of musical creation is already a formal proposition that must go beyond the simple framework of existing forms (creation is not a repetition of the existing or a variation on the existing. The repetition of form, the variations on already known forms, is what we call academicism: a kind of prison of beauty). But how can form be constantly renewed? How, in short, can new expectations be created, disappointed or exceeded within the work? This is the onerous task of the composer, who must plunge, like the poet, "into the depths of the unknown to find something new[29]".

---

[29] Pour out your poison that it may refresh us!
This fire burns our brains so fiercely, we wish to plunge
To the abyss' depths, Heaven or Hell, does it matter?
To the depths of the Unknown to find something new!
Charles Baudelaire, *Les Fleurs du Mal, Le Voyage*

This brings us back to Kant's famous dictum that "genius is the talent (natural gift) that gives art its rules[30]". In music, and in art in general, the rules and standards are never definitively established. It is always the artists who, returning "to the fountain of intuition", create new rules as they create new works. We could certainly argue that certain theories imposed their restrictive framework on great works. In the seventeenth century, classicism, for example, which was characterised by a quest for balance, measure and harmony inherited from the works of Greek and Roman antiquity, was one of the most telling examples of normative rigidity in art. The guardians of the temple of classicism imposed on theatrical creation the famous rule of the three unities: unity of time (the action had to take place over a twenty-four hour day), unity of place (the action had to take place in a restricted geographical setting) and unity of action (a single main plot, with no complex subplots). The rules of classicism — theorised (later) by Nicolas Boileau in *The Art of Poetry* (1674) — also required verisimilitude, propriety (decency and morality) and clear, pure language. The genres (tragic, comic) had to be clearly separated, and the works had to be didactic. In short, classicism had all the characteristics of academicism. The rigidity of its framework and the absurd rigidity of its aims should have marked it with the seal of the most certain and definitive sterility. Yet it was during the classical period that France produced three of its greatest poets and playwrights: Molière, Racine and Corneille (who, to say the least, produced more than minor works). How can we explain the emergence of such geniuses within a

---

[30] Immanuel Kant, *Critique of the Faculty of Judgment*, § 46

theoretical framework that seemed so constrained and corseted?

It should first be pointed out that, although they probably served as a general framework for the so-called "classical" works of Molière, Racine and Corneille, the rules of classicism were frequently adapted or transgressed. Molière, for example, mixed the tragic and comic genres, as in Dom Juan, and only imperfectly respected the unity of time and place. What's more, by criticising the mores and institutions of his time, he departed from the traditional ideal of propriety. Similarly, in Racine, the complexity of the plots and the violence of the passions departed from the strict principles of classicism. And in Corneille, unity of action, verisimilitude and decorum were not systematically respected. Jean Chapelain, an influential member of the Académie française, was particularly critical of Le *Cid*. In his work *Sentiments de l'Académie sur la tragi-comédie du Cid* (1637), he criticised Corneille for numerous breaches of the rules of decorum and verisimilitude. The Académie française itself published a report criticising *Le Cid* for its lack of respect for unity of time, place and action, as well as for its treatment of honour and love, which was deemed implausible. Nicolas Boileau, although not a direct contemporary of the first performance of *Le Cid*, also later criticised Corneille for not respecting the classical rules. The interest of classical masterpieces thus undoubtedly lay as much in accepting the framework as in going beyond it, in other words in transgressing the rules it laid down. Musical classicism suffered a similar fate: the great "classical" composers (Haydn, Mozart, Beethoven) were also (like the playwrights) those who departed from the strict rules of classicism in the structure of their works, their rhythmic innovations and the liberation of musical motifs. Composition, in the theatre as in music, could not really be conceived within the rigid framework of a regulatory *corpus* that had to be scrupulously adhered to. It was always at the same time (in the case of *at least* the great works) about going beyond the framework and renewing the form. This formal renewal was certainly not anarchic or anomic. The artist is the one who invents the new rules (who finds the new forms). He does not submit to a *corpus of* old dogmas; his creative action is in this sense an action of surpassing.

It is interesting to note that, for Kant, artistic genius is above all a natural gift. By instituting new rules, genius raises itself to the level of nature itself: it is in a way its child, capable of producing, in its image, a new reality (*Born a poor young, country boy/Mother Nature's son/All day long, I'm sitting, singing songs for everyone...* sing the Beatles[31]). It is precisely because artists are part of a *natura naturans* that they are able to give art its own rules. In the context of artistic creation, the rule does not derive from a pre-existing intuition of reality; it is the fruit of the productive imagination, in other words a spontaneous generation of forms, proposed by the imagination and ordered by the understanding. Genius, and with it all artistic creation, invents forms and destroys them in a perpetual movement of formal surpassing. Artistic creation is thus a process of

---

[31] *Mother Nature's Son*, White Album, The Beatles, 1968: "Born poor and young, country boy, Mother Nature's Son, All day I sit, singing songs for everyone."

continuous renewal, giving rise to a new formalism — both the formalism of the "motif" and the formalism understood as the internal coherence of the work — with its own logic and its own rules.

In this respect, Ernst Cassirer is right to note that "in the particularity of the linguistic function, there again emerges the universal *symbolic* function that unfolds, as *immanent legality* (emphasis added), in art and in mythical and religious consciousness, in language and in knowledge[32]." Like *logos*, art is immanent legality in that it creates its own rules, its own constraints, its own coherence. Unlike common language, art — and music in particular — is not a prisoner of the forms it generates. The creation of music is both a formal proposition and a transcendence of form. In this sense, it is "convulsive", in the sense that André Breton meant it when he concluded *L'Amour fou (Mad Love)* with the words: "beauty will be convulsive or will not be". To create is above all to rebel against convention and conventionality. Creation cannot be a simple application of a formal rule, but an incessant surpassing, a movement of rupture and renewal. In our view, the convulsion takes place in the artist's inner back-and-forth between the intuition of the artistic motif — an aesthetic intuition, irreducible to analysis — and its formal expression. It is in this tension, between intuitive emergence and the structuring of form, that the very essence of creation lies. The convulsion of beauty lies precisely in this refusal of a pre-existing formalism: it is an over-coming in act of the norm. In

---

[32] Ernst Cassirer, *The Philosophy of Symbolic Forms*, Volume I, *Language*, Ch. II, *A Moment of Artistic Expression: Sensibility*

this sense, creation is a movement of emancipation, an attempt to escape the tyranny of normality, in the words of David Bowie. However, as we have emphasised, music and musical composition are not anomic. When the artist creates a rule — even a new one — he paradoxically finds himself subject to it. The rule becomes an open prison, a framework from which he tries to free himself while remaining indissolubly bound to it. This paradox of the rule is particularly explicit in musical interpretation. In interpreting a melody, the musician follows a score, which constitutes the mechanical structure, the skeleton of the work. However, their role is not limited to faithful performance: they must bring this structure to life. In this process, the performer's sensitivity, a mark of his incarnation and finitude, seeks to go beyond the strict mechanics of the work, to make the score meaningful without betraying its intention. The performer is therefore a creator in his own right, confronted with a rule that he did not institute, but with which he must come to terms. He can neither submit blindly to it nor turn away from it completely. Interpretation thus becomes a constantly renewed struggle between the musician, who seeks to breathe life into the work, and the score, which imposes a structuring framework on him while remaining a fixed form from which he must emancipate himself without denying it.

The composer is also, albeit in a different way, an interpreter, an executor of the rules he himself creates. He is both its creator and its first servant, immediately subject to this framework which he can, however, break or transcend at any moment — as shown, for example, by changes of rhythm or tonality. In this way, the work of art, and more particularly the work of music, becomes the site of a perpetual tension between the rule and its transcendence, the norm and its alteration, constantly oscillating between structure and freedom, constraint and transgression. In this way, it is specifically human, in the sense that it is a meeting point between sensibility and form, within which formalism becomes both a mode of expression and an object of ceaseless surpassing. It is indirectly in this sense that Nietzsche referred to the coexistence, within the work of art, of Apollonian and Dionysian forces[33]. The Apollonian is what we call "form" (the norm, the rule, the fixed shape of the finished work) while the Dionysian is what we call the anarchic imagination (the form at work, not yet organised or synthesised). In artistic creation, the imagination can be called "Dionysian" insofar as it is first and foremost a power of life, an anarchic creative activity not yet synthesised by the representation of a concrete (artistic) form that is the work, the result of an autonomous creative process[34]. This fusion, within the work, of formlessness (the anarchic power of the imagination) and form (the work, the definitively limited, fixed and meaningful form) is precisely what gives the impression to the listener or spectator that the work is a demonstration.

---

[33] See Friedrich Nietzsche, *The Birth of Tragedy*

[34] In *Poetics,* Aristotle insists on the autonomous nature of artistic creation. A work of art does not owe allegiance to historical events; it is the creation of universal truths governed by internal rules (which would be taken up and formalised in seventeenth-century France). The work of art, and tragedy in particular, also has its own purpose, which is independent of its function (cathartic in the case of tragedy).

It is a demonstration, not only as a presentation, an exhibition (the work shows, presents, demonstrates in the Latin sense of the term *demonstrare*), but also insofar as it unfolds according to its own autonomous logic, in which the listener takes a certain pleasure. Yet the aesthetic pleasure of the work does not derive specifically from its internal logic (as we suggested earlier, we do not derive the same pleasure from solving an equation as we do from listening to the *Goldberg Variations*, for example). The demonstration, then, is not so much in the formal unfolding of the work (a formal unfolding which, in certain respects, could be seen as a form of mechanics) as in the monstration, exhibition and development of the motif of the work, the motif that drives it and makes it great. In this respect, music is a double protest against nonsense: firstly, insofar as it is a demonstration of formal coherence (formalisable, mechanisable) and secondly, and above all, insofar as it is an exhibition of the motif (of the form) which the creator, through his sensitivity (through his sensitive incarnation) mediates and relays. The musical work thus stands at the crossroads of two worlds: the world of formal coherence on the one hand (that of peaceful *logos* and mathematics), and the world of sensibility on the other (that of embodiment, of the precarious life that must be protected and defended, and also that of the tragic). In this sense, it is the tip of the mantle of the causality of reality, the reflection of the structure of truth.

A TRUTH WITHOUT CORRESPONDENCE

> But it is precisely this that is only profoundly human; it makes no attempt to appear so, or at least to appear real. It remains a work of art.
>
> André Gide, *Les Faux-monnayeurs (The Counterfeiters)*, 1925

7.

ART IS MIMESIS WITHOUT AN OBJECT — Music, as a non-figurative yet signifying art, lies at the heart of the problem of art. Although music shows nothing more than itself (if it is not made up of signs pointing to a set of external meanings), it is nonetheless linked to the problem of truth. For the artist, for the composer and for the creator, there is such a thing as musical *truth*. We have seen that, in the context of scientific discourse, the certainty of having 'found' a truth has to be confronted retroactively with the experience of reality. The schemes of the scientist's imagination are only valid insofar as they correspond to a certain arrangement of facts. Nothing of the sort, however, in the case of musical creation. The musician and the artist (including, in reality, the figurative painter) have no factual basis for comparison with which to assert that they have 'found it', i.e. that they have acquired new, objective knowledge. Artistic forms do not correspond to reality. They can certainly reproduce parts of reality, but what is properly artistic in form is not *mimesis*, i.e. the imitation of reality. This idea of non-mimetic art, which has been at the heart of the problematic of art since Antiquity, finds an interesting formulation in Jean Arp. In *Jours effeuillés*[35] (1966), for example, Arp wrote: "My collages were made entirely of paper, and were neither drawn nor painted. They were not speculative; I was haunted by the idea of making something absolute. Cubism introduced trompe-l'œil into its paper collages, whereas I used paper to construct my plastic realities. It is clear from Jean Arp's description of his artistic activity that collages are not experienced in the mode of *mimesis*: they are not speculative; in other words, they do not postulate some correspondence. On the contrary, Jean Arp intended to present "plastic realities" that were not dependent on any form of imitation: "I was haunted," he wrote, "by the idea of something absolute". He added later: "These collages were static, symmetrical constructions, porticoes of pathetic vegetation". The series of works that Arp undertook marked the beginning of what he would later call "concrete art" — anonymous art that did not copy nature, but produced it, like "a plant that produces a fruit[36]". The artist, like nature, does not copy, but is nature in action (la *natura naturans*). This shift from *mimesis* to *poesis*, also advocated by the Dadaists, became the central idea in Arp's work and led him, in 1917, to adopt a new biomorphic style, which the artist described as "decisive forms". For example, he explains: "In Ascona, I used a brush and Indian ink to draw broken branches, roots, grasses and stones that the lake had washed ashore. Finally, I simplified these forms and united their essence in moving ovals, symbols of the

---

[35] Jean Arp, *Jours effeuillés, Poèmes, essais, souvenirs, 1920-1965*, 1966, Gallimard, p. 420 and pp. 430 ff. (French Edition)

[36] Jean Arp, *Art concret*, 1944, p. 183 (French Edition)

metamorphosis and becoming of bodies[37]. Jean Arp's approach was to find and present fundamental forms. This does not mean identifying more or less complex forms in order to determine their numerical properties. Just as the musician is not a mathematician, the sculptor is not a geometer. They do not produce geometric structures, but from the outset propose forms that are meaningful in themselves (we will come back to this notion of the meaning of forms). Where the geometer presents ideal (pre-signifying) patterns that structure his apprehension and understanding of reality, the sculptor presents concrete, finished forms that are already significant in themselves. In other words, artistic forms are units of meaning that resonate within our own sensibility (within our own network of meanings). This resonance is in fact based on some correspondence: the motif, imperfectly expressed and relayed by the work of art, constitutes a sensitive projection by the artist, the (re)production of an abstract vision nourished both by observation of the world and by a synthesis of the signifier. In a sense, the work *is* the artist: it emanates from his innermost being, from that non-formal part of himself — the part that is not easily recounted, to borrow an idea from Paul Ricœur, and to which the artist does not have immediate access, the work of art never being a simple autobiography. It is thus a *mimesis* without an object, or perhaps even a *mimesis* of the subject himself, a kind of photographic negative of his being. This resonance, which condenses and structures the artist's *self* in the work, in turn summons the spectator's or listener's self,

---

[37] Jean Arp, Wegweiser/Jalons, written in June 1950 in Ascona, in *Jours effeuillés*, 1966, p. 357 (French Edition)

establishing an echo between the intimate history of the recipient of the work and his or her own network of meanings. The aesthetic experience thus becomes the site of a silent encounter between two subjectivities in search of a shared meaning.

This idea of resonance, of the tuning of deep structures, undoubtedly sheds light on the notion of artistic discovery that André Breton developed in particular in *Nadja* (1928) and *L'Amour fou* (1937). For Breton, it was a chance, unforeseen and often marvellous discovery that most often played an essential role in the creative process. Far from being the simple fruit of a mastered intention, the creative act appears as a cross between chance and necessity, through which the artist, in search of forms and meanings, encounters what he was not yet looking for. This discovery, which resonates with his inner world, comes to him with disturbing clarity, as if the work were revealing itself to its creator (note that we are not far removed from the notion of serendipity that we discussed in Book I in the context of the philosophy of knowledge, see Book I, § 38 — *Eureka!*). While evoking Rimbaud's power of incantation (again, the reference to music and resonance, the word incantation coming from the Latin *incantare* meaning "to chant magic formulas"), André Breton wrote in a footnote to the 1963 reprint of *Nadja*[38]: "Nothing less, the word incantation must be taken literally. As far as I was concerned, the outside world was at all times in composition with his world, which, better still, formed a grid over it: on my daily route, on the edge of a city that was Nantes, dazzling correspond-

---

[38] André Breton, *Nadja* (French Edition)

ences were established with his, elsewhere. A corner of a villa, the edge of a garden, I could 'recognise' as if through his eye; creatures that seemed very much alive a second earlier suddenly slipped into his wake, and so on. André Breton entered into a kind of "resonance" with Rimbaud's work by seeing reality as he would see it through the poet's eye (art, said Zola, is "nature seen through a temperament"). This experience of Rimbaud's poetry also suggested a new series of correspondences (apart from the angle of the villas and their overhanging gardens, which Breton thought he "recognised"). In the passage immediately following this note, Breton meets a young girl who "without preamble" offers to recite *Le dormeur du val* (*The Sleeper in the Valley*) to him. The hero then recalls a Sunday he spent with a friend at the Saint-Ouen flea market (where he bought a curious object, a kind of white semi-cylinder, of no significance to him). His attention was drawn to a copy of the *Complete Works* by Rimbaud lost in a "thin display of rags, yellowed photographs from the last century, worthless books and an iron spoon[39]". Flipping through the book, Breton found two interleaved leaves, a type-written copy of a free-form poem and pencil notes of reflections on Nietzsche. The book was not for sale,

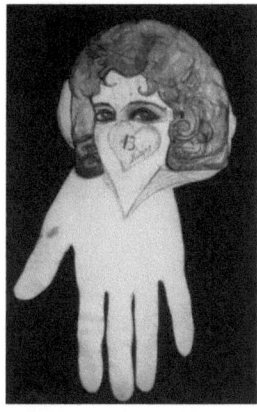

Self-portrait, Nadja, Henri Manuel, illustration by *Nadja*

---

[39] Ibid.

and it was then that a "young girl, very laughing" burst into André Breton's walk at. She started talking about Shelley, Nietzsche, Rimbaud, the Surrealists and *Le paysan de Paris* (*Paris Peasant*). This episode suddenly reminded the hero of another: "the suggestion made one day to a lady, in front of me, that she gives the 'Surrealist Centre' one of the astonishing sky-blue gloves she wore when she visited us at this 'Centre[40]." In the memory of this new episode, the woman agrees to take off her glove, which plunges the hero into an erotic-aesthetic panic: "I don't know what could have been for me at that moment, what could have been so frighteningly, wonderfully decisive in the thought of that glove leaving that hand forever[41]. The episode takes an even more intense turn when the woman plans to leave a bronze glove she owns where she had placed her blue glove: "a woman's glove too, with a bent wrist, fingers without thickness, a glove that I have never been able to stop lifting, always surprised by its weight". Shortly after this episode, Louis Aragon pointed out to André Breton that a hotel sign bearing the words "RED HOUSE" in red letters was made up of letters arranged in such a way that, at a certain angle to the road, "HOUSE" was erased and "POLICE" read "POLICE". This optical illusion, says Breton, would have been of no importance if the same day, one or two hours later, the lady with the glove had not led him past a changing painting in the house she had just rented. It was an old engraving," Breton wrote, "which, seen from the front, depicted a tiger, but which, if you took a few steps away, depicted an angel or a vase, depending on

---

[40] Ibid.
[41] Ibid.

whether you turned to the right or the left of the engraving. André Breton concludes: "Finally, I mention these two facts because for me, in these conditions, their connection was inevitable and because it seems to me particularly impossible to establish a rational correlation between one and the other[42]. André Breton's ramblings thus led him to establish correspondences not between a discourse and its object, as in the case of rational knowledge or the physical sciences, for example, but between objects or situations that have no *a priori* logical correlation between them. Breton's surrealism is based on the idea that reality has a wider meaning than that attributed to it by strict logical rationality, giving objects a significance that goes beyond their mere function or appearance. In short, André Breton makes objects 'supersignificant', so to speak. Everyday experience, which at first glance may seem banal and prosaic — a stroll through the streets of Nantes, the flea market in Saint-Ouen, a bronze glove, the illuminated sign in a hotel... — is transformed into a poetic experience by an over-investment of meaning. Reality only really becomes 'my reality' when it becomes part of my own network of resonances and poetic meanings, which are not based on logical links but exclusively on aesthetic and metaphorical associations. In artistic activity, it is the mind's capacity to establish links (schemas) that is at work. The reality of the experience of objects always surpasses the objects themselves (their prosaic nature, their use, their function). This network of correspondence, which is the work of the narrator's 'deep *self*', resonates with the reader only insofar as the latter is

---

[42] Ibid., p. 61

able to extricate himself from a purely utilitarian vision of reality. At the end of the passage we have quoted at length, André Breton makes an interesting point about this notion of the availability of the *self*: "the event," he writes, "from which everyone has the right to expect the revelation of the meaning of his own life, that event which perhaps I have not yet found, but on the path of which I am searching, *does not come at the price of work*[43]." The revelation of meaning, writes Breton, "does not come at the price of work" (André Breton's emphasis). It does not appear to the mind of the person whose brain is occupied with the task (either because it is anaesthetised by labour, or because its attention is monopolised by an analytical or mechanical task). It can only be done during a moment of rambling (we find this idea of rambling presiding over the discovery of great philosophical or scientific theories).

8.

COMPOSITION OR THE SEARCH FOR BEAUTY? — Until now, we have defended the idea that the artistic motif (theme, form) is communicated to the artist or composer in the form of a revelation, requiring a kind of semi-passivity of consciousness, the artist's mind having to make itself both available to the proposals that come to it (or that it suggests to itself) and ready to recognise and grasp these proposals within itself. This idea of a work 'revealed' to the artist, which is to be set against our non-formal conception of creation and understanding (we use the term formal here in the sense of analytical and logical formalism), raises the

---

[43] Ibid., p. 61, emphasis by André Breton.

question of the artist's role in creation. Is the composer of music, for example, an assembler (in the sense of the word compose, from the Latin *ponere* meaning 'to place' and *cum* meaning 'with') or a passive messenger of forms that reveal themselves to him or her?

If we accept the idea that the themes, motifs or primitive forms of the work are somehow 'revealed' to the artist (that they are the work of the imagination and of an operation of aesthetic synthesis of the mind rather than of a conscious analytical effort), we must at the same time recognise that the general structure of the work of art, and particularly of the musical work, is also the manifestation of an analytical effort of reason which retroactively and consciously criticises the first aesthetic intuitions of the imagination. In the creative process, the artist, like the scientist, removes himself[44] to consider his work in terms of its meaning and overall coherence (in the same way that the scientist tried to ensure the coherence and communicability of his theory by considering it as outside himself). For the artist, the retroactive consideration of the work concerns the value of the aesthetic forms (what is the intention of the form, what abstract meanings does it direct me towards?) as well as the arrangement of the forms between them (which is, in this respect, his work as a composer). This is why we believe that the work and the creative process in general should not be reduced to the mere revelation of 'pre-existing' forms. If, in fact, one of the artist's skills is to put his 'superficial self' in the background in order to facilitate

---

[44] What objections, for example, might my peers make to my theory?

the perception of the artistic form or motif, his activity is not reduced to the capture of such forms. The artist is certainly, like Rimbaud's seer, a kind of receptacle for forms (he becomes the spectator, as Rimbaud said, of the forms that are created within him), but he is also *the one* who organises these forms among themselves: it is he who gives them their overall coherence within a work. Thus, a work of art is always the combined product of passivity (the aesthetic moment of receiving the form) and the artist's conscious activity (the moment of organising the motif(s) into a meaningful construction). Moreover, the artist's state of passivity is already a form of activity. Like the scientist who is about to make a discovery (and whose consciousness is in a state of availability, as we showed in Book I), the artist is not passively open to any form that might present itself to him; he already knows that he is looking for *something*. The state of availability in which he finds himself is therefore always already conditioned (consciously or unconsciously) by this search. So, even if they are not necessarily in an active state when they encounter the form, artists are not open to all the possibilities: they are already unconsciously testing hypotheses. It's only when he has reached a favourable combination that the hypothesis tested appears to him to be 'the right one'. But this combination could not be achieved by pure analytical reasoning. It did not follow from a set of axioms or a determined chain of logic. The combination that the artist was looking for could not, however, be given to him analytically; it could not be deduced from a set of axioms or a set of determined hypotheses. This is precisely why the artist needed to withdraw from his research (to leave behind the analytical mode of his immediate consciousness).

In this quest for form lies one of the great tensions of the creative process. The artist never evolves in an aesthetic vacuum but always finds himself inscribed in a "state of the arts", in other words a set of pre-existing forms and works that influence, consciously or unconsciously, his work. Faced with this heritage, the artist oscillates between two opposing attitudes. The first is to embrace the history of art, to immerse himself in it to the point of making it a matrix for his work, at the risk of falling into the easy trap of repetition or pastiche (creation becomes a simple variation on already established forms). The second is to attempt to wipe the slate clean of all influence (assuming such an act was possible), in order to seek only the genius that resides deep within him, at the risk of becoming trapped in a kind of *ego* conformism (I am unique... like everyone else). Thus, the tension between heritage and innovation, between influence and rupture, is one of the fundamental dilemmas of artistic creation.

Innovation, however, is not enough to qualify art. If innovation does not resonate with either the artist's deepest *self* or that of the listener or spectator, it is condemned to remain a dead, arid structure, devoid of concrete meaning. In short, in musical composition there is always a search for adequacy and correspondence, even if this correspondence is without object (it is not a correspondence with a fact that we could verify experimentally, but rather it is a correspondence with the vision of form that the artist seeks to materialise in the work). Experimental research in music, if it is a necessary activity for going beyond conventional forms, must not, in our opinion, become locked into a kind of self-referential complacency (a complacency that can paradoxically lapse into a form of conformism). In other words, it seems to us that an art that is nothing more than a 'rupture' or destruction of form runs the risk of signifying nothing (just a series of experiments unconnected with any vision or form that the artist is trying to make meaningful[45]). In our opinion, this risk of conformism through excessive anti-conformism is present in all forms of artistic expression that focus above all on the purely 'formal' or 'stylistic' aspects of the work (as if the form of expression alone could constitute the object of art). This is undoubtedly the criticism that could be levelled, for example, at the famous doctrine of "art for art's sake" espoused by Leconte de Lisle and those who followed him as the Parnassians[46]. The decisive importance given to form, combined with a doctrine of separation — that we consider artificial — between "form and content" was to result, according to the Parnassians, in the erasure of the *ego* and all sentimentality in order, they said, to adopt a more universal and objective perspective (here we find the gesture of Francis Ponge, only this gesture is unfortunately disconnected, in the Parnassian theory, from any concrete reality[47]). In a way, the Parnassian approach to art is reminiscent of the Hilbertian

---

[45] Take, for example, Yoko Ono's interminable solos, the artistic content of which, I confess, escapes me.

[46] Doctrine according to which art, and poetry in particular, should aim for purely formal perfection (strict use of the rules of classical versification, including metre and rhyme).

[47] And with good reason, since the Parnassians often described a borrowed reality in their poems (themes inspired by a fantasised Antiquity, conventional poetic figures, etc.).

approach to mathematics: it is all about form and the extension of form. But isn't the Parnassian conception of 'pure' form illusory? Can we really detach form from its conditions of historical emergence in the same way that we detach a sign from its meaning?

If the sign itself is always a sign of something, then formalism (the formal expression of art, in other words, the rules of art) is also dependent on a 'state of the arts'. It seems to us illusory to claim that the history of art is progressing towards an increasingly perfect or ideal mode of expression. On the contrary, it seems to us that form is always dependent on what it represents, i.e. the reality it supports. In this respect, the classical alexandrine (with a caesura at the hemistiche), considered by the Parnassians to be the ideal form in poetry (for objective reasons[48] which we can certainly discuss) does not necessarily constitute the unsurpassable horizon of poetic expression. The poet, historically situated, is the heir to the history of art. He is free, however, to evolve the forms of expression (think, for example, of Baudelaire's irregular use of the alexandrine or Verlaine's use of the odd verse[49]). The

---

[48] Harmony, balance, symmetry, musicality...

[49] We are of course referring to Verlaine's famous poem, *Art Poétique:*

Music first and foremost!
In your verse, Choose those meters odd of syllable,
Supple in the air, vague, flexible,
Free of pounding beat, heavy or terse.

A few lines later, Verlaine makes a thinly veiled critical reference to the Parnassians:

idea of perfect form, in the sense of that sought by Parnassus, is therefore, for us, a chimera, a figment of the imagination. Artistic form (in the sense of the style of the work, its formal conditions of expression) is never pure or perfect. The perfection of expression, from the point of view of our problematic of signification, has no real object. Art, in fact, is not a search for the best possible form to express a reality in the most faithful or ideal way possible; it is always already directly intuitive of a signifying form and the organisation of this form within the work (the artistic narrative). To ask the question of the perfection of form, in the same way as to question exclusively the conditions of its surpassing in the work, amounts in a way to putting the cart before (or without) the horse: form alone is devoid of meaning.

Take vain Eloquence and wring its neck!
Best you keep your Rhyme sober and sound,
Lest it wander, reinless and unbound—
How far? Who can say? —if not in check!

Music or the Language of Being

— Have you noticed that the whole point of modern music is to make tolerable, even pleasant, certain chords that we initially thought were discordant?

— Precisely, I retorted, everything must finally give in and be reduced to harmony.

— To harmony! he repeated, shrugging his shoulders. All I see is an addiction to evil, to sin. Sensitivity is dulled; purity is dulled; reactions become less vivid; we tolerate, we accept...

— Yet you don't claim to restrict music to the expression of serenity? In that case, a single chord would suffice: a continuous perfect chord.

— A continuous perfect chord; yes, that's it: a continuous perfect chord... But our whole universe is plagued by discord, he added sadly.

I took my leave of him. He accompanied me to the door and, kissing me, whispered again:

— Oh, how we have to wait for the resolution of the agreement!

André Gide, *Les Faux-monnayeurs* (*The Counterfeiters*), 1925

9.

MUSIC AS A NETWORK OF MEANINGS — Music, as a non-representational art form, has a special status among the arts as a whole. While we have attempted to separate the problematic of art from that of *mimesis*, and have consequently put forward the idea (relatively classic in philosophy) that what is truly artistic in a work is not imitation (*mimesis*) but genuine creation (*poesis*), We should nevertheless note that music, unlike the other arts (with the possible exception of dance and, to a certain extent, architecture), is not an intermediated art (and cannot be intermediated). The note, the rhythm, designate nothing other than themselves. They are both the signifier and the signified. If, as we believe, music, like all the arts, rises to the level of signification, it is not insofar as musical notes or phrases refer to an external signification, but necessarily (if we accept to consider the problem of signification in the context of musical creation) insofar as they refer to an internal, intrinsic signification. In Book I, in particular, we constantly attempted to demonstrate, on the contrary, that the problem of signification must necessarily be seen through the prism of *radical* dualism and the 'signified-signifier' pair. How, then, are we to understand the idea that there can be an internal meaning to a melody (a melody that designates nothing outside itself)? Here we are at the heart of one of the most fundamental problems of dualism. If we reduce dualism to the problem of the duality between the signifier and the signified, we expose ourselves to a number of objections, not least the claim that the *radical* dualism between the signifier and the signified is not a dualism at all, precisely insofar as it can be formalised by a mathematical function of the type "$f(x) = y$", in which $f(x)$ is the signified (a function of reality x) and y is the signifier (the y designation of a reality x). In reality, the dualism of the "signifier-signified" pair is based on a more fundamental and non-formalisable dualism, the "animate-inanimate" dualism, which itself implies the "thinking matter-thought matter" dualism. This *radical* dualism, which is the subject of the first chapters of Book I, is in fact the dualism with which the musical work confronts us. When we speak of an internal signification of the work, our proposal is somewhat inappropriate. Admittedly, the meaning of the work can be said to be 'internal' insofar as it is not the sign of something other than itself (as a painting of an English landscape might be), but this does not mean that the meaning is autonomous or self-referential. On the contrary, it is a matter of intentionality (for the composer or artist) and interpretation of the thing itself. In this way, the meaning of a musical work is understood within a dualistic structure of intentionality and interpretation, which lies at the heart of the creation and reception of artistic works (the composer being not only the creator but also, as we have already mentioned, the first listener of his work, albeit in a different way, it goes without saying, from the listener, who is totally external to the work).

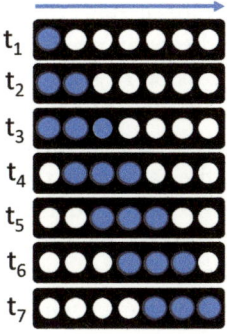

To illustrate our point, let's imagine a set of blue lights, arranged next to each other and lighting up successively, each in turn, so that we have the impression that three blue dots forming a line move from the left to the right of the figure, as illustrated in the diagram opposite. If we look at things from a strictly factual point of view, divorced from any problem of meaning, we actually see blue lights going on and off at set intervals. As a result, there is no blue line running across the figure from left to right (it should be noted, moreover, that we will find it very difficult to fix on one or more lights in order to consider them in their unitary flashing, since our consciousness unwittingly makes a signifying connection). From a "de-anthropologised" point of view, then, there is no through-line. But is this the right 'point of view'? If we do indeed have the impression of seeing a blue line crossing a figure, it is in all probability because the intention of the engineer who designed this system was to make us perceive this line, in the same way that when we look at our television screen we immediately see images and not a set of dots that light up, go out or change colour. We have therefore clearly identified two distinct levels here, the factual and material level, which is that of scientific discourse (there is no blue line, just luminous lights that go on and off at regular intervals) and the level of meaning (which is also that of interpretation, a level that we can only reach by accepting the intentionality of the engineer and the signifying projection made by the spectator when viewing the device). From the point of view of science, however, there would be a great danger in not considering "this level of meaning". If a scientist from another planet were to arrive on Earth with the task of studying this curious instrument that sends out a quantity of light signals per second, he would no doubt have the greatest difficulty in understanding the operation and purpose of the object if he himself did not rise to the level of meaning (to the level of what 'mean', for humans, the whole of these points, which would mean that the extraterrestrial scientist would have to understand the way in which their connection is operated by the spectator and intentionally regulated by the engineer[50]).

The same is partly true of music. While a single sound has no meaning in itself, a succession of sounds forms a melody, a musical phrase, in other words a structured and coherent unit that expresses a complete musical idea (just as a succession of pixels forms a global image that can only be apprehended in its meaningful dimension). The signifying link between the notes is made by both the composer and the listener, who

---

[50] If our extraterrestrial scientist were a good statistician, he would no doubt see that the juxtaposition of colours and intensities would end up drawing shapes and groups of shapes. Statistical analysis could thus give him the keys to formalism without first having to deal with the problem of meaning. However, it should be noted that (i) the efficiency ratio between energy expended and result would be very unfavourable if the scientist first rejected the problem of signification (the analytical and deductive method involves a much greater expenditure of energy than the intuitive method of formal recognition), (ii) as soon as the scientist identifies shapes using his analytical and statistical method, he will *de facto* reach the level of signification, the identification of shapes already being a first step towards signifiance.

immediately receives the composition as a signifying proposition[51]. In *Les neurones enchantés*, Jean-Pierre Changeux himself admits this signifying dimension of music: "in the perception of music," he writes, "and in musical delight, there is a content of meaning that does not exist in the simple production of sounds[52]". The term 'delight' used by Jean-Pierre Changeux still seems to us to be very closely linked to the lexical field of pleasure, i.e. the simple reaction to a positive *stimulus*. In the rest of the passage we quote, Jean-Pierre Changeux confirms this orientation: "re-flection on this organisation leads us, *of course*[53], to try to go further in understanding the central nervous mechanisms involved in the perception of music[54]." This return to the materiality of signification (to its material supports, i.e. also to the material effect produced on us by the melody), testifies to the misunderstanding of the problem of signification, a misunderstanding that results in a systematic attempt to reduce the problem to its material translation (which is only part of the problem, We should certainly not neglect this part, but it will not help us to understand the question of meaning in isolation, just as considering blue points of light in their rhythmic alternation will not help us to

---

[51] In *Les neurones enchantés*, Pierre Boulez exclaimed: "Absolutely! As if an E flat were an absolute E flat! Whereas it is relative in relation to everything that happens around it, to everything that enhances it", Op. cit., p. 126. Unfortunately, this does not prevent him from largely ignoring the problem of the meaning of the work

[52] Op. cit., p. 109

[53] Emphasis ours

[54] Ibid.

understand the question of the perception of a blue line). While Jean-Pierre Changeux admits that "our brain is not simply an ear, but [that] it reconstructs an organisation perceived in a chosen way, which it analyses[55]", he never really takes note of the epistemological implications of this ability to reconstruct and link elements together (although he does account for their complex material manifestations).

Music, being originally linked to the question of meaning, is the very negation of reductionism. This means that we cannot reduce music to the effect it produces on the spectator (according to a set of *stimuli* that would either fulfil or disappoint the listener's expectations) without going through the problematic of meaning, an intrinsically dual problematic (which calls upon the idea we have of the melody as well as its immediate perception). If the spectator is moved or happy, if he feels cheated or even if he feels angry, it is not because he will have the impression of being in the position of a fairground animal who is amused by being rewarded or disappointed, but because he will make free use of his (*ideal*) faculty of judging. By elevating himself to the level of meaning, man transcends the simple status of animality (the animal itself, moreover, transcends the strict mechanistic and materialist vision of the reductionists). In Volume III of *The Philosophy of Symbolic Forms* (1929), Ernst Cassirer, referring to the idea of "symbolic prevalence" in the perception of forms, writes: "Pure visibility can never be thought of outside a given form of 'vision' and independently of it; as a 'sensitive' experience it is always already the bearer

---

[55] Ibid., p. 115

of a meaning and in some way at the service of it[56]". In other words, for Cassirer, "visibility" (the fact that a sentient being can perceive *something*) is immediately linked to "vision", i.e. to the signifying projection of the sentient being onto things (this refers back to our developments on consciousness in Book I, see in particular the chapter entitled *What is a thing?*) We cannot understand sentient perception without immediately linking it to the question of meaning. For animals, as for the most elementary forms of life, the world is immediately perceived in the mode of differentiation, i.e. meaning. While this differentiation is not conscious in elementary forms of life, it becomes conscious in evolved animals, who conceive of themselves as differentiated entities to be defended. It is this conscious — or unconscious — differentiation of the organism in relation to what is external to it that gives rise to the problem of meaning, which is linked to the fundamental issues of survival and reproduction. The probability of survival of living organisms depends on the 'quality' of their decoding (their ability to give a global and orderly account of the world). As the organism becomes more complex, the decoding system in turn becomes more complex and more global. The sentient being then acquires greater and greater freedom in relation to the world around it (see Book I, § 19, *Degrees of Freedom*). While the relationship between sentient beings and things is already of a dual and significant nature, it is the human ability to rise to the level of the problem of signification that differentiates us from the most evolved animals (the great primates in particular). In his book *Objective Knowledge*, Karl

---

[56] Op. cit., Ch. 5, *Symbolic Pregnance*

Popper refers to man's ability to make use of the superior faculties of language (see Book I, § 20, *The idea as non-matter acting on matter*). These superior faculties include, in particular, the function of description and argumentation[57]. When man listens to a melody, therefore, he is not only in the position of the animal being rewarded or frustrated (this search for reward and flight from pain being directly linked to the animal's most fundamental instincts), he is also and above all in the position of exercising a critical judgement (i.e. a retroactive judgement, calling on his "higher faculties" as Popper defines them) on the work of art. It is this retroactive critical judgement (even if, in reality, it is almost concomitant with listening to the work) that provides, beyond the initial emotion of pleasure or displeasure, the emotion that is properly aesthetic. Aesthetic emotion is thus linked to a retroactive judgement that is made when the work is listened to (with a slight time lag in reality, as the critical judgement is consubstantial with listening or viewing[58]), this judgement amplifying, attenuating or

---

[57] Human languages, Popper explains, share with animal languages the two 'lower' functions of language, which include self-expression and the exchange of signals. Beyond these two functions, however, human language has many other functions, the two most important of which are, for Popper, the descriptive function and the argumentation function. The descriptive function of human language gives rise to the regulatory idea of *truth*, i.e. the idea that a description can correspond to the facts.

[58] We are talking here about critical judgement in the broad sense, not just aesthetic judgement. Like Cassirer, who

modifying the initial sensation of pleasure or displeasure[59].

If we affirm that aesthetic judgement is by nature retroactive, it is because we link it to the fundamental problem of signification. In the *Critique of Judgement*, Kant, clearly wishing to separate aesthetic pleasure from utilitarian feelings of pleasure, insisted on the disinterested nature of aesthetic judgement. In the same way, Kant asserted, that we must not be too hungry to judge the quality of a dish (a man who devours his dinner after fasting for three days is hardly in a position to appreciate its quality), we must judge a work not according to the immediate, self-interested pleasure it gives us (an immediacy that would bring into play considerations of personal interest and prevent our judgment from postulating universality), but according to its intrinsic beauty, appreciated for itself and not for its consequences or uses. So, according to Kant, aesthetic judgement must be *disinterested*. It seems to us, in contrast to this Kantian vision, that aesthetic pleasure, while it cannot be reduced to utilitarian pleasure (which could be, for example, that of the animal), is the sign of a commitment, of an adherence of being, in other words of a fundamental *interest* in the

---

asserted that visibility cannot be conceived outside the problem of signifying vision, we assert that perception is quasi-concomitant with judgement. Perception, for the sentient being, being originally linked to its survival, leads to a concrete response that does not necessarily take the form of a reflex (perception of movement leading, for example, to a reaction of flight).

[59] This immediacy is already part of the process of learning music, as we will see in the next chapter.

work (in the Latin sense of the word interest, which comes from *interesse*, *inter*: between, among, *esse*: to be). If we take aesthetic pleasure in a work of art, it is not, in our view, because we rise above our own self-interest, but rather because, by putting ourselves in tune with the work, we show a fundamental interest in it, a commitment to it that is a total and *ideal* engagement of our being. In our view, the potentially universal (or universalisable) character of the work does not rest so much on our muted interest in it, but rather on our ability to transcend our 'superficial' interests — that is, our immediate inclinations, our aesthetic prejudices, our attraction to certain facilities. In other words, aesthetic pleasure is intrinsically linked to an understanding of the work, not of what the work *wants to say* (or of the 'message' it transmits, as we sometimes rather naively hear people say) but of what it is, *in itself* and *for ourselves*. As we have said, understanding a work of art is in this sense a tuning of our sensibilities that summons our deepest *selves*, tracing a path of correspondence between man and artist, but also between men in general.

In fact, as we have said, although music is not directly part of the duality of the signifier-signified pair, it is nonetheless part of the overall field of signifiance. Notes, rhythms and breaks have no meaning of their own (they do not refer to an external correspondence), but they nonetheless form what we literally call 'musical phrases', which 'tell' a story within an overall structure in which motifs and themes appear, disappear and are repeated. This story can only be told if it is received as a meaningful story. Like the phrases of ordinary language, the musical phrase expresses something within a frame of reference (the scale, the harmony, the framework of the musical narrative) shared by the composer and the listener, a frame of reference that can occasionally be changed and exceeded within the work itself. This frame of reference can only be understood and integrated from an *external* point of view (that of the creator and the listener). As sentient beings, we are not prisoners of a framework; we are precisely the extra-framework. It is only on this condition that we can understand the music, resonate with it (the analogy between "resonate" and "reason" is interesting in this respect). The listener is thus in a kind of borderline position: at once summoned by the immediacy of the melody, by the sensations and feelings it provokes in him, and at the same time an external witness to these sensations: "the sensation analysed," wrote Remy de Gourmont, "diamond dust[60]"!

10.

HISTORICITY OF MUSIC — Melody, as the primitive and meaningful link between sounds that in isolation signify nothing, is for us the clue to the possibility of a transcendence: that of meaninglessness. By linking together particularities that in themselves are devoid of meaning (sound, vibration), it is in effect a proposition that tends towards the absolute and the universal. Mathematics, like all formal systems, needs foundations that are external to it. It is only on this condition that they can claim consistency and coherence. As we

---

[60] Remy de Gourmont, *Sixtine, roman de la vie cérébrale*, XI. *Poussière de diamant,* Nouvelle Librairie Parisienne, Albert Savine Editeur, Paris, 1890, p. 80 (French)

discussed at length in Book I, language and logical systems in general are always the expression or formalisation of *something*. The numeral is thus linked to a concrete or abstract unit, with "1", for example, referring to the external idea of unity (which is not contained as such in the sign "1", Arabic numerals, unlike Roman numerals, for example, which are completely free of any concrete meaning — while the Roman numeral 'II' evokes duality through the juxtaposition of two 'I's, this is not the case with the numeral '2'), '2' refers to the duality or addition of two units, and so on. Musical sound, on the other hand, is not the sound of *something*; it is a raw vibration that is given to the person who perceives it immediately and, so to speak, "without ulterior motive". Even more than mathematics, music, as a purely linking activity devoid of underpinnings, postulates a form of absolute truth insofar as it designates nothing external to itself (nothing that is not already contained within itself). It is pure architectural activity, the shaping of a *priori* insignificant matter. This signifying shaping, although it postulates a form of absolute (in the sense that it is relative to nothing outside itself) is, paradoxically, no less linked to our ability to *make things signify*, that is, to what most profoundly constitutes our sensitive subjectivity. On the one hand, then, music is a purely architectural activity (which is not compromised by the problem of adequacy); on the other, it is a purely subjective activity (it is the purest and most primitive manifestation of our ability to link things together, in other words, to make them meaningful). The musical work is, in other words, the meeting place between the purely subjective (creation, sensitivity) and the purely objective (legal, formal architecture). It is, in a way, objectified subjectivity, in other words, pure and immediate signification. If, however, we admit that music, as a non-mediated art (which possesses a meaning that does not operate in the mode of adequacy with an external reference), postulates a form of absolute, we nonetheless admit, paradoxically, that it is a historical form of ex-pression. Wouldn't it be paradoxical, however, to consider music as a historical absolute? Isn't the absolute precisely that which should escape historicity, that which, in other words, should apply at all times and in all places?

We must not misunderstand the meaning of the word "absolute". What are we saying when we use the word "absolute" to describe music? We certainly do not mean to assert that music is an eternal truth, a kind of Platonic idea, solitary and immortal. On the contrary, we have seen that music, as a pure architecture of forms that are insignificant in themselves (the vibrations we perceive as sounds), relies entirely on our ability to link sounds, rhythms and forms, and therefore on our ability to make meaningful what is not immediately meaningful (to insert meaning into the apparent meaninglessness of matter). The 'absolute' character of music is not to be understood within the traditional framework of philosophical absoluteness as that which exists in and of itself and which admits of no restrictions or limitations. On the contrary, we have seen that music is intimately linked to the subjective reception of signals intentionally produced by the artist. If we speak of the absoluteness of music, then, it is not in the sense of an apodictic, unsurpassable truth. The absolute character of music is not supported by its totally objective character, but on the contrary by its purely subjective definition (insofar as subjectivity does not suffer here from a compromise with a reality that it would be a question of expressing faithfully). If, for all that, we can account for what music is in an objective way (music is a science of relationships, it always plays with a rule that it creates or destroys), it becomes meaningful only through the subject who feels it within himself, without relating it to anything known outside himself.

This potential absoluteness of music can only be understood and attained by a movement of withdrawal of the *ego* in favour of what we have called the deep *self* (the self freed from its preoccupations, its immediate interests, from everything that makes up the everyday *self*). It is only by making our ego *available* that we can really enter into the problem of the meaning of music (what it is in itself, what it is for us). Thus, as a pure manifestation of the most fundamental subjectivity, music immediately places itself in the (historical) field of signification. The signifying world is in fact always already historical (it precedes us and determines us as human beings; we always inherit a history, if only that of language, for example).

Music, too, despite its absolute nature *for us*, has a history. First and foremost, it depends on the material forms in which sound is emitted. From the bone flutes of prehistoric man to modern synthesizers, musical sounds have followed the evolution of instrumental techniques[61]. Similarly, harmonies, from the first

---

[61] I recommend a very instructive visit to the Musical Instrument Museum in Phoenix, Arizona, which has a

musical manifestations (voice and percussion before 40,000 BC, appearance of the first instruments around 40,000 BC), to contemporary harmonies, have undergone a slow historical development: development of musical theories based on intervals and scales that are probably pentatonic or heptatonic in Egypt (3000 BC - 500 BC.) and in ancient Greece (Pythagorean scale), monodic music (Gregorian chant) in the Middle Ages, polyphony between the twelfth and the fourteenth centuries in Europe, extension of complex polyphony in the Renaissance (mass, motet, chanson), development of instrumental music and court dances in the seventeenth and eighteenth centuries (increasing use of major and minor modes), development of tonal harmony in the Baroque period, opera, the sonata, the concerto and the suite, the symphony during the Classical period (1750 - 1820) and new harmonic languages that we have already commented on in the twentieth and twenty first centuries (atonality, dodecaphony, minimalism, electronic music, etc.). Whether through its timbre (its material manifestations) or its harmonic forms, music is not, and never has been, a timeless absolute. It is always rooted in the means and forms of expression specific to a given period. However, this historical anchoring of musical works does not mean that their scope is strictly circumscribed to their time, nor that they cannot retain a value beyond the context in which they were created. We must be careful not to fall into the aporias of Marx's or Hippolyte Taine's theories on art. The fact that music depends on the material instruments of expression of

---

collection of over 7,000 musical instruments from 200 countries.

an era does not mean that it should be analysed through the single prism of historical materialism and class struggle (Marxism), nor that it is essential to reduce works, as Hippolyte Taine does, to historical social or racial determinants (the artist's character and national traits, cultural and ethnic origin, etc.). Music is not simply the reflection and illustration of an era, as clothing fashions would be, for example. If it can be said to be historical, it is not only as a material *product* of history (a material product that could be used to date an era, in the same way that the use of stone, bronze and iron are used, for example, to date the eras of the same name) but also and above all insofar as it is precisely a particular *expression* of the history of mankind, the scope of which goes beyond history itself. Thus, for example, Mozart's *Requiem*, while undoubtedly influenced by the material, social, psychological and historical conditions in which it was created, cannot, in our opinion, be reduced to these determining criteria. We could certainly point out, for example, that on the harmonic level, the *Requiem* relies on minor keys, which were quite widely used at the end of the eighteenth century to express intense, dark and dramatic emotions (in this respect, fashion has not changed that much). Passages alternating between major and minor keys were also relatively common at the time, as was the use of counterpoint techniques such as fugues and imitations (the *Kyrie*, for example, is a double fugue), showing the influence of the Baroque tradition, which was still very much alive at the end of the eighteenth century. We might also point out that the *Requiem* was written in 1791, two years after the French Revolution, at a time of political and social upheaval. It was also the end of Mozart's life, marked by great personal and financial difficulties[62]. Yet no historical, psychological, societal or social reading really captures what the *Requiem* is and why it remains one of the most performed works in the world today. In fact, if the *Requiem* retains its significant power for us, people of the twenty-first century, it is not as a historical relic or a contingent manifestation of a musical style belonging to a bygone era. The timeless ("absolute") character of the *Requiem* lies above all in its profound relationship to the human condition. *For us,* the *Requiem* is the work of human questioning in the face of death, the quest for redemption, the hope of transcendence. Listening to the *Requiem*, we come face to face with our own finitude, while at the same time experiencing a sense of belonging to a timeless community: that of mortals. Music, if it does not signify anything in itself, always refers us to a specific network of meanings. It establishes a form of "signifying universe[63]" that may remain linked to a specific era, but whose scope

---

[62] From the point of view of music history, the *Requiem* could be seen as the turning point and transition between the classical style and the nascent Romanticism. The dramatic use of choir, soloists and orchestra prefigures the great choral works of the nineteenth century.

[63] This universe does not necessarily have to correspond in every respect to the artist's intentions. As soon as the artist completes his work, it becomes an object, no longer entirely his own, but enters the shifting universe of meanings for others. How many times have we been captivated by a melody without understanding the words? How many times, in fact, have we been disappointed by the lyrics or by the intention of a piece of music that we have interpreted according to our own sensibility, different from that of the composer?

extends beyond the historical specificities of its expression. When we listen to Mozart's *Requiem*, we are immersed in the 'signifying universe' of pre-romantic Europe at the end of the eighteenth century, in the same way that when we listen to *Jumpy Jack Flash*[64], we can feel as if we were born in the middle of a crossfire hurricane ("*I was born, in a crossfire hurricane*" sings Mick Jagger) or as if we were a Londoner in the 1960s (even if we weren't born in 1960 and have never been to England). But if music, by virtue of its historicity, refers us to an era (as a synthetic expression of the era, but also as a symbol of a period that it helped to define), it also refers us to our personal history: it echoes periods in our lives, events, particular moments in our history. Music, as the art of duration par excellence (music is a kind of concrete materialisation of duration), is thus an art of time, of the history of mankind as well as of our own personal histories, whose meaningful architecture it disrupts.

11.

FREEDOM AND CREATION — In *Reason, Truth and History* (1981), Hilary Putnam described a thought experiment in which an ant, moving randomly across the sand, drew, purely by chance, a figure that ended up resembling the portrait of Winston Churchill. Putnam's question is: "Did the ant draw Churchill? To this question, Putnam replied that, despite the resemblance of the drawing to a portrait of Churchill, it was incorrect to assert that the ant had "drawn" Churchill. The ant has no intention of creating an image and has

---

[64] The Rolling Stones

no knowledge of Churchill. This thought experiment is Putnam's way of demonstrating that meaning is not simply a matter of correspondence or physical resemblance. Meaning requires intentionality — that is, the intention or awareness of creating something specific. If we now imagined a bird singing a melody that we thought was a masterpiece, could we say that the bird created the melody? Probably not, and for the same reasons. Most of the time, birds sing to mark out a territory, to attract a mate during the breeding season, to signal danger or to identify themselves within a community, not to create a work of artistic significance and scope. So, when, for example, Franz Liszt says that a melody in his symphonic poem *The Preludes* was inspired by the song of a bird he heard on a walk, the bird in question would seem to us to have little grounds for asking him for copyright. Creation, and particularly artistic creation, is from the outset linked to the problem of meaning. It is from this perspective alone that we can envisage artistic creation as a free act (an act which is undoubtedly the manifestation of its material conditions, but which is also an overcoming of these conditions), a new intentional and meaningful creation whose comprehension cannot be explained by its formalism alone, insofar as, precisely, it is not a matter of argumentation or critical sense[65].

---

[65] Music, art, does not refer directly to critical argumentation (it is not a question of applying an existing rule in order to understand the music, to "feel" it). The composer appeals to our free capacity to judge, not by applicative capacity (in the sense, for example, of judging an offence or a deviation from

12.

CREATION AND FORMALISM — In the *Critique of Judgement* (Analysis of Beauty), Immanuel Kant points out the displeasure we might feel if we were one day to be fooled by a man who, by an artificial process, imitated the song of a bird to perfection: Here, no doubt," he writes, "we confuse our sympathy for the joyful nature of a small animal that is dear to us with the beauty of its song, for imitated by man to perfection (as sometimes happens with the song of the nightingale), it seems to our ear quite insipid[66]." If we experience this feeling of disappointment and insipidity, it is precisely because, writes Kant, the freedom of the bird that sings its random notes (a freedom for which we have some sympathy, although it is not in itself an artistic act) seems greater to us than that of the person who slavishly imitates them[67]. If, on the other hand, Kant explains, we were to judge the artistic interest of a bird's song without considering the natural sympathy we feel for this little being, we would surely be disappointed. Interestingly, the beginning of the passage we're quoting deals with regularity in art: "any stiffness in regularity (which comes close to mathema-

---

an established rule) but by prospective capacity (in the sense of sensing the emergence of a form that is not entirely known to us and that we are nonetheless trying to make meaningful to ourselves).

[66] Op. cit., *Analytic of Beauty*, § 1-22, *General remark on the first section of the analytic*.

[67] "Even the song of birds, which we cannot reduce to any musical rule, seems to include more freedom and for this reason to contain more for taste than human song, which is directed according to all the rules of the musical art", Ibid.

tical regularity)," writes Kant, "is in itself contrary to good taste: it is that one does not promise to occupy oneself at length in its contemplation, but that it is boring, unless its aim is expressly knowledge or a specific practical end[68]." The interest we take in art (and music in particular) is not the result of the regularities it offers us. On the contrary, these regularities can become distressing to our ears (as the regularities of a bird's song would become if it were reproduced perfectly and "pseudo-randomly" by some technical process). On the contrary, Kant explains, the work of art must be the manifestation of a free occupation of the faculties of the mind, an occupation in which "the understanding is at the service of the imagination and not the imagination at the service of the imagination[69]".

In the field of artistic creation, artificial intelligence, as we know it today, is like the man who, by some subterfuge, imitates the song of the nightingale. Artificial intelligence is still pure formalism, a meaning-

---

[68] Ibid.

[69] "Regularity, which leads to the concept of an object, is undoubtedly the indispensable condition (*conditio sine qua non*) for grasping the object in a single representation and determining the diversity in its form. From the point of view of knowledge, this determination is an end; and in relation to this, it is always linked to satisfaction (which accompanies the realisation of a project, even a merely problematic one). It is then only a question of the approval given to a satisfactory solution of a problem, and not of a free occupation, without a determined end, of the faculties of the mind with what we call beauty and in which the understanding is at the service of the imagination and not the imagination at the service of the imagination", Ibid.

less synthesis of meaningful musical works. The machine, as a force for formalisation and synthesis, creates nothing (it is totally devoid of creative intent) but is content to aggregate meaningful content. It thus gives the illusion of creation, just as the man imitating the nightingale gave us the disappointing impression of being a nightingale. Creation is not, and cannot be, simply a synthesis of what already exists. It is meaningful insofar as it is linked to an authentic, sensitive experience of the world, an experience that is the source of all creation. Otherwise, it is doomed to be a repetition, a stammering, a bad copy of man[70]. Just as we cannot think of the activity of knowing and understanding the world outside the problem of incarnation (the world is known for me, in me, a sensitive and incarnate being), we can only think of artistic activity in its sensitive dimension, i.e. as immanent meaning (an immanent meaning that mathematics, for example, does not possess).

---

[70] These repetitions, stutterings and bad copies are unfortunately also the work of human artists...

Music as movement between levels of meaning

13.

MUSIC IS INHERENTLY MULTI-LAYERED — As a reflection and production of the human mind's activity of linking, music, although it is the manifestation of a rule and a formal system in its own right, is not reducible to any formalism or mathematical game. The musician is not, as Leibniz thought, a sort of unconscious mathematician. Rather, as the creator of his own rules, the composer is the one who stands above the systems (the equal, as it were, of la *natura naturans*). In *Les neurones enchantés*, Pierre Boulez states: "I'm very interested in creating hierarchies that are exploited for a certain time before falling into another hierarchy, and the first hierarchy is erased[71]. While the composer creates the rules that are then imposed on him, he is also free to undo them. He is not a prisoner of any normative rigidity (since he himself is the standard-setter). In this respect, the composer is human in the true sense of the word, as Pierre Boulez asserts a little further on in his conversation with Jean-Pierre Changeux: "from the point of view of sound," he says, "everything that is highly hierarchical is a product of man[72]." Artistic creation, and particularly musical creation, while being the creation of a framework, is also the possibility of breaking and destroying the framework. It rests in this way on a formal balance between continuity (the continuity of the rule necessary

---

[71] Op. cit., p. 23
[72] Ibid., p. 91

to the coherence of the work and which also makes it communicable) and rupture (rupture which is the sign of this freedom with regard to the rule which can sometimes border on madness or genius). The composer always has the capacity to change perspective in order to shed new light on his work, and this change of perspective can take the form of a regulatory accident or a radical change of rule within the work. Musical creation is thus the symbol of the free play of the imagination (not devoid of coherence and internal architecture). It is "non-referential", has no object, and therefore no correspondent (it is purely the activity of producing new forms). Imagination (the "madwoman of the house") has the ability to think the true and the false together and temporarily frees itself from the rules of coherence. In a way, it is Gödel's devil. It can activate all the detonators without detonating the bomb...

14.

MOVING BETWEEN LEVELS OF MEANING — Beauty is often to be found in the semi-voluntary acts of linking different musical phrases, in the in-between verses (what, in a song, we call with a particularly appropriate term: the "bridge"), in the passage from one level of meaning to another, in other words in all the intervals that do not yet belong to a defined form, but operate as a junction between two forms. Beauty is in the intervals.

15.

GOING BEYOND FORMS AND BEYOND LEVELS — In musical creation, imagination, the free capacity to create unconstrained (but standardised) forms, is a manifestation of the human spirit's ability to rise to higher levels of meaning (through imagination, through aesthetic intuition), in other words not to remain captive to a certain formalism, to a fossilised formal logic. This transcendence of formalism, an authentic "creator of forms", is made possible by what constitutes our sensitivity (what makes us human, what makes us not, and what makes it impossible for us to reduce ourselves to complex algorithms, however subtle). Musical creation, and artistic creation in general, are the manifestation of this capacity to step outside ourselves, to tear ourselves away from our immediate *ego*. They are a sign of our sensitive openness to the world. Paul Cézanne's relationship with the Montagne Sainte-Victoire, the subject of nearly eighty of his works, is an example of this sensitive openness to the world: "I feel good there, I can see clearly, there's air[73]", Cézanne is quoted as saying when he painted the mountain. The painter wanted to capture the mountain from every angle, at every hour and in every season, in every light, in all its colours, brilliance and vibrations. In his eyes, the mountain is a being endowed with life, with which he communicates (with which he echoes, with which he puts himself "in tune"). Each of its aspects corresponds to a different state of mind, a new sensitivity. As he explained to his friend Joachim

---

[73] Reported by Gustave Coquiot: Cézanne, Ollendorf, Paris, 1919.

Gasquet at: "The great classical countries, our Provence, Greece and Italy as I imagine them, are those where clarity is spiritualised, where a landscape is a floating smile of acute intelligence... Look at Sainte-Victoire. What impetus, what imperious thirst for sun, and what melancholy, in the evening, when all that heaviness falls away! Those blocks were made of fire.

Paul Cézanne (1839-1906), *Mont Sainte-Victoire*, 1888-1890, oil on canvas

There is still fire in them. During the day, the shadows seem to recoil with a shudder, to be afraid of them [...]; when the great clouds pass, the shadows that fall from them quiver on the rocks, as if burnt, drunk immediately by a mouth of fire[74]." The Montagne Sainte-

---

[74] Remarks reported by Joachim Gasquet in Cézanne, Bernheim-jeune, Paris, 1921.

Victoire, the emblem of Cézanne's native Provence, is approached by the painter through a confrontation that is both sensitive and intimate, where two solitudes meet: that of the artist himself and that which he attributes to the mountain, which becomes the mirror of his own interiority. In the representation of the mountain, it is Cézanne's spirit and his sensitive rooting in the world that takes shape and materialises (the imprint that the living mountain leaves on the artist's sensibility). Maurice Merleau-Ponty, in *L'Œil et l'esprit (The Eye and the Mind)*, emphasises this co-relationship between perception and embodiment, insisting that seeing is not simply a passive act of receiving images (as we already discussed in Book I), but an active engagement with the world. In this sense, the artist becomes the mediator of this living perception, translating into his work the dynamic exchange between his gaze and the presence of the world. They are not content to let the form freeze into a worn-out metaphor, like that of common language. On the contrary, he engages in a perpetual renewal of form, which can only happen if reality enters into a sensitive resonance with it at every moment. A human body," writes Merleau-Ponty, "is there when, between the seeing and the visible, between the touching and the touched, between one eye and the other, between the hand and the hand, a kind of recrossing takes place, when the spark of the sensing-sensible is ignited, when that fire begins that will not cease to burn, until some accident of the body undoes what no accident would have sufficed to do... Now, as soon as this strange system of exchanges is given, all the problems of painting are there. They illustrate the enigma of the body, and it justifies them. Since things and my body are made of the same fabric, it is necessary for my vision to take place in them in some way, or else for their manifest visibility to be doubled in it by a secret visibility: "nature is inside", said Cézanne[75]. Here, Merleau-Ponty insists on the coappearance between vision and incarnation, between touching and touched (between legislating and legislated, we might add, following the tracks we traced in Book I.). He sees painting as the place where two materialities come together sensitively: that of raw matter (the rock of the mountain, the painter's painting) and that of spiritualised matter (the painter's abstract representation made concrete on the canvas). It is this spiritualisation of matter (matter made meaningful) that, according to Merleau-Ponty, enables communication, the spiritual resonance of matter within us: "Quality, light, colour, depth, which are there before us, are there only because they awaken an echo in our body, because it welcomes them. This internal[76] *equivalent*, this carnal formula of their presence that things arouse in me, why shouldn't they in turn arouse a trace, still visible, where any other gaze will find the motifs that support its inspection of the world[77]?" Cézanne transformed our perception of the mountains by using colour, form and composition to reveal hidden aspects of reality. He showed how the mountain is not a simple accumulation of visual details, but a living, dynamic presence. He "thinks in painting", says Merleau-Ponty: "essence and existence, imaginary and

---

[75] Op. cit., in *L'Œil et l'Esprit (The Eye and the Mind)*, Ch. II (French Edition)
[76] Emphasis ours
[77] Ibid.

real, visible and invisible, painting blurs all our categories by deploying its dreamlike universe of carnal essences, effective resemblances and mute meanings[78]." For Merleau-Ponty, painting is thus understood in its signifying dimension (the "mute significations" that are signifying without, however, relating to a precise signification), this significance being made possible only by incarnation (by the co-belonging between matter and spirit). To paint his subject, the artist himself must understand what it means *to him*. This is undoubtedly why Cézanne remained for a long time "without being able, without knowing how to paint Sainte-Victoire". As he noted in 1905 in a letter to Emile Bernard, "time and reflection gradually modify the vision, and finally understanding comes to us". However, the vision is never definitive, which no doubt explains Paul Cézanne's determination to return to his subject again and again: the creation of the work is always a form of betrayal of the vision. "The poem is the realised love of desire that remains desire[79]": René Char's famous aphorism could just as easily be applied to painting. The work of art is a kind of love realised, but it does not exhaust aesthetic vision and artistic activity. It is only one of its frozen forms. This is why we can affirm, with André Breton, that beauty must be "convulsive". Beauty is convulsive, trembling, in the sense that it never settles definitively into a given form. Convulsion is the symptom of this relationship between form and sensibility. The renewal of form by sensibility causes reality to tremble, just as Cézanne causes Mont Sainte-Victoire to tremble (think of the

---

[78] Ibid.
[79] René Char, *Fureur et Mystère*, 1948

large cubic blocks that seem to make the mountain spring out of itself in some of his representations).

16.

THE CRISIS OF CREATION — Is there today a crisis in musical creation (or a crisis in creation in general)? Everyone is free to judge. If this crisis does exist (as we believe it does), it undoubtedly has something to do with the crisis of truth that characterises our era. In many respects, musical creation is a quest for truth, a quest that requires us to transcend the immediate interests of the *ego* (on this point, Kant was right to speak of disinterestedness, but in our opinion this disinterestedness is the condition for encountering a deeper and more "primitive" *interest* of being). The crisis of truth, like the crisis of creation, is the manifestation of this inability to step outside oneself, outside one's immediate concerns, outside one's egotistical quest for recognition, a quest that leads more often to repetition than to creation.

MUSIC AND TIME

17.

MUSIC AND DURATION — As Jean-Pierre Changeux points out in *Les neurones enchantés*, unlike the figurative arts, music is characterised by its stretching over time: "Another feature common to music and language," he says, "is the capacity to integrate duration. So, the overall meaning of a proposition generally only becomes apparent after it has unfolded completely over time. Working memory intervenes and allows the meaning to be telescoped into a meaningful form. Isn't the same true for the perception of melody and "chord", which is formed at the end of the process in our working memory[80] ? Jean-Pierre Changeux is right to point out that the resolute moment of agreement can only occur because a certain dramatic (or aesthetic) tension has been built up over time. By tuning in to the composer's intentions, we perceive this contrast as a significant moment. It is memory, Changeux asserts, that "allows signifieds to be telescoped into a form that makes sense". In our opinion, Jean-Pierre Changeux is right to emphasise the retrospective nature of meaning. It is the listener who gives meaning to the musical phrase, that meaning being in some way 'reconstructed' by memory (and by 'projective' consciousness) *after* the phrase has been listened to. This time lag between the perception of the phrase and its reconstruction by consciousness is a first indication of the intermediary nature of aesthetic feeling, which is not the result of immediate pleasure as might be the perception of a

---

[80] Op. cit., p. 43

pleasant sound (the wind in the leaves, the sea ebbing, birds singing[81]). On the contrary, the aesthetic feeling emerges from a retrospective and retroactive analysis of the melody. When we listen to a melody, we are not only in the immediacy of its unfolding, but always at the same time in a slight analytical shift. This shift may be prospective, marked by the expectation of a resolution, but it is above all retrospective: as we listen, we mentally replay the preceding moments, as if we were replaying the musical sequence in our minds (we are "replaying the tape"). The aesthetic feeling is retroactive in that the listener is not content with passive reception; he acts on the melody by reconstructing it internally, reinterpreting it and giving it meaning. (Two examples come to mind to illustrate this activity of the mind in the perception of the melody: first, the natural tendency of most music lovers to overplay the music in their heads, to make it 'over-significant' by accentuating this or that already-familiar passage). When they listen to the melody again, they often realise that they have exaggerated the dramatic intensity — they are "projecting". Secondly, the worried projective attitude that we sometimes adopt when we first listen to a melody. When we first listen to a melody, we involuntarily, consciously or unconsciously, make projections about the melody, projections that are only possible to the extent that we

---

[81] Although we could still contest the purely sensible and "non-intermediated" nature of these pleasant impressions, see on this subject the analyses in Book I on the questioning of the theory of sense data, in particular the chapter *What is a thing?*

have already retrospectively integrated the overall meaning of the melody.)

In our opinion, the birth of aesthetic feeling is always the result of a slight analytical gap between the perception and the understanding of music (the integration of the melody, the phrase or the work into a signifying system, even if this system has no concrete referent), so it does not seem entirely relevant to us to speak of "aesthetic affect" to qualify our emotional relationship to music, as the American musicologist Leonard B. Meyer does, for example, in *Emotion and Meaning in Music* (1956). Even if affect is undeniably part of aesthetic feeling or emotion, we feel that it is an abuse to reduce aesthetic feeling to affect (this qualification aims to reduce aesthetic feeling to its immediate emotional manifestation, i.e. to deny the subject his or her ability to make an aesthetic judgement, a judgement that conditions his or her listening and guides his or her affect). Musical creation is not a learned mechanism designed to produce in the listener a feeling that he or she would describe as "beautiful". Would we say, for example, that a poem "arouses emotions", as if it were a matter of the poet pulling the levers of "sadness", "nostalgia" or "sweet melancholy"? In other words, is it the emotion aroused by the poem that allows us to conclude that it is beautiful, or is it its beauty that arouses a feeling of aesthetic emotion, a beauty that can only be felt and understood through critical judgement?

Hermann von Helmholtz was one of the first, in *On the Sensations of Tone as a Physiological Basis for the Theory of Music* (1863), to attempt to establish a scientific basis for the relationship between the physiology of hearing and musical perception. He described in detail the anatomical structure of the ear, in particular that of the inner ear where sound vibrations are transformed into nerve signals. He introduced the theory of resonators — one of the foundations of modern acoustics[82] — according to which the fibres of the basilar membrane of the cochlea resonate at different frequencies, enabling tones to be dis-criminated. By exploring the notion of fundamental frequency and harmonics, he showed how complex sounds can be broken down into simple components. Helmholtz's work led him to explain consonance in terms of coincidence of harmonics (coincidences that create pleasant sensations) and dissonance in terms of interference of harmonics (which create un-pleasant sensations by producing beats or auditory conflicts). The musical perception of the timbre of a sound (its quality or colour) was similarly explained in terms of the presence and relative intensity of harmonics. Despite his fundamental intention of identifying the physiological causes of musical perception, Helmholtz never really

---

[82] Subsequent research confirmed that the basilar membrane is tonotopic, meaning that different sound frequencies cause maximum vibrations at different positions along the membrane. This observation supports the fundamental idea of Helmholtz's theory. However, this theory simplifies the complexity of the cochlea. For example, it does not take full account of the active role played by the outer hair cells in amplifying and fine-tuning the response of the basilar membrane. Furthermore, Helmholtz did not have access to modern knowledge about neural processing in the auditory pathway. Today, we know that sound perception involves complex processes in hair cells, auditory neurons and the auditory cortex.

claimed to reduce musical perception to these physiological causes. On the contrary, he developed a semiotic theory of perception that recognised the signifying dimension of musical perception ("Sensations are what we call the impressions on our senses, in so far as they come to our consciousness as states of our own body, especially of our nervous apparatus; we call them perceptions when we form out of them the representation of outer objects.", he wrote, for example, in *On the Sensations of Tone as a Physiological Basis for the Theory of Music*[83]). Here again we are confronted with the problem of reducing sensation and feeling (all our affective and cognitive systems) to pure materiality. However, with music, the problem of reduction takes on a new dimension and acuity. Indeed, no theory is more ill-suited to music than the reductionist theory based on the principle of action and reaction to a given set of *stimuli* or signals. Even the most radical materialists, in their analysis of music, have thus had to make concessions to meaning, these concessions being themselves always more or less linked to the temporal character of music, to its sequencing, to its duration and to the history that we make meaningful to ourselves through our own projective and meaningful perception of time.

Listening to a melody requires openness and immediate availability, as well as an effort at feedback, projection and synthesis (we see the melody as a coherent and meaningful whole). The aesthetic judgement, as a judgement in the time of the very temporality at work is therefore not a matter of pure affect. It is not simply

---

[83] Helmholtz: *Tonempfindungen*, 1870, p. 101

the sensitive manifestation of a seizure (a certain vibration which, for a set of objective reasons, pleases the ear). As a signifying projection, listening is always an "activity of listening", an activity that requires attention "over time" (listening to a musical work is not a matter of passive and pleasant perception, as listening to the song of the robin might be). This conception of the work in terms of its duration and the intentional temporal relationship it establishes with the listener brings us back to a passage in Volume III of Cassirer's *Philosophy of Symbolic Forms*: "The self that intuits itself as being 'in time' is not understood as a simple sum of static states, but as an essence that, extending forward in time, aspires from the present to the future. The musical work is precisely the concrete manifestation of the extension of the *self* in time. It is the linking together of forms at the same time as the synthesis in time of a succession of states (in this, it is the reflection of the *ego*'s operation of synthesis).

18.

MUSIC AND EXPECTATION — In *Emotion and Meaning in Music* (1956), Leonard B. Meyer makes musical expectation one of the key triggers of what he calls musical affect. This theory of affect is based primarily on a physiological approach to music, as illustrated by this reference to the Canadian neuropsychologist Donald Hebb, famous for his work on artificial neural networks: "According to Hebb," writes Meyer, "the difference between pleasant and unpleasant emotions lies in the fact that pleasant emotions (or, in our terminology, pleasant emotional experiences) are always resolved." They depend "on first arousing apprehension, then dispelling it. (Hebb, 1952)[84]." In the rest of the passage we quote, Meyer slightly qualifies Hebb's position by pointing out that the pleasant character of an emotion seems to reside less in the resolution itself than in the belief in a resolution. Meyer thus abandons the idea of the immediacy of musical affect (which is undoubtedly a first step towards recognising the signifying dimension of music) in favour of the idea that music plays with anticipations (an idea that we find in Jean-Pierre Changeux and Pierre Boulez and that we ourselves have, in a sense, defended). However, for Leonard B. Meyer, musical anticipation is not seen as part of a general problematic of signification, but is, on the contrary, interpreted as an extension of the mechanistic and physiological theory of music (signification being understood as one of the results of this mechanism). Leonard B. Meyer, for example, repeatedly emphasises the feeling of expectation, seeing in it "direct analogies in experiences in general[85]". For him, "in music, the state of suspense involves an awareness of the powerlessness of man in face of the unknown[86]." Music must not stray too far from this rule, which Meyer seems to regard as immutable: "the unexpected shall not be confused with the surprising. For when expectation is aroused, the unexpected is always considered to be a possibility, and, though it remains the less expected of several alternatives, it is not a complete surprise[87]." For Meyer,

---

[84] *Emotions and Meanings in Music*, 1956, The University of Chicago Press, Ltd., London, p. 19

[85] Ibid., p. 28

[86] Ibid., p. 29

[87] Ibid., p. 29

the work is linked to a general system of beliefs. It elicits a form of mental synthesis that the listener makes immediately (something we agree with, see previous chapter). However, as Meyer explains, if this mental synthesis does not take place directly, three things can happen: "(1) The mind may suspend judgement, so to speak, trusting that what follows will clarify the meaning of the unexpected consequent. (2) If no clarification takes place, the mind may reject the whole *stimulus,* and an irritation will set in. (3) The unexpected consequent may be seen as a purposeful blunder[88]." We can see here how Meyer attempts to reduce the whole problem of meaning to the material issues underlying meaning (exactly what we call "reductionism"). So, on the one hand, the state of suspense, says Meyer, "involves an awareness of the powerlessness of man in face of the unknown" (the problem of meaning); on the other, the "mind" reacts to a "stimulus" that it either accepts (pleasure) or rejects (irritation, even annoyance).

In his theoretical approach to music, Meyer does not, however, tell us how a simple *stimulus* could contain a meaning such as "man's helplessness in the face of the unknown". By asserting that man feels helpless or powerless in the face of the unknown and that he therefore seeks to return to the "known", Meyer does not explain (i) how man can progress in knowledge, (ii) nor how this idea that man is powerless in the face of the unknown could have been formed in Meyer (if not through an effort of analysis and detachment from himself and from man in general that we call precisely

---

[88] Ibid., p. 29

the signifying effort of analysis and synthesis). In reality, this notion of "man's powerlessness in the face of the unknown" is not, contrary to what Meyer suggests, a physiological and material problematic, but already an *ideal* problematic (this very idea of "man's powerlessness in the face of the unknown"), which while based on processes, i.e. a material dynamic (and not a *stimulus* which implies a form of passivity, of Pavlovian reaction) cannot be reduced to it (as we tried to show in Book I). In other words, if Meyer is able to formulate the idea that man is powerless in the face of the unknown, it is because he [Meyer] is able to look at himself objectively (as an object), i.e. from a higher level $(n+1)$ than the level (n) of man who is 'simply' powerless in the face of the unknown. This change of level, which is a synthetic contemplation of the previous level, is what we call "meaning". As soon as man has the capacity to rise above himself, he enters the realm of what we call "signifiance". And what is music if not the ladder of meaning that enables us to rise above ourselves ("Everybody is looking for the ladder" sings Prince in the song *The Ladder*[89]), to contemplate ourselves both as subjects (the listening subject) and as objects in the process of listening? To speak in this way of a *musical stimulus* to which *musical affect* reacts is in fact, for us, devoid of meaning[90]. There

---

[89] *Everybody's looking 4 the ladder / Everybody wants salvation of the soul*

Prince, *The Ladder*, *Around the World in a Day* album, Prince and the Revolution, 1985

[90] See Leonard B. Meyer: "Affect, or emotion-felt, is aroused when an expectation— a tendency to respond— (here we see

is no *stimulus* that is properly musical, to which would correspond a cerebral compartment that would be automatically activated once seized by this *stimulus* and that we would call "musical affect". While Meyer is right to emphasise music's fundamental relationship with time, and therefore with duration, expectation and anticipation, he is wrong, in our opinion, to reduce the problem of expectation to its physiological manifestations alone (expectation is not necessarily the manifestation of a physiological or physical need, the problem of expectation also concerns the universe of meaning: when a sentence begins, we are as if in suspense, waiting for its meaningful resolution, for its meaning, which is given to us only *in time*).

It seems to us, moreover, that Leonard Meyer, like Jean-Pierre Changeux and Pierre Boulez, overestimates the importance of the problem of expectation and its resolution within the musical work. The example frequently cited by theorists of "musical physiology", that of the imbalance created by a dominant chord which, at the end of a work or musical sequence, calls for a tonic chord to re-establish the harmonic balance, is in this respect highly illustrative of the reductionist conception of this theoretical approach. First, the transition from dominant to tonic is not an absolute necessity (it appeared relatively late in eighteenth-century Western music). Furthermore, the dominant/tonic pairing is a formal proposition that

---

how Meyer is a prisoner of the Pavlovian problem of reflexology, of action-reaction), activated by the musical stimulus situation, is temporarily inhibited or definitively blocked", Ibid. p. 31

means nothing in itself. It only makes sense in the context of an overall narrative. While the harmonic proposition may appear dated or fossilised (our ears are accustomed to it by listening to hundreds or thousands of works that use this harmonic device), it must be restored to the general dynamic of a work which, although it may use means of expression already well known to the public, cannot be reduced to the spread of these means (the work is not a synthesis of tried and tested auditory automatisms, it is not an attempt at Pavlovian conditioning). If the work, as narrative fiction, can arouse questions and expectations, it is not so much through a game of conditioning (action/reaction, stimulus/emotion) as precisely through its narrative, signifying purpose: the suspense created by the work is a signifying suspense, not a physiological or physical one.

Reducing the musical work to the action/reaction or stimulus/emotion pair is therefore problematic for us, not only insofar as it is an erroneous interpretation of the problem of expectation (which relates to the problem of meaning and not to a supposed physiological or physical determination of the listener, i.e. to a form of conditioning), but also insofar as this problem does not, in our opinion, constitute the fundamental mainspring of music, or even of artistic creation in general. To reduce the musical experience to this mechanism alone would be to neglect all the perceptive, expressive and formal richness that makes a musical work unique. Music, no more than poetry, literature, painting or sculpture, cannot be reduced to a game of satisfying or frustrating anticipations or expectations. Above all, it is a bridge of meaning between the artist and the reality he is trying to make audible or visible.

If, despite everything, we wish to address the issue of expectation in music (which is only one aspect of it), we must not confine this expectation to a form of restless agitation or a feverish expectation of resolution. For example, we need to distinguish between short time (that of the bar or phrase) and medium and long time (that of the narrative). We also need to define what expectation is, and how it is constructed or manifests itself in the general narrative of the work. In our opinion, this characterisation of expectation (this understanding of the problem of expectation) requires us to consider the problem of meaning in its non-reducibility to the immediacy of a simple musical *stimulus*.

19.

NARRATION AND RUPTURE — As we have said, the problem of time in music is linked to the fundamental problem of being and signification. Music, as a non-referential language, is the manifestation of a form of "immanent signifiance": it is, therefore, dependent on the rules that are those of any signifying system (rules that themselves contain linking and sequencing operations that derive from our sensitive intuition of time). However, if the coherent formal system generated by the artist is dependent on its own rules (since, from a musical point of view, it *is* the rule, the immanent manifestation of the rule), the artist is not bound to submit to any predefined rule. He remains free at any time to change the rules of the melody, to introduce breaks or accidents (rhythmic, chromatic, stylistic changes...). The artist is precisely the one who plays with the rule at the same time as playing with the rule. It is precisely in this game, in the break with a rule that he himself has established, that the most significant moments of the work (the moments most 'invested' with meaning) are hidden, in our opinion.

Creation is therefore not so much an exercise in satisfying or disappointing expectations that the artist has voluntarily or involuntarily raised; it is first and foremost an evocative search, an attempt to freely decipher the world by contributing to its invention. This attempt may take the form of narrative tension, or it may be characterised by a relative absence of tension (what dramatic tension is there, for example, in Charles Trenet's *La mer*? The song is certainly not linear and has its own twists and turns and meanings, but it cannot be said to be the scene of any particular dramatic tension). Moreover, the narrative tension may be resolved within the work, or it may remain deliberately unresolved (the Doors song *Riders on the Storm*, for example, does not really offer a resolution within the work, but rather remains in a form of disquieting strangeness). The moments of radical change in the work — which may well occur outside of any particular dramatic tension — are thus evidence of the composer's freedom, a freedom exercised not in reference to a particular expectation, but within the framework of a general narrative. In *Sometimes it Snows in April*, for example, Prince makes this kind of significant break:

In the second line of the excerpt from the score we are presenting here, the artist introduces a chromatic movement that takes us from the scale 'A major' to the

From 2:48 for chromatic break

(Ctrl + Click on the image for online version)

scale 'B flat major' before finally returning to the tonic (F) of the scale 'F major'. It's true that chromatic movements are widespread in Western music. Thus, it's hardly surprising to find them in a Prince song. Johann Sebastian Bach, for example, made frequent use of them, especially in his fugues, such as those in The *Well-Tempered Clavier*. In his chorales and cantatas, chromaticism often appeared in moments of transition or dramatic intensification. In Bach's case, however, its use was so extensive that it became part of a more systematic logic. A particularly attentive musicologist could undoubtedly identify an underlying structure and show that Bach's chromaticism was not merely an expressive device, but a fundamental element of his musical language, part of a wider formal logic[91]. Nothing of the sort, however, with Prince. In the song *Sometimes it Snows in April*, there is no hint of the chromatic movement that takes place in the middle of the phrase: "*sometimes* I wish[92], *that life was never ending, and all good things they say never last*". Here, the chromatic break is (and can only be) a signifying break. It occurs precisely between "*I*" and "*wish*". It is at this precise point that the song breaks off before ending with the bitter observation that "*all good things they say, never last*". Ironically (and perhaps a sign of the fundamental importance of this break for the artist), Prince died on 21 April 2016 in Paisley Park, near Minneapolis, in his recording studio complex. A strange snowfall occurred at the end of the day.

The composer is thus never a prisoner of form, form always being for him a means rather than an end (hence the artificiality, as we pointed out, of the distinction between form and content, an artificiality that is all the more apparent in music, which is an entirely formal art, but which is not reduced, paradoxically, to its mere coherence — form expresses something more than

---

[91] We believe that in Bach, as in Prince, the use of chromaticism is, despite its more 'systematic' character, intrinsically significant (that it is the fruit of the artist's intention rather than the constraint of the general system in which the artist finds himself unwillingly caught). We could also mention Bach's rhythmic breaks, such as the one at the end of the first Goldberg variation (Aria), which Glenn Gould particularly accentuated in his 1981 recording (as opposed to the 1956 recording, which, while already having an intuition of the break, does not yet fully mention it).

[92] Chromatic break, underlined.

formalism). In a sense, the introduction of the unexpected into a narrative that raises its own expectations makes us aware of the non-mechanical nature of the world. The unexpected is certainly not the incongruous. In this sense, we can partly subscribe to the assertion that the artist's creative freedom is not total (it is not absolute[93], it remains constrained, although this constraint continues to offer him an intensive infinity of possibilities). The works, as we have said, offer their own directions and possibilities. We nevertheless defend the idea that they are part of intentional and meaningful narrative ensembles. It is precisely these ensembles that place the listener, spectator or reader in a narrative, the short narrative, that of the sentence or bar, the median narrative, that of the part or chapter, the long narrative, that of the work. If we leave out the narrative, and thus the signifying dimension of the work and its internal movements, it then becomes impossible for us to think about aesthetic emotion in a coherent way (this is the limit of materialist approaches, such as Meyer's, which intend to settle more or less on the idea of an "aesthetic affect" that would be triggered by a *stimulus* of an aesthetic nature — which in our opinion is meaningless, there is nothing like a musical *stimulus*, for example: a *stimulus* is a *stimulus*, it cannot receive any intrinsic qualification, the musical or non-musical nature of the *stimulus* is determined by our interpretation of the *stimulus*, i.e. by an act of signifying binding that is not contained in the *stimulus*, but is an act of the "meaning-making machine" that is our brain). Within the

---

[93] In Book I we showed the contradictions arising from this idea of absoluteness.

narrative, the break is always a break in something, in other words, in a signifying construction.

The Magic Mountain (1924) is a spectacular example of this kind of break. In Thomas Mann's famous novel, Hans Castorp, a young German engineer, lands in a sanatorium in the Swiss mountains, where his cousin Joachim Ziemssen has been staying for several years to treat his tuberculosis. Hans Castorp, whose condition is unclear, initially plans to stay in the sanatorium for only a few days. As the days go by, however, time expands. The pages that began as hours become days, weeks and then years. Time passes and Hans Castorp is still there, as if trapped in a fascinating, anaesthetising routine filled only by a few friendly, philosophical discussions. Week after week, Hans Castorp's discharge is postponed, as the doctors do not consider him fit to return to "those below". A reluctant, then vaguely consenting captive, Castorp eventually lets himself be carried away by the rhythm of the changing times and seasons, which he comments on at length, lying beside his cousin on his "excellent deckchair". Nothing disturbs this peaceful harmony apart from an unwelcome woman who has the unpleasant habit of suddenly opening and slamming the doors when she arrives at the sanatorium restaurant. At first annoyed by this woman who, with irritating regularity, appears noisily behind his back, Hans Castorp ends up taking an interest in her, her entourage and the people sitting at her table. This interest soon turns into fascination and then obsession. The young woman's name is Clawdia Chauchat. She is a Russian woman with "Kyrgyz eyes". She is married to a Russian civil servant with whom she seems to have little contact. She is beautiful, fascinating and, like everyone else, ill. For the five hundred pages that make up the first part of the novel, Hans Castorp barely speaks to the young Russian woman. Running into her in a corridor or coming out of a doctor's consultation, however, upsets him, sometimes for days on end. He now waits every day for the moment when Clawdia bursts noisily into the dining room. Manoeuvring skilfully with his tablemates, he managed to position himself where he could observe her more easily. Hans Castorp's life comes to revolve around his passion for Clawdia, until one carnival night (imagine the sadness of a mardi gras in a sanatorium from which most of the inmates will never emerge alive?) when Hans Castorp, intoxicated by the party and perhaps a little by the alcohol, finally dares to approach Clawdia. The party is in full swing, and a game thrown by the host gives Hans the pretext he's been waiting for: "Do you by any chance have a pencil?" he asks Clawdia (we can imagine the superhuman effort this request takes from the hero, who is livid, "deathly pale", writes Thomas Mann). "Me?" replies the sick woman with the bare arms. Yes. Yes, perhaps. What follows is a surreal conversation lasting several pages, during which Hans Castorp confesses his passion to the woman he has never dared speak to. Clawdia knows how to express herself perfectly in German, but isn't this change of language — dare we say this "chromatic break" — better suited to the discourse of love? French becomes the official language of a Russian and a German lost in the middle of the Swiss mountains). Finally, when the boarders have already deserted the party, Hans Castorp, "rambling in his creaky armchair", "almost gets down on one knee", shaking all over and stammering to

Clawdia: "*I love you, I have always loved you, for you are the You of my life, my dream, my destiny, my need, my eternal desire*[94] ...", "*Come, come!*" she replies simply, "*if your teachers could only see you...*". Then comes this passage, which is probably the narrative climax of *The Magic Mountain* (at the very end of Part One). Clawdia has to leave the Magic Mountain, she has decided to return to Dagestan, but she doesn't quite push Hans away:

"You are indeed a gallant suitor, one who knows how to woo in a very profound, German fashion."

And she set her paper hat on his head[95].

"Adieu, my Carnival Prince! I can predict that you'll see a nasty rise in your fever chart this evening."

Then she glided out of her chair, glided across the carpet to the door, where she stopped and turned halfway back to him, one bare arm raised, a hand on the hinge. Over her shoulder she said softly:

"Don't forget to give me back my pencil."

And she left.

I'm almost reluctant to comment on this passage, which in fact stands on its own. The situation is both grotesque and grandiose. Hans is younger than Clawdia, and he becomes infatuated with her through an incongruous and absurd combination of circumstances. She's ill, married, and obviously quite detached (though not totally insensitive... She puts her hat on his head). All he knows of her is her image. This

---

[94] Italics indicate French in the text.
[95] His Carnival hat.

image, insignificant at first, becomes obsessive as the days go by. She is the figure of eternal desire, the embodiment of fundamental otherness (dare we say duality again?): the "You of my life". "Adieu", she says, in a sentence that consecrates the break-up as much as the union, since she adds "my Carnaval Prince". Virtually nothing is said, and yet everything is said. Clawdia is like Chimène in *The Cid* who, almost with a sigh, concedes the famous "go, I don't hate you". Then, at the height of this dramatic and amorous intensity, Clawdia, in a dreamlike, theatrical movement, adds softly, gracefully turning around and raising her bare arm: "*Don't forget to give me back my pencil*". What could be more prosaic than the appearance of this seemingly insignificant pencil at the heart of this decisive moment? The summit has been reached. It's a peak as well as a break. We realise that the descent has begun. Like Flaubert who, at the end of *L'Education sentimentale (Sentimental Education)*, concludes the last interview between Madame Arnoux and Frédéric with the disastrous and sublime "And that was all" ("Et ce fut tout[96]."), Thomas Mann writes, as if to complete a story that has not begun and will never begin: "and she left".

---

[96] It should also be noted that Frédéric, like Hans, stops at the threshold of a story that was only a dream and which he probably never really wanted to materialise in flesh and blood: "Frédéric suspected that Madame Arnoux had come to offer herself; and his lust was stronger than ever, furious, enraged. However, he felt something inexpressible, a repulsion, like the fear of incest. Another fear stopped him, the fear of being disgusted by it later. Besides, what an embarrassment that would be! And both out of prudence

Narration, like the world, has immutable rules and yet has no established rules. With Thomas Mann, there will be no happy resolution. We will never return to the tonic of the major scale. Music, art, is both the rule (without which the world would be nothing, a nothingness) and the breaking of the rule (without which the world would be pure mechanism, another form of nothingness). This rupture ("*don't forget to give me back my pencil*") is only possible if it arises in a signifying universe (almost saturated with meaning in Thomas Mann's work), in other words a dual, living, human world[97].

20.

MUSIC AND THE FUNDAMENTAL DIMENSIONS OF THE HUMAN BEING — Music brings together the three fundamental dimensions of the human being: sensitivity, reason and finitude. Despite its formal manifestation, music is not limited to a simple set of structural arrangements. On the contrary, it constitutes a network of immanent meanings, addressed simultaneously to the composer, the performer and the listener. Although these meanings do not always overlap, they nevertheless find a common anchor (the musical 'signal', the score), the interpretation of which varies according to the history, sensibility and state of

---

and in order not to degrade his ideal, he turned on his heels and began to light a cigarette. She gazed at him in wonder.

[97] The pencil episode is not without significance, of course. In *The Magic Mountain*, it also refers to the hero's childhood and his relationship with his classmate Pribislav Hippe, the mode of encounter being similar (borrowing a pencil).

mind of each of the actors in the musical experience. So, although these meanings may unfold in different directions, they emerge from the same source, conveyed by a universally shared language.

However, this language is never articulated in a linear fashion. Like any signifying system, it unfolds on several interlocking levels, superimposing layers of meaning that interact, mutually modifying each other and thus enriching the experience of the work. Significance arises solely from this dynamic superimposition, through the interweaving of referential and recursive loops. In turn, these loops only become meaningful if they generate some correspondence with a subjective experience — since meaning can never be autonomous or detached from an experience. It is in this way that we can affirm that art, and music in particular, engages the essential dimensions of being: it summons what is most primitive and fundamental in us, establishing a dialogue between formal structures and the intimate experience of the listener.

Music as internal separation

Art as the resolution of an internal conflict: what is the nature of the conflict?

21.

WHAT IS THE NATURE OF THE CONFLICT? — In his first manifesto, André Breton gave the following definition of Surrealism: "Surrealism is based on the belief in the superior reality of certain hitherto neglected forms of association, in the omnipotence of dreams, in the disinterested play of thought. It tends to definitively ruin all other psychic mechanisms and to replace them in solving the main problems of life[98]." A few years later, in *L'Amour fou*, Breton wrote: "I am intimately convinced that any perception recorded in the most involuntary way, such as, for example, words spoken out of turn, carries within it the solution, symbolic or otherwise, of a difficulty with oneself[99]." Here we have the fundamental idea that art is a form of open conflict, the externalisation of an internal difficulty that carries within it the possibility of resolution. Conflict is literally a (dual) confrontation between the inside and the outside (conflict comes from the Latin *conflictus*, which is the past participle of the verb *confligere*, composed of the prefix "con-" meaning together and "*fligere*" meaning to strike). The word conflict thus expresses the idea of a "clash"

---

[98] André Breton, *Manifeste du surréalisme* [1924] in *Manifestes du surréalisme*, Paris, Folio Essais, Pauvert éditeur, 1962, p. 36 (French Edition)
[99] André Breton, Op. cit., p. 22

between two realities). It is from this confrontation between two heterogeneous realities (the image of our *ideal*, synthetic unity and the world outside us, which goes beyond the boundaries of our *ego*) that the work of art is born[100]. Once again, it is through the image of a woman that this new formulation of truth reaches Breton[101]. In addition to the example of the passer-by that Breton develops in his first Manifesto[102], we think again of Nadja and the character of Jacqueline Lamba in *L'Amour fou*, or the seductive women in *Poisson soluble*. In both *Nadja* and *L'Amour fou*, the relationship

---

[100] André Breton's ideas are reminiscent of slightly earlier developments by Sigmund Freud, in particular his vision of art as the sublimation of the id and sexual drives, see in particular *Three Essays on the Theory of Sexuality* (1905) and *The Ego and the Id* (1923).

[101] On the image of women in the modern definition of truth, see Geoffroy de Clisson, *L'image de la femme ou le renversement symboliste de l'idée de vérité* (2013).

[102] "He hardly dares to express himself and, if he does, it's only to say that this idea or that woman has an effect on him. What effect, he would be unable to say, but this is the measure of his subjectivism, and nothing more. This idea, this woman disturbs him, inclining him to be less severe. She has the effect of isolating him for a second from his solvent and depositing him in the sky, the beautiful precipitate that he can be, that he is. In despair, he then invokes chance, a deity more obscure than the others, to whom he attributes all his errors. Who's to say that the angle from which this idea that touches him presents itself, what he loves in this woman's eye, isn't precisely what ties him to his dream, chains him to data that through his own fault he has lost? And if it were otherwise, what might he not be capable of? I would like to give him the key to this corridor", Op. cit., p. 23. (French Edition).

with the beloved is based on chance encounters and coincidences that are not coincidences at all. The construction of the two works, apparently unstructured, is made up of phantasmagorical parts, dream narratives and narrative breaks mixed with photography and poetry. The truth of the image is not generated by the logical or chronological coherence of the discourse. On the contrary, reality adapts to human temporality. It is when two temporalities come together that there is a real "encounter". From then on, this encounter no longer really belongs to reality; it is surreal insofar as it takes place in the form of a reunion between dream and reality: "I believe," writes Breton, "in the future resolution of these two states, apparently so contradictory, which are dream and reality, into a kind of absolute reality, *surreality*, so to speak. It is to reconquer this reality that I am going, certain that I will not succeed, but too unconcerned about my death not to anticipate the joys of such a possession[103]." The image created by the chance encounter is reminiscent of what the Symbolists called an "apparition". It is in the image that the random yet necessary meeting occurs, from which poetic truth suddenly emerges. This is what André Breton said in a tribute to Saint-Pol-Roux, whom he described in his first manifesto as a "surrealist in the symbol[104]": "It appears more and more", he wrote, "that the generating element par excellence of this world that, in place of the old, we intend to make our own, is none other than what poets call 'the image'. The vanity of ideas cannot escape even

---

[103] André Breton, Manifeste du Surréalisme (*Manifesto of Surrealism*), 1924, p. 24 (French Edition)
[104] Op. cit., p. 38 (French Edition)

the most cursory examination. The best-chosen modes of literary expression, always more or less conventional, impose a discipline on the mind to which I am convinced it does not lend itself well. Only the image, in its unexpected and sudden nature, gives me the measure of possible liberation, and this liberation is so complete that it frightens me. It is through the power of images that, in the course of time, the 'real' revolutions may well be accomplished[105]." With the Surrealists, we see how truth moves from the idea to the image. The image, however, is still an idea, an idea mediated not by language, but by a presentation which, although unmediated, remains significant (see Book I on the productive imagination and its active role in the formation of images).

Like the surrealist image or language, music stands as a third term, an intermediary space between reality and being. It is both an externalisation of form for the composer and an invitation to exteriority for the listener. It is undoubtedly this in-between position that gives it its magnetism. Music does not resolve an inner conflict simply by alternating between tension and resolution. It operates at a deeper level: it is the mediated symbol of the *ego*'s encounter with the world, a fluid articulation between subjective interiority and a reality that eludes it, making sensitive what would otherwise remain elusive. In this respect, the cathartic virtue of theatre — and tragedy in particular — as described it in *Poetics*, and which we so often evoke, does not seem to us to be a simple mechanism of

---

[105] André Breton, *Hommage à Saint-Pol-Roux* (1935), *Anciennetés*, pp. 24-25 (French Edition)

liberation or emotional purification. If, in the cathartic mechanism described by Aristotle, we find this idea of conflict between interiority and exteriority (an interplay of projection and reception that results from the terrifying representation of passions and tragic situations in a non-passionate, safe, 'neutral' setting), it seems to us that we should not reserve the notion of *catharsis* for tragic representations, but extend it to all forms of art.

Like theatre, music invites the listener or spectator to step outside themselves, to adhere to a form that temporarily suspends their superficial *self* — that is, their opinions, their concerns, their daily worries, the conjunctural projection of their existence. This movement of adhesion links him to a deeper *self*, capable of resonating with the otherness of the artistic forms he receives. Paradoxically, this otherness seems familiar to him, like an echo of the common ground of humanity, a foundation of the universal. So, in their relationship with the work, viewers are not so much looking for a restitution of reality as a liberation, an openness to a truth that is not exhausted in the simple designation of things (a sword, for example, can very well be represented by a piece of pointed wood without altering the viewer's adherence to it). The key, then, lies less in material verisimilitude than in the ability of the forms to absorb the everyday *self*. It is in this sense that, to use Henri Gouhier's expression in *Le théâtre et l'existence* (*Theatre and Existence*), if the spectator "holds as true[106]" what takes place on stage, it is not out of credulity, but because he opens himself up to a truth of another order. This is not a naïve adherence to the factual, but an immersion in the truth of the artistic form, a truth which, through its evocative power, momentarily extracts the individual from himself.

In music, as in theatre, truth is not based on a simple adherence to the facts, but on a *commitment to the form*, a resonance of the deepest *self* with the narrative that is offered. This tuning in is not the result of a search for correspondence with reality — like the demand for verisimilitude — but of an immersion in the form itself. So, in a theatre or cinema, we don't need to see a rabid dog appear for us to feel a sense of fear or terror. A nine-headed hydra in a narrative that we know is fictional can provoke a reaction that is just as intense, if not more so, than that provoked by an aggressive dog barking at our neighbour's gate. The terror experienced in these two contexts will certainly not be identical in its implications, because we don't instinctively run away from a theatre or a cinema (although it can happen...). However, the sensation that runs through us is expressed in almost the same way: an impulse to withdraw, to look away, even to hide our eyes from what is happening in front of us. Unlike 'real' terror, however, the terror aroused by the nine-headed hydra will be linked to an overall narrative, in short, it will be a contextual terror (the image of the hydra would

---

[106] In fact, Henri Gouhier probably borrowed the notion of "holding as true" from Samuel Taylor Coleridge, who in his *Biographia Literaria* (1817) uses the expression "suspension of disbelief".

undoubtedly be less terrifying if it were presented to us outside any narrative context, but the rabid dog is always just as frightening, with or without horror music, for example). What matters in the work of art is above all our acceptance of a narrative form, an immersive acceptance that makes us momentarily forget our own position (we cease to perceive ourselves fully as spectators sitting in a cinema, theatre or concert hall, to become one with the narrative). This engagement goes beyond the simple intensity of the immediate emotions that the work arouses — whether fear, terror, tenderness or pity. It is based above all on a suspension of the *self* in favour of the work unfolding before it.

However, although the work of art is an invitation to formal adhesion, it cannot be reduced to this proposition of adhesion. The work of art is not a flycatcher, and the viewer is not the pigeon who was fooled by Zeuxis's realistic grapes[107]. In the work, form is both proposed and distanced (to produce form is already to separate it from oneself; to receive form is to understand that it is proposed as a signifying *medium*). The spectator's or listener's adherence to this form is not entirely the same as the pigeon's adherence to the form of Zeuxis's grapes. It is both adherence ("holding it to be true", acceptance of the proposition) and distancing. What's important about a work of art is not

---

[107] Zeuxis of Iraclia was a famous Greek painter of the fifth century BC, known for his ability to create works of art so realistic that they could fool the senses. The most famous anecdote relates that he painted grapes so realistic that birds tried to peck them.

so much its realism or the reactions it immediately arouses in us (a desire to drink, for example, triggered by an advert for *Coca-Cola*), but the reflection it engenders by echoing our own internal system of meanings. For us, this is where art's cathartic virtue lies: as an open manifestation of conflict (the question), the work of art is a formal proposal for resolving (better understanding) this conflict[108]. In our opinion, aesthetic feeling proceeds precisely from this mechanism. It is an infra-rational resolution of a conflict I am in with myself. As a signifying response to the work, aesthetic feeling is not necessarily reduced to an experience of beauty.

In the wake of Edmund Burke, the Romantics were among the first to theorise the aesthetic appeal of terror, darkness and the ugly, in reaction to the theoretical rigidity of classicism. It is true that ancient tragedy had already paved the way, but it was Burke who proposed the first systematic conceptualisation, analysing the determinants of the category of the sublime. For Burke, the feeling of the sublime was aroused by the terror inspired by a representation, its

---

[108] The resolution of the conflict I am in with myself, in the sense of André Breton's expression, is therefore due to the fact that, firstly, the work of art has forced me to leave behind my superficial and immediate self and, secondly, to the fact that it has offered me one or more forms (representational or narrative) that have resonated with my deeper self, that have meant something to it, and that, sometimes, have made it confusingly envisage the answer to a question it had not directly asked itself.

power, its obscurity and its grandeur[109]. Sublime representations were thus supposed to provoke feelings of admiration, awe and respect. By dissociating aesthetic feeling from the idea of the beautiful, Burke opened the way to a reflection on the significance of art and its relationship to truth. However, his classification of aesthetic experiences according to the feelings they were supposed to provoke maintained him in a sentimentalist vision of art, where the work was defined above all by its emotional impact rather than its signifying power. In our view, this classification of aesthetic feelings was based on an artificial distinction. Many of the affects that Burke described as 'sublime' were not really distinguishable from the emotions associated with beauty, except by the intensity or context in which they occurred. Burke's separation of these two categories — the beautiful, associated with harmony and gentleness, and the sublime, associated with terror and grandeur — thus seems arbitrary to us, in that it was based more on a typology of emotional reactions than on a real ontological differentiation between the beautiful and the sublime (a differentiation that Kant would make in the *Critique of Judgement*, by considering the sublime in its dynamic dimension of transcending form). The merit of Burke's philosophy, however, was to link art to the problem of its active reception by the spectator, i.e. to the problem of correspondence. With Burke, the theory of art left its classical framework (art as respect for rules, as a theory of harmony and beauty) and entered into the general problem of signification, that is, duality and

---

[109] His reflections would influence Kantian theories of the sublime, see The *Critique of Judgement*.

correspondence. This conception of art opened the way to the idea of a truth specific to the work, not in the sense that it corresponded to a concrete reality that we had to copy or attain (art as *mimesis*), but in that it echoed in us a fundamental reality, a way of being in the world that was both singular and universal. The idea of the truth of the work of art — which is not, strictly speaking, a thesis of Burke's, but a direction suggested by his philosophy — does not, therefore, belong to the classical theory of truth as adequation, but is more akin to a conception of truth as correspondence, a truth proper to form itself.

If this truth is aesthetic in nature, it is not primarily linked to beauty, but to meaning, i.e. signification (in this respect, "aesthetics" is more humanist than "beauty"; it does not postulate beauty or harmony as a necessity; beauty can, on the contrary, derive from "meaning"). It is this truth that the painter, sculptor or musician tirelessly seeks. It is also this truth that resolves the internal conflict in the viewer. However, this resolution does not occur within the work itself, but through the external mediation it offers. There is nothing didactic about the work: it imposes no fixed rules, does not demand that a happy outcome be built into it, nor does it function as a therapy. By leaving their immediate, superficial *selves* behind for a moment, the spectators gain a better understanding of themselves through the work. They find not so much an explicit answer as a diffuse intuition of a question they had not yet formulated. In this sense, the work acts as an infra-rational resolution to the conflict. Art can thus offer both a resolvable conflict, where beauty and harmony appear as signs of appeasement (for example, the return to the tonic in music marks a conventional resolution), and an insoluble conflict, where the work exposes the tragedy, the absence of meaning, the destruction of all expectation, an unsettling strangeness that offers no denouement (think, for example, of the often repetitive music of horror films, which has its troughs and *climaxes*, but most of the time offers no logical resolution). In both cases, the work of art remains within the formal framework of aesthetics. It does not attempt to go beyond form, which is why we think that the Kantian distinction between aesthetics and the sublime is more effective than Burke's: the sublime is generated by going beyond form, by defeating the imagination of the spectator, who is unable to synthesise the form or forms presented to him[110]. The

---

[110] See Kant, *Critique of Judgement*. For Kant, the mathematical sublime concerns the experience of infinity and magnitude beyond all measure. It manifests itself when the human mind attempts to understand objects or concepts of such immensity that they escape all ordinary measurement. For example, contemplating the vast starry sky or gigantic mountains can evoke this feeling. For Kant, the mathematical sublime highlights the capacity of the human mind to conceive of the infinite, even if the senses cannot grasp its totality.

For Kant, the dynamic sublime is linked to natural power and force (here we find the influence of Burke). It arises when man is confronted with formidable and potentially destructive natural forces, such as storms, hurricanes, erupting volcanoes or raging oceans. This kind of sublime arouses admiration mixed with awe in the face of nature's power. However, this fear is tempered by the fact that the

difference between the aesthetic and the sublime is of the same nature as the one we feel when we are confronted with a landscape whose limits we cannot envisage — the ocean, the mountain tops lost in the clouds, and to the representation of this same landscape within the formal framework of a work — we think, for example, of the famous *Wanderer Above the Sea of Fog* by Caspar David Friedrich, a work often cited by philosophy students as belonging to the "sublime" even though it possesses all the codes of classical aesthetics. Admittedly, the dis-tinction within aesthetics between the beautiful and the sublime remains, but this distinction is no longer directly linked, as it was for Burke, to the "category of feelings" aroused by the mountain

Wanderer Above the Sea of Fog (*Der Wanderer über dem Nebelmeer*), Caspar David Friedrich, 1818, Oil on

---

viewer knows that he or she is safe, allowing the power of nature to be felt without actually being threatened.

For Kant, the two types of sublime share certain characteristics: they provoke a feeling of surpassing ordinary human capacities for perception or understanding. They also involve reflection on the limits of our own minds and our ability to grasp the infinite or resist natural forces. The sublime involves both reason, which attempts to conceptualise what is beyond the senses, and imagination, which strives to represent immensity or power.

landscape and its formal representation, for ex-ample, in Friedrich. For Kant, the feeling of the sublime[111] arises from the failure of the imagination — which is incapable of synthesising what is conveyed to it by sensory intuition — but it is not linked to any particular emotional theme. Terror, fear, strangeness, obscurity or even the confrontation with death are not constitutive of the Kantian sublime, since these emotions can just as easily be aroused by works of formal aesthetics. In the aesthetics of the sublime, as in the aesthetics of the beautiful, what we call *aesthetics* is not an absolute property of things themselves (in the same way that, in the philosophy of knowledge, concepts were not properties of things in themselves). The notion of aesthetics always refers to a relationship between an object and the way in which we perceive it in a meaningful way. However, this relationship goes beyond the simple utilitarian function of everyday objects. The artistic object can never be reduced entirely to a trivial object, even when it is hijacked or reinvested (as in André Breton's "trouvailles", for example).

What thus qualifies our relationship to the work and to aesthetics in general (which goes beyond the strict framework of the work) is the relationship of signifiance that we maintain with it. Aesthetic feeling is always linked to the emotional interpretation of an exteriority that we perceive as intentional. When we

---

[111] It would probably be more accurate to speak, not of a feeling of the sublime, but of a sensation of the sublime, the sensation being a more passive experience than the feeling (referring to this defensive attitude of being overwhelmed).

come face to face with nature, whether immense or untamed, and when we confront works of art (pictorial or musical), it is in reality always ourselves that we are confronted with. The *self* in aesthetic confrontation is no longer, however, the egotistical *self* of everyday life, but a *self* installed outside itself, looking at itself from the outside as it contemplates the mediating otherness of the work or nature that denies it. This is what *catharsis* is for us: the possibility of anaesthetising the everyday *self* in order to tune in to a more fundamental *self*, freed from its internal conflicts.

LOOKING INWARD — SPLITTING THE *SELF* IN TWO

22.

MUSIC AND FORMALISM: IMAGINATION AND CRITICISM — Musical creation, like the scientific enterprise, is the result of two distinct movements. First, it is an intellectual (or abstract) intuition of a form, followed by a critical and retroactive selection of the form. In the scientific approach, critical selection is based on the criterion of correspondence with the facts. Abstract intuition finds a concrete formulation in the theory, and the results of this theory are then compared with the set of facts that the theory is supposed to describe. In artistic creation (and in musical creation in particular), the critical moment is not a comparative moment (the music is not confronted with any kind of reality that would confirm or invalidate it) but a moment of pure aesthetic evaluation of form (what does form mean? What is the place of form within the work?) Artistic creation is thus defined by this tension between the forms presented to the *self* by the imagination (or by a kind of abstract intuition of forms) and the selection of forms that is the work of critical reason (the word criticism here having its original meaning, from the Greek κρίνω meaning to separate, to judge, to sort, i.e. to separate the good from the bad). It is therefore, so to speak, the result of a "splitting of the *self* into two", of a confrontation between the intuitive *self* (the almost "passive" *self*, one might say, the forms presenting themselves in a sense freely to our consciousness without our active intervention) and the critical *self* (the "active" self, the one that evaluates, judges and sorts). This tension between these two moments of artistic creation can be analysed as a form of dislocation of the *self*, the artist being the site of a temporary confrontation between the form and the critical and evaluative power that judges the form from the point of view of its aesthetic significance. Criticism is thus a process of iterative loops (which proceeds from recursivity in reverse); it is criticism of the work at the same time as criticism of the evaluator, and in an upward spiral, criticism of itself (see on this subject Book I, § 56 — *Should we abandon the principle of causality?*, footnote on quantum superposition states: as soon as measurement comes into play, it disturbs the phenomenon it is trying to analyse in the same way, in the critical process of creation, the evaluator, by observing the work in progress within himself, disturbs the creative process; this disturbance is nevertheless the *sine qua non* of the concrete realisation of the work. The evaluation of the work does not stop there, however; when he evaluates the work, the artist is also evaluating himself as an evaluator, and so on in a form of upward spiral reminiscent of the critical spiral of the evaluative process of knowledge, which starts from the subjective and sensitive to arrive at a form of objective concreteness). In composing his work, the artist is in a sense composing himself, exposing his deepest *self*. This exposure and definition of the *self* is as much the result of passivity (the passivity required to rid oneself of the everyday, trivial *self*) as it is an autonomous, conscious act (the artist's activity of selection, of composing, sorting, pruning and exposing). It might be objected that automatic writing, which was given pride of place by the Surrealists, seems to contradict the idea of critical feedback between the work and its creator (the idea of automatism seems to exclude all critical feedback from the outset). To this we reply, on the one hand, that it seems illusory to claim to achieve an authentically and purely 'irrational' production, since critical reason is 'always already there', including in altered states of consciousness (hypnosis, trance, psychotropic drugs, etc.): the critical *ego*, if inhibited, is never totally suppressed[112]) and, secondly, that the mode of artistic expression (in this case automatic writing) is already part of a significant critical choice (just as John Cage's work *4'33* was part of the same significant choice).

23.

ART AS "*PRE-LOGOS*" — The artist, like any sentient being, is first and foremost the receiver of the forms that present themselves to them (those "TSF waves" that Guillaume Apollinaire refers to when he compares the poet to a kind of transistor). But he is not just a being who is content to feel and express forms. As a rational being (capable of structuring and understanding meaningful data), the artist is also genuinely *active* in the world. He evaluates, selects and organises forms, integrating them into a meaningful

---

[112] In hypnotic states, for example, the subject's critical faculties are generally altered but not entirely eliminated. Hypnosis induces an altered state of consciousness, often described as a state of heightened concentration or deep relaxation, in which the subject is more receptive to suggestions. However, even in this state, they retain a degree of self-awareness and, in most cases, will not do anything that goes against their moral values or fundamental will.

whole that we call a "work[113]". The work of art is therefore as much the product of a receptive passivity as of an emitting activity. In this way, it reveals the dual structure of the sensitive and rational being, both from the point of view of our sensitive relationship to the world (the sensitivity of the being presupposes its belonging as much as its separation from the world, separation from that which is not me) and from the point of view of our critical relationship with all signifying forms (rational criticism pre-supposes an overcoming of sensitive immediacy, a conscious recognition of the *self* as a separate being, capable of formulating, through the *logos*, signifying propositions about things). The gradual structuring of the forms of language thus went hand in hand with the advent of critical discourse, of which the fifth century in Athens — so often referred to by historians and Hellenists as the "century of *logos*", due in particular to the significant development of rational and philosophical thought — was one of the most brilliant illustrations[114]. But critical

---

[113] In French, the word "œuvre" comes from the Latin *opera*, which is the plural of *opus*, meaning "work" or "work". The Latin word *opera* gave rise to the French word œuvre, via the Old French *ovre*, which also meant "work", "work" and indicated the idea of an accomplishment, an activity.

[114] That Sophist relativism (although this is not really the subject of this book, it would be advisable here to define Sophism properly and not to subject all Sophists to the traditional vindictiveness of rationalists, see Jacqueline de Romilly's *Les sophistes* on this subject) appeared at roughly the same time as the philosophy of Socrates and Plato is, moreover, not very surprising, just as it is not entirely surprising that Athenian society, open to public controversy

discourse — and this is one of the important lessons to be learned from our theory of art — was not, and never has been, in itself a producer of knowledge. To produce knowledge, you have to go through forms and meanings. Without form (i.e. without this duality between the sentient being and the world, form being a signifying representation of the world by the sentient being), there can be no significations, and without significations, there is hardly any possibility of knowledge. This is the essential limit of reason: without sensible intermediation, reason runs on empty and can no longer produce knowledge[115]. It is always the senses that transmit to us the matter that the understanding (consciousness) puts into form and on which reason issues judgements. Reason, without the help of sensibility and imagination, cannot produce new knowledge.

---

and confrontation between discourses, was the historic setting for the advent of the world's first democracy. In a sense, critical discourse about things gave rise to its own criticism. This emergence of criticism of critical discourse at the same time as critical discourse itself is somewhat paradoxical, since it seems to implicitly validate the relativism from which the first critical discourse was precisely trying to extricate itself. The critique of critical discourse often seems to be a less naïve and more advanced version of the first critical discourse. This, however, is an illusion to which we must not give in: he who speaks last is not necessarily right...
[115] "All our knowledge begins with the senses, passes from there to the understanding and ends with reason. Immanuel Kant, *Critique of Pure Reason, Transcendental Logic, Second Division, Transcendental Dialectic, On Reason as the Seat of Transcendental Appearance.*

If we accept, however, that the work of art is the combined result of formal imagination and critical reason, would it not be somewhat logical to assert that it can be the vehicle of a form of knowledge? As we have said, the work of art, as a concrete and voluntary realisation, is not and cannot be the fruit of a pure combination of circumstances (the form of which would be the result of that *happy* chance which sees, for example, a colony of ants form the face of Winston Churchill on the sand, as in the example of Putnam that we quoted a little earlier in § 11). The work of art is necessarily the result of an action mediated and communicated in a concrete form. As a conscious and voluntary action, it always carries a meaning, a significance. It is, so to speak, already a "language" or a "pre-language", not insofar as it designates a concrete reality in the mode of adequation, but insofar as it is the presentation of an organised formal structure. In music, this organisation manifests itself at several levels: in the rhythm, first of all (the first musical works were often rhythmic works, using percussion instruments), in the metre, the measure, the harmony, the tonality, the arrangement, the theme, the melodic lines, the general narrative, the interpretation, the accidents: everything in music is structure, everything is therefore potential signification. The accidents of structure themselves are signifiers (as is organised chaos, from the moment it is the work of a self-conscious artist who presents his work for what it signifies, see § 3 — *Music and Chance*). This structure, this musical *logos*, is by its very nature the bearer of meaning: it is the signifying manifestation of the confrontation of organised finitude[116] with sensible reality. However, we need to clear up a fairly common misunderstanding here: the fact that musical *logos* (and artistic logos in general) is in fact a signifying language does not mean that it has anything concrete to say about the world. Artistic *logos*, and musical *logos* in particular, are not *logos* of designation, they are *logos* of structure, the manifestation of a pre-linguistic coherence (a grammar without nouns or adjectives, without concrete sensible embodiment[117]). This is why artistic *logos* are not, most of the time, univocal. On the contrary, it is more often than not evocative of a multiple reality (a reality that is not yet fixed in a concrete meaning). The work is certainly not open to all possible meanings or interpretations (the per-formers and actors are also, so

---

[116] to the sentient organism, if one prefers, but the rational sentient organism, having reached consciousness of itself and of others.

[117] The question undoubtedly becomes thornier and more ambiguous the closer we get to artistic forms that use common language. While poetry remains structurally close to the musical work, the novel is undoubtedly the most ambiguous literary form. It seems to us, however, that a work of art consists in (actively) bringing together one or more formal intuitions revealed by the imagination. Texts with a 'message' or a 'commitment' do not seem to us to fall directly within the general idea of a work of art as we defend it, but rather within the didactic or argumentative genre. Nevertheless, we know that some great works have been the fruit of partisan commitment, or have served a political idea or message. It seems to us, however, that these works were not limited to the communication of content and transcended didacticism or the theories (political or artistic) that they claimed to defend or illustrate.

to speak, under the tacit surveillance of the work). However, the meaning of the work is by its very nature open to multiple meanings. In reality, it arises from the encounter between two structures, firstly that of the artist, as initiator or sender of the work, and secondly that of the spectator, listener or reader, as receiver of the work. The encounter between the same signal and different receivers produces distinct effects[118] while remaining within a coherent interpretative halo (the signal being "identical", it cannot, *a priori*, be perceived in diametrically opposed ways, in the same way that the same object — the same sensitive reality — cannot be perceived sometimes as a chair, sometimes as a fork). So, when we speak of the 'truth' of a work of art, we are in no way referring to the validity of a particular idea that it expresses, but rather to the *multiple reality* from which it springs and which it carries along in its wake. The work of art is not, therefore, about bringing to light a truth hidden from the eyes of the world, or revealing what would constitute, in Heidegger's words, "the thingness of the thing[119]". When Van Gogh paints a pair of leather clogs, he is not necessarily referring univocally to the hard work of the peasant woman who returns home in the evening after humbly tilling the land of her ancestors, the same land that modern industry — of which Descartes is forever the disgraced father— has soiled and scorned. Nor does he

---

[118] This reminds me of the image of the rocking horse, used by several economists (Knut Wicksell, Ragnar Frisch, Johan Åckerman) in the 1920s and 1930s to describe the way in which structurally different economies could react in different ways to the same economic shock.

[119] See Martin Heidegger, *Off the Beaten Track*, 1950

necessarily have in mind the muted revolt of the German peasantry, the people with their backs bent, who, because of their daily and age-old proximity to the nourishing earth ("that which does not lie"), hold the ultimate secret of "being there", forgetting themselves in order to become one with their history, their nation, their people and their destiny. The truth of Van Gogh's work has in fact, contrary to what Heidegger tries to

A pair of leather clogs, Vincent Van Gogh, 1889, oil on canvas

see in it, no properly political or subversive content. It is not the illustration of an idea (it is not an allegory), it is the representation of the idea itself, its concrete manifestation. As such, it expresses nothing less and nothing more than itself; it is a pure presentation that opens up to a multiplicity of meanings.

The fact remains, however, that Van Gogh's series of shoes has something to do with the idea of truth. It is certainly not the idea of a truth-designation (of which didactic art is yet another avatar) but of a truth which, preceding concrete language (that of truth-correspondence) skips over the question of adequacy to focus on the question of meaning. In the series of shoes, Van Gogh describes pairs of shoes as he sees them, as they are constituted in his history, in the system of meanings he has slowly built up for himself. The shoes are therefore a kind of concrete manifestation of what Van Gogh sees in himself (like Rimbaud, who becomes a seer "*through a long, immense and reasoned disruption of all the senses*" of what is happening inside him, of the work that is being born there). The truth of the work lies precisely in its fidelity to the internal and signifying form that it embodies, as much as to the external coherence of the work that enables it to be communicated (let's remember Brouwer's distinction between the two moments of mathematics: the moment of intuition and the moment of mathematical communication, which is the moment of formalisation and communicability).

While we could take up Heidegger's idea that the work of art makes visible the 'underpinning of the object' (that which makes the object the object, that which founds, as Heidegger puts it, its 'thingness'), we need to make it clear that this 'underpinning' towards which the work points is neither ontological nor didactic: the work of art is first and foremost the expression of a signifying experience, the point from which one or more signifying directions radiate. It is not the unveiling of a hidden or profound meaning, as Heidegger suggests, but rather an invitation to reflect on our relationship with the visible through the *medium of* the artist's eye.

When we look at Van Gogh's clogs or series of old shoes with laces, we are observing reality *through* Van Gogh's *eye*. This transparent observation in turn teaches us something about the shoe, in the same way that we learn something about the tree by confronting Mondrian's (increasingly abstract and structural) series of trees. However, no more than with Van Gogh's shoes, we learn something of what the tree is *profoundly* or *primitively* through Mondrian's painting. Mondrian's tree series does not reveal the deeper structure of reality but rather provokes in us a feeling of (intensive) enlargement of reality. Through Mondrian's tree series (as well as through Van Gogh's shoe series), we learn

1. *Apple tree, pointillist version*, Piet Mondrian, 1908-1909, oil on panel, 2. *red tree*, Piet Mondrian, 1908-1910, oil on canvas, 3. *horizontal tree*, Piet Mondrian, 1911, oil on canvas, 4. *apple tree in blossom*, Piet Mondrian, 1912, oil on canvas

something about what trees are. This knowledge, however, was not contained in our prior experience of trees. It is in this way that we can speak of an extension of our knowledge, this extension being achieved by the signifying addition of a reality that remained unknown (albeit familiar) to us.

For both Van Gogh and Mondrian, however, the work of art did not point to an external reality (the work is not a signpost). The truth of what it expresses is entirely contained within the work. If we speak of *truth* in relation to the work of art, then, it is not in a Heideggerian sense, that is to say in a sense that, whatever Heidegger may say, would go beyond the work itself (the work as indicator or vector of an ideological or political message) but rather in a Plotinian sense: truth as manifestation of the multiplicity of the One (multiplicity of creation, reception and interpretation linked by the uniqueness of the work). As a concrete manifestation of this multiplicity, the work of art is also, once again, the sign of separation: separation first between the artist and the world, then separation within the artist's own creative solitude (the artist who sees himself created, who is his own evaluator), separation finally between the artist and his public: the work of art is the fundamental testimony of our dual relationship to the world.

Art as Play — A Shifted Discourse on Reality: Irony

> These Greeks were superficial — from profundity!
>
> Friedrich Nietzsche, *The Gay Science*, 1882

24.

The process of artistic creation, like to a certain extent the process of scientific discovery, is one of internal dissociation. This capacity for dissociation is reflected in the artist's sense of formal criticism as well as his habit of distancing himself (from himself and his work). The distance — that is, the space that separates the artist from himself, from his work, from the forms he glimpses or projects — is what we call "play", in the sense that we might say that a mechanical part "has play" (that it moves, that it is out of place, that it creaks). The artist is thus the one "who doesn't *fit*, who doesn't fit entirely into a global mechanism, in the same way as we would fit into an organic society in which each of the components has a fixed and determined place. The artist is the part that 'plays' in the overall mechanism, as much as the one who creates the game, who invents new rules and a new space. In art, there is the idea that nothing is serious (that nothing is "for real", as the kids say). Art, as the creation of a new space, a new universe, is originally understood in terms of "recreation", of taking time off, in other words of temporarily distancing oneself from reality. (René Girard, for example, theorises that there is a relevant link between cult and culture, with the invention of the sacred, with its rites and prohibitions, protecting mankind from mimetic violence and thus making possible the "hominisation" and evolution of culture, which is initially understood as a kind of appendage to cult[120]). However, even in its religious themes and formalism, art remains the manifestation of an "other side of reality". This "sidewaysness" is not always expressed ironically or playfully — although examples of such playful expression can be found as early as the Middle Ages, for example in the margins of illuminated manuscripts, where grotesque figures are sometimes to be found, anthropomorphic animals or scenes from everyday life that seem unrelated to the sacred text, the humour of fabliaux, the gargoyles of Gothic cathedrals, not to mention the formal explosion of the Renaissance, Jerome Bosch, the Italian Mannerists, vanities... — but it nevertheless opens up a new space that is properly "surreal" in the sense that this (mystical) space was not yet contained within reality.

With the decline of religious themes in art, the same space that had been saturated by sacred figures became larger and freer. This cracking open of the sacred can be seen *in concreto* in many of the works of the Italian Renaissance. Whereas the Middle Ages were dominated by flat tints on golden backgrounds — golden backgrounds that were themselves the symbol of divine light and eternity, a celestial reality that never changes — the Renaissance saw the emergence, within its religious representations themselves, of a double

---

[120] See in particular René Girard, *La violence et le sacré* (*Violence and the Sacred*), 1972 and *Des choses cachées depuis la fondation du monde* (*Things Hidden Since the Foundation of the World*), 1978.

breach that is, in our opinion, the combined fruit of the invention of perspective and the appearance of the background. Attributed to the Italian architect and artist Filippo Brunelleschi[121] in the 1420s, linear perspective soon made its appearance in painting. Masaccio's *Holy Trinity* (c. 1427), a fresco in the church of Santa Maria Novella in Florence, is considered to be one of the first concrete applications of the principles of linear perspective in art. In Masaccio's work, God the Father, Christ crucified, and the Holy Spirit are accompanied by holy figures and the figures of his patrons. Behind Christ, a sort of deep chapel with an inverted barrel vault opens out between two columns. With this second plane created by perspective, Christ's Calvary is no longer the sole subject of the painting. The (sacred) foreground is, as it were, "set against" a secular background. At the heart of the work there are now two infinities, the first represented by Christ himself, the second symbolised by the vanishing point of perspective, a vanishing point that is at eye level with a standing spectator, located at the bottom of Christ's cross, just above the sarcophagus, and which opens onto an earthly infinity. This double competition between the sacred figure (introduction of a background, introduction of a terrestrial infinity made by man for man, at man's height) within the work itself is the concrete manifestation of what we have called

---

[121] Brunelleschi carried out a famous experiment in Florence to prove the principles of perspective: he painted an image of the façade of the Baptistery of Florence using a vanishing point perspective, then showed the image through a mirror to demonstrate how converging lines created a realistic illusion of depth.

"play" (play as recreation, as dismissal, play as the creation of a new space). Beginning with Masaccio's work, the background became a theme in its own right in Italian painting. Numerous representations of the Madonna and Child (Sandro Botticelli's Madonna Campana in 1467, Leonardo da Vinci's Madonna of the Carnation in 1473, Giovanni Antonio Boltraffio's Madonna Litta in 1490, Cima da Conegliano's Madonna and Child in 1496, Raphael's Madonna Esterházy in 1508, etc.), for example, show a glimpse of the background in the second half of the painting.), for example, offer glimpses of landscapes, monuments, mountains or the Italian countryside in the background, through a doorway, vault or window. The viewer's eye is guided and drawn outwards, away from the main subject of the painting (in the same way that our eye, in a more trivial way, is irresistibly drawn to the television screens in certain bars or restaurants, even if the programme being shown is of no particular interest to us).

Holy Trinity, Masaccio, c. 1426-1428, fresco

The invention of perspective introduces an *imbalance*, so to speak, into the work. The vanishing point is in fact a tipping point towards man (it should be noted in this respect that it was from the Renaissance onwards

1. *The Madonna Campana*, Sandro Botticelli, 1467, tempera on panel 2. *The Madonna with the Carnation*, Leonardo da Vinci, 1473, oil on panel 3. *The Madonna Litta*, Giovanni Antonio Boltraffio, 1490, tempera on panel transferred to canvas 4. *The Madonna and Child*, Cima da Conegliano, 1496, oil on panel 5. The Madonna Esterházy, Raphael, oil on canvas 1508

that the figure of the "artist" emerged, and it was also from the Renaissance onwards that artists began to sign their works — the first known example is Giotto di Bondone in the fourteenth century, but it was from the fifteenth century onwards that the act of an artist signing his work began to become widespread). The work of art, first and foremost a concrete manifestation of exteriority and decentring (the opening up of an external space), was therefore also historically *the medium* through which man refocused on himself. By taking himself as the theme and subject of his works (think of Leonardo da Vinci's famous *Vitruvian Man*, which depicts a naked man in two superimposed positions, inscribed in a circle and a square), man completed the historical loop of self-awareness, a loop he had himself inaugurated by representing figures that were purely external to him.

It is not our intention here to take up the famous Hegelian theory that art reflects the development of the human spirit, evolving from symbolic materiality towards an ever more marked expression of interiority and subjectivity — a characteristic, according to Hegel, of medieval and modern Christian art. Nor do we subscribe to the Hegelian idea that art, although it expresses the spirit through a sensible form and constitutes an essential stage in its historical development, is destined to be overtaken by philosophy[122]. Our perspective differs in that we do not see art as being "in tow of the spirit", i.e. as a soluble phenomenon through which the spirit passes "from above" or "behind" man's back. On the contrary, we see it as one of the fundamental sources of the dissociation between man and the world, a dissociation that is not only historical, as Hegel thought, but also individual, inherent in the cognitive development of each human being — hence, in our view, the fundamental role of artistic activities in the development of the child (see in particular the analyses of Jean Piaget[123], Lev Vygotski, Howard Gardner,

---

[122] Hegel sees philosophy as the ultimate manifestation of the absolute, a purely rational and conceptual understanding of the world in which art plays only a secondary role.

[123] According to Piaget, art, particularly drawing, helps to structure children's thinking at every stage of their cognitive development, in particular by enabling them to substitute symbolic representation for concrete action (see Piaget, *La formation du symbole chez l'enfant*, *The Child's Conception of Space*, 1945). Piaget distinguishes two stages in this respect:

- The pre-operational stage (2-7 years) in which the child begins to use symbols to represent objects in the real world. Drawing becomes an essential tool for expressing ideas and feelings. Through art, children develop their ability to manipulate abstract concepts, while developing their sense of symbolic representation (symbolic play).
- The concrete operations stage (7-11 years), in which children begin to understand more complex concepts such as perspective and proportion in drawing. Artistic activities help to reinforce cognitive skills such as spatialisation, categorisation and recognition of relationships between objects.

More generally, Piaget saw art as a tool enabling children to explore the world through mental representations, thereby facilitating the development of their symbolic thinking. His work with the Swiss psychologist Bärbel Inhelder also analysed the way in which children represented their own bodies (see in particular *c*, 1948). According to Piaget and Inhelder, the evolution of children's drawings follows a progressive cognitive development that reflects a growing awareness of the self. The evolution of children's drawings of the human figure— from simple heads with legs— to more complex and detailed representations of the body, for example, shows progress in bodily self-awareness. The child begins to understand that he or she has a distinct body, with different parts, and becomes capable of representing it more realistically. By structuring their drawings, children also learn to perceive themselves as a subject distinct from their environment, with their own identity

Piaget also attaches great importance to creative play in children's development (see Piaget, *La formation du symbole chez l'enfant*, *The Formation of the Symbol in Childhood*, 1945). As we pointed out earlier, art is precisely a form of symbolic play for children. Through play, children learn to differentiate their point of view from that of others and to situate themselves in the social world. By creating works of art or stories, children experience different perspectives, which contributes to their social awareness and understanding that they are individuals among others (see the work of Lev Vygotski on this subject, particularly his 1925 thesis entitled *Psychology of Art*). Through their artistic creations, children explore their ideas and emotions. These activities help them to reflect on themselves as individuals with thoughts, feelings and a distinct subjectivity.

Piaget also insists on the concept of equilibration (see in particular *L'équilibration des structures cognitives, The Equilibration of Cognitive Structures*, Piaget, 1975), a process by which the child seeks to establish a balance between assimilation (integrating new information into existing mental structures) and accommodation (adapting mental structures to integrate new information). For Piaget, art is an area in which the child is constantly experimenting with this balance. When children create a work of art, they explore the world in their own way, then try to organise and represent it according to their mental schemas. This process of striking a balance between what they already know and what they discover in their environment helps them to develop a sense of self, i.e. to recognise themselves as subjects capable of producing unique, personal representations.

For Piaget, art is thus an activity in which children exercise their autonomy by making independent creative decisions, choosing shapes, colours, subjects and techniques to express their ideas and emotions. This process of creative autonomy helps children to develop reflective awareness and autonomous thinking, which is one of the ultimate goals of learning and cognitive development.

Elliot Eisner...). In short, art is not only the historical testimony to the development of the mind, but also, as a dissociative and identifying force, the driving force behind that development. The process of distancing that lies at the root of all artistic activity is a good illustration of the idea of "play" that we mentioned earlier, in a sense similar to that which Wittgenstein employed in his *Philosophical Investigations* on language.

For Wittgenstein in *Philosophical Investigations* (1953, posthumous), language is in fact understood as a 'game' insofar as it responds to rules that depend on specific contexts. Like us, Wittgenstein uses the metaphor of a game to show that language should not be understood as a rigid system of rules or fixed representations in which the meaning of words is defined once and for all, but as an *activity*, a game of the mind, which alone makes and breaks meanings. Each 'language game' has its own rules and conventions that determine how words and phrases are used. For example, the language used in an informal conversation is different from that used in a scientific or legal context. The rules of each language set are established by social practices and contexts of use[124]. In each context or language set,

---

[124] One example springs to mind. In a French comedy, the main character (who is "French by adoption" in the film in question), having got himself into a tricky situation, exclaims: "an Academy is happening to me...". The term "Academy" has never been defined for us, the viewer, as corresponding to the idea of a delicate or inextricable situation. In fact, the form of expression is not even metaphorical, as the concept of an academy has nothing whatsoever to do with the meaning in which it is used by the character. Yet the context

words have specific meanings based on the practices and rules of that context. For example, the word 'bench' can mean a seat in a park or a financial institution, depending on the language game in which it is used. Individuals are free to invent new spaces, new games and new rules (which is the only way that language can evolve). We must therefore be of trying to find universal essences or definitions of language. People learn language not so much by learning definitions, but by participating in language games[125].

In the same way, the individual involved in the process of artistic creation finds himself absorbed in the active dynamics of play. Play is both a creator of spaces (new spaces that generate new rules of their own) and a dynamiter of dead metaphors. This is why there is a

---

makes it easy to understand the new meaning of the word "Academy". In fact, the character could have used any word he clearly didn't understand. It's the context that defines the meaning of the word, not the other way round.

[125] In Paragraph 23 of *Philosophical Investigations*, Wittgenstein gives a list of examples representing the multiplicity of language games: " Forming and testing a hypothesis — Presenting the results of an experiment in tables and diagrams — Making up a story; and reading it — Play-acting — Singing catches — Guessing riddles — Making a joke; telling it — Solving a problem in practical arithmetic — Translating from one language into another — Asking, thanking, cursing, greeting, praying. — It is interesting to compare the multiplicity of the tools in language and of the ways they are used, the multiplicity of kinds of word and sentence, with what logicians have said about the structure of language.", Ludwig Wittgenstein, Philosophical Investigations, trad. G.E.M Anscombe, Basil Blackwell, 1958, p. 128

"history of art", a history that is by its very nature evolutionary, since art cannot be limited to the indefinite repetition of the "already known" (or the "already seen"). There is also in this dynamic approach to language and art the idea that nothing is fixed, that everything is dynamic and playful. Art is a shift in relation to reality, a play with form, within form, a relaxation, a recreation, a dismissal of the world at the same time as an awakening of self-awareness, an awakening that is both happy and painful: happy insofar as it is a revelation of our creative power, unhappy insofar as it is also an understanding of our differentiation from the world, a perception of our limits (properly a "delimitation"), in other words an awareness of our finitude.

The final scene of Sergio Leone's famous Western *The Good, the Bad and the Ugly* (1966) is a good illustration of this artistic dynamic. Art, divested of the question of religion, dispossessed even of the question of man, remains this activity of dissociation, of ironic displacement from the world. In Sergio Leone's cinema, man is no longer idealised, as in the time of Raphael and Leonardo da Vinci. He has descended from the nimbus of the Sistine Chapel and abandoned the circle that was the symbol of his perfectibility — if not his perfection — to become a disillusioned, sneering, grating figure. The Good is not much gentler than the Bad, nor much more virtuous the Ugly. All three embody a brutal humanity, eaten away by greed and original immorality. Their final confrontation, in a cemetery lost in the middle of the desert, evokes a classic figure of vanity: a setting where, under the sweltering sun, dramatic tension and grotesquerie mingle in a play of glances and expectations, revealing all the cruel and derisory absurdity of the human condition. The Good Guy (Clint Eastwood, *aka* Blondin), with his hand on his gun, watches the Bad Guy (Lee Van Cleef, *aka* Sentenza) out of the corner of his eye, who in turn divides his gaze between the Good Guy and the Ugly (Eli Wallach, *aka* Tuco). Ennio Morricone's music, sublime in its factitious grandiloquence, accompanies the resolution of the plot. In reality, everything in this scene sounds wrong (a bizarre situation, characters who are nothing more than caricatures of themselves, the endless length of the scene, music that is inappropriate because of its over-

(Ctrl + Click on the image for online version)

significance) and yet everything rings true. The film's final scene is in fact an illustration of the idea that art is not subservient to reality, that the artist creates his own space, his own parallel reality (which can sometimes adopt the codes of our reality, and sometimes deviate from it without causing us any problem).

The cemetery scene is in fact the site of a triple distancing (a triple play or triple spatial creation): Firstly, the director distances himself from his characters (who are treated as "types", the close-ups of their eyes accentuating the idea that their entire identity is contained in a form of theatrical exteriority), and secondly, he distances himself from the scene itself, This is underlined by the grandiloquence of Ennio Morricone's music (in a way reminiscent of the scene in *New York Stories* entitled *Œdipus Wrecks*, in which Woody Allen's Sheldon Mills eats his chicken, lost in thought, to classical music that is totally out of sync with the action...).); and finally, distancing ourselves from the art itself, which, by becoming the object and setting of the comedy, is immediately and entirely revealed for what it is: a farce, a game, a flippant and superficial buffoonery, out of all depth.

ART AS TRANSUBJECTIVE HUMANISM — THE OTHER CORRESPONDENCE — RELIGIO

ART AND COMMUNITY

25.

ART AND RELIGION — As we have said, art, as an activity that dissociates the *self* from the world, is a process of identifying the *self*, of becoming aware of its autonomous and separate nature. In so doing, it is also a vehicle for the discovery of otherness (a kind of gentle, symbolic otherness). In the process of artistic creation, I discover myself as a dissociated evaluator (I am the one who creates as well as the one who evaluates) in a form of otherness, of exteriority to myself. This exteriority is itself the symbol of the other who is both the other *me* and the other assessor. Art is therefore properly an activity that connects me to myself at the same time as it connects me to others. The work is intended for the other, be it the other *me*, who selects, criticises and evaluates, or the other than me, who is radically external to me. In this respect, the artist's approach (unlike that of the aesthete) is essentially altruistic: it is a projection towards otherness. This "projection towards otherness" (which in a sense resembles Brouwer's concrete formulation of mathematical equations, which is the condition of their communicability) is not necessarily a projection towards the other (who is external to me), but it is a projection towards an external figure who is the aesthete, the evaluator. The artist, in his creative process, is in a schizophrenic position; he is the theatre of a splitting of the *ego*: he must at once rid himself of the critical *ego* and communicate to it the dynamics of his creation in a form that is acceptable, that is to say evaluable. In reality, the artist is already trying, in his creative process, to woo the approval of the aesthete within him. Creation is the embodiment of this bond. The binding dimension of aesthetic judgement had already been clearly perceived by Kant, when in the *Critique of Judgement* he indicated that aesthetic judgement proceeded from a subjective universality, a universality which (not being objective) could only be based on an implicit communication with others. For Kant, aesthetic common sense was precisely this capacity to judge by taking into account the (fictitious) point of view of others[126], — it is what Kant described as the act of "thinking in the place of all others" ("*sich in die Stelle jedes anderen denken*"), the maxim of enlarged thinking[127].

---

[126] When we make a judgement of taste, we must be capable, according to Kant, of "abstracting" ourselves from our own subjective situation and considering the point of view of others by adopting a kind of "disinterested" position (we prefer this term to the idea of disinvestment from the immediate *self*).

[127] See Kant, *Critique of the Faculty of Judgement*, the three maxims of thought. Expanded thinking is part of the maxim of aesthetic judgement, whereby we try to imagine how our judgement might be perceived by others who share with us this universal faculty of judging, albeit subjectively.

These are the maxims: 1. think for yourself; 2. think in the place of everyone else; 3. always think in accordance with yourself.

In aesthetic judgement or appreciation (whether this appreciation is internal or external to the artist) there is therefore the germ of the idea of a link, of a community of judgement (not in the sense that we should all like the same thing according to our community affiliation or our social class, as Pierre Bourdieu theorised, in our opinion excessively, in a 1979 work entitled *La distinction, critique sociale du jugement, Distinction: A Social Critique of the Judgment of Taste*, but rather in the sense that judgements of taste would create *de facto* communities of affinity, links of aesthetic convergence). This is also the bond we are talking about in the religious art we mentioned in the previous chapter. Art is religious insofar as it stems from this binding dynamic. The term religion (need we remind you?) comes from the Latin *religio*, which derives from the

---

The first maxim is unprejudiced thinking, the second is expanded thinking, and the third is consequential thinking.

The first maxim is that reason is never passive. Prejudice is the tendency towards passivity and consequently towards the heteronomy of reason [...].

As far as the second maxim of thought is concerned, we are well accustomed to calling narrow-minded (narrow-minded, the opposite of broad-minded) anyone whose talents are not sufficient for any important purpose (especially one that requires great strength of application). [...]

It is the third maxim, that of the consequent way of thinking, which is the most difficult to put into practice; it can only be done by linking the first two maxims and after having acquired a mastery made perfect by repeated exercise. The first of these maxims can be said to be the maxim of the understanding, the second that of the faculty of judging, and the third that of reason.

verb *religare*, meaning to bind or link[128]. Religion is therefore the locus of the dual relationship between "man and God" and "man and man", while art is both the space and the symbol of this dual relationship. It was undoubtedly because art was the locus of the binding dynamic that it became one of the vectors of religion (in polytheistic religions and then in the Catholic religion in particular). Thus, art was not simply a vehicle for religion (in the sense that it was invested with the mission of communicating and transmitting religion), it was the very dynamic of the bond that holds religions together.

26.

HISTORICISM IN ART, HISTORICISM IN MUSIC — Art has an ambivalent position in human history. As a manifestation of the ontological separation between man and the world, and at the same time an ex-pression of this man-world relationship, it claims a form of timelessness and universalism. However, as a marker of the evolution of this relationship, art is also a historical and temporal manifestation of the relationship between man and the world, and between man and man. This is

---

[128] The Latin root of the term "religion" and its exact origin have been the subject of debate among linguists and historians. The most widely accepted theory is that "religion" comes from the Latin *religio*, derived from the verb *religare*, meaning "to bind" or "to link". However, some researchers suggest that *religio* could also be related to *relegere*, another Latin verb meaning "to reread" or "to consider carefully". This interpretation emphasises the idea of 'repetition' and 'reflection' on religious rites and practices.

why there is a 'history of art', just as there is a history of languages or a history of ideas (see § 10 of this book — *Historicity of music*). As an autonomous discipline, art is also subject to the problem of historicism. On the one hand, art is dependent on the historical conditions in which it develops (the issues and preoccupations of the time); on the other, it depends on its own evolution, i.e. its internal movement, its innovations, the direction of its productions, i.e. its artists. It is impossible to repeat indefinitely what has already been done or said ("Everything has been said, and we have come too late in the more than seven thousand years that there have been men who think", laments La Bruyère in *Les Caractères*). In this respect, art remains intrinsically linked to the time of history, the time of the history of mankind, and also the time of the artist's personal history. The difficulty of creation lies precisely in this ambivalence. The artist, as a historical creature (the history of mankind, his personal history) is dependent on this relationship to the history of art, that is to say to art that is, in short, "already there". But if the artist confines himself to the strict observance of an overwhelming tradition, he remains incapable of creating. He then remains, so to speak, in a purely formal and synthetic relationship with what exists (as can be the case with artificial intelligences which claim to "create" works of art when all they can do — for the moment — is produce a formalism, a synthesis of what exists). The artist is thus at once caught in the dilemma of recognising tradition and demanding a break with it, a demand that cannot either constitute a recipe that would preside over creation, as is unfortunately sometimes the case — it is not in fact enough to break with tradition in order to innovate.

The basis of artistic creativity lies precisely in the non-formal relationship that the artist maintains with the world and with others (again, we use the expression "non-formal" not in the sense of "not embodied in a form" but rather in the sense of "not subject to a formal communication mechanism, a logical formalism"). This non-formal relationship, which is in fact the very structure of duality, characterises the state of openness of the sentient being, openness to the world, openness to itself and to others. Art is therefore a formal manifestation of historicity, but this manifestation does not start from form (from formal and historical synthesis) but from a kind of non-formal impulse towards otherness: the self (the otherness of the *self*), the world, others. The history of art is as much the result of this impulse of the sentient being towards otherness (an impulse that is properly "aesthetic", pre-rational) as it is one of the components of this otherness that makes the artist. It is thus received by the sentient being open to the world, not in what is formal and repeatable, but on the contrary in what is radically other, external to the subject. The artist is thus open to the state of the arts (just as he is open to the sensibility as a whole) not in order to make a synthesis of it, which would be a form of repetition, but in order to renew it in a formalism whose rules he himself defines — the artist gives his rules to art, he does not inherit them from a history that precedes him.

Universalism of Art — Universalism of Death

27.

I TOO AM IN ARCADIA — What is art and how can a work of art interest us, in other words connect with our "deepest *self*", as we suggested earlier? We have begun to try to answer this question— and to provide, I hope, some answers — by suggesting that art is the symptom of man's, the artist's, openness to otherness. But what exactly is the nature of this link between the artist and the world? In our previous comments, we emphasised the 'intermediary' role of the artist, his capacity to receive and transmit (Apollinaire's TSF waves), his ability to look at and observe the world, to allow himself to be seized by things (think, once again, of Rimbaud's letter entitled *Le voyant*). It seemed to us that artistic activity was precisely linked to this state of openness to things, to the artist's readiness to feel them in a different mode from that of the "everyday *self*" (which we contrasted with the "deep *self*"). Contrary to the idea sometimes conveyed of the artist as being 'solitary', 'apart from the world', 'in his ivory tower', it seemed to us, on the contrary, that his main quality had to do with this state of openness to the world, this sensitivity to things.

The artist does not stand above or beside the world, but in the midst of things (he literally takes their *side*, to paraphrase the famous title of Francis Ponge's collection[129]) and people. This central position of the artist in relation to the world is particularly striking in a painting by Nicolas Poussin — undoubtedly one of the most famous — entitled *The Shepherds of Arcadia* (1638), in which three shepherds and a woman stand before a stone tomb in the heart of a pastoral landscape.

Nicolas Poussin, *Et in Arcadia ego* (second version), 1638, oil on canvas

The woman stands slightly back, observing the scene with a serene, almost detached attitude. The shepherds, dressed in classical tunics, are absorbed by the inscription engraved on the tomb, while one of them points to the words, seeming to decipher them: "*Et in Arcadia ego*": I too am in Arcadia. At the very heart of

---

[129] Francis Ponge, *Le parti pris des choses* (*The Nature of Things*)

Arcadia, a mythical pastoral paradise, a place of harmony and happiness, hovers the shadow of finitude and death. If art can be understood as an attempt to overcome finitude (in the same way as knowledge), it is also the expression of this finitude. In Poussin's painting, the tomb, a massive and tragic symbol of finitude, is placed at the centre of the work, in the middle of a landscape that will no doubt outlive its protagonists. The shepherds turn their questioning gaze towards an enigmatic woman (the figure of truth?), who, with one hand on her hip and the other on the shoulder of one of them, seems to be unconcerned by their concern. The artist is among these men, sharing their anguish; he too is in Arcadia, subject to the same doubts and dominated by the same suffering. This, then, is what links the artist to mankind: sensitivity, finitude (the second being the consequence of the first), the intimate certainty of the tragic nature of life and, at the same time, the awareness of his profound relationship to others, to those who share his condition as a human and mortal being. In this way, the work of art bears witness, not so much to an interiority[130] that wants to be exteriorised, but to a

---

[130] Hannah Arendt has written in several places that "if the interior were to appear, we would all resemble each other" (see, for example, *The Life of the Mind* and *The Crisis of Culture*). According to Arendt, the work of art is not so much the fruit of the expression of an "interiority", which is something we partly agree with. It should be noted, however, that the notion of man's openness to which she repeatedly refers (and which refers to the German neologism 'Erschlossenheit', which in Heideggerian philosophy means 'state of being open') is difficult to conceive without the idea of interiority.

relationship, an openness to the world and to others, an openness that can very well be experienced in a negative mode, as in Fernand Khnopff's painting *I Lock my Door upon Myself* ; in this case, the negative mode always refers back to the problem of opening and closing, interiority and exteriority[131] (of what, in short, is me or is not me). In this way, the work of art always means, more or less, "you're not alone[132]" (or "come and get me..."). In reality, there is a form of agreement — or "communion", to use a term often employed — between the artist and the person who receives him as such, in other words, the person who understands and shares his intentions.

Fernand Khnopff, *I lock My Door Upon Myself*, 1891, oil on canvas

---

[131] In fact, the title of Khnopff's painting refers to a line by Christina Rossetti entitled *Who Shall Deliver Me?* which brings us back to the issue of the relationship with the other, experienced here in a negative light.

[132] *"Oh, no love! You're not alone"*, cries David Bowie in the song *Rock'n Roll Suicide* (1972), before adding: *"I've had my share so I'll help you with the pain"*. The artist "suffers with" his creatures.

This 'agreement' is also experienced within the artist as a form of harmony, a correspondence between his *ideal* intention and his work, however imperfect it may be. To take up a Platonic idea, the material production of the work is always seen as a form of degradation of the idea (Plato even speaks of a double degradation, using the example of the bed made by the craftsman, which would already be a degradation of the idea of a bed, while the bed represented by the artist would be a degradation of the bed made[133]). This brings to mind a passage from a book by Thomas Bernhard entitled *Old Masters* (1985), in which the hero, an inflexible disciple of a decadent aesthete, declares, quoting his master: "Art is the greatest and at the same time the most repulsive thing, he said. But we must persuade ourselves that great art, sublime art, exists, he said, otherwise we despair. Even if we know that all art ends up clumsy and ridiculous and in the dustbin of history, like everything else, we must, *with perfect assurance*, believe in great art and sublime art, he said." In this passage by Thomas Bernhard, we find the Platonic idea of the degraded and imperfect nature of the work ("all art ends in awkwardness"). But there is also the idea that great art, "sublime" art, exists, even if this *ideal* existence (in which we must believe "with perfect assurance") has perhaps never yet manifested itself in our world. The extreme contradiction that Thomas

---

[133] See Plato, *The Republic*, Book X: this Platonic view of art seems to us to be based on an erroneous idea of art, which in Plato would rest above all on the idea of μίμησις, i.e. copying, artistic activity being primitively understood in *The Republic* as an activity of copying the idea or copying the materialisation of the idea (the bed).

Bernard's hero describes in his analysis of art ("that which is greatest and at the same time most repugnant") is of particular interest to us insofar as it points to this dichotomy of art, which is at once the surpassing of finitude, the ideal ("that which is greatest") and the desolate attempt to materialise this surpassing. The work of art is literally repugnant, because it is materiality, the human (all too human?) expression of an impossible perfection. But isn't it precisely this impossible quest for perfection that makes art great? Indeed, isn't art born of this impossibility? Doesn't the work itself become a 'work' because of its shortcomings and im-perfections?

We tried to develop a similar idea earlier, when we analysed the role of signifying ruptures in the narrative of great musical works (see *Music and Time*, § 19 — *Narration and rupture*). Ruptures in the narrative (chromaticism, rhythmic breaks, etc.) are, as we have said, what constitute the (human) signifying character of the work. Over and above the significance of these deliberate breaks, it is sometimes possible to perceive, in the line spacing and connections between two musical phrases, moments of hesitation on the part of the artist. It is precisely these moments of anxiety, these sometimes-clumsy attempts to restart a musical line that seems to be running out of steam or going astray, that constitute, in our view, the very essence of creative genius. David Bowie's song *Life on Mars* (1971) is one of many examples — of what we are trying to describe here. In the song's lyrics, David Bowie tells the story of a young girl disillusioned with reality, who seeks escape through cinema and popular culture. The question "*Is there life on Mars?* is not just an existential one: it also expresses our aspiration to another reality, one that is wider and more meaningful, beyond the narrow world of everyday life. At the heart of the song, between the fourth and fifth verses, Bowie introduces a deliberate break, what is commonly known as a "bridge" — a term borrowed from the "harmonic bridges" or "modular transitions" of classical music, later taken up by jazz and big band in the early twentieth century, before becoming a staple of blues and rock'n'roll.

(Ctrl + Click on the image for online version)

As the first part of the song draws to a close, just after the first chorus ("*Sailors fighting in the dance hall — Oh man, look at those cavemen go — It's the freakiest show...*"), a short instrumental sequence underlines the tragedy of this "*God-awful small affair*". In the video, Bowie closes his eyes, grips his arm and swings his foot slightly in a posture of suspended

expectation. It is at this precise moment that the break occurs. The rhythm slows down, the piano chords muffled before Bowie's voice picks up again: "*It's on America's tortured brow — That Mickey Mouse has grown up a cow*". It is in this uneasy transition, in this almost tangible hesitation, that greatness is revealed.

As Pascal said, "Continuity is disgusting in every-thing; greatness needs to be left behind in order to be felt[134]." Greatness thus lies in differentiation, in the ebb and flow of melody, similar to the movement of waves, as Pascal points out in fragment no. 2/7 of the *Pensées diverses*, whose layout we have tried to respect below:

"Nature acts by progress. *Itus et reditus*, it passes and returns, then goes further, then twice as far, then more than ever, etc.".

The sea flows like this. The sun seems to walk like this:

The artist, in these moments of anxiety — which are, in short, nothing other than the moments when the form,

---

[134] The exact quotation from Pascal's *Pensées* is: « La grandeur a besoin d'être quittée pour être sentie. La continuité dégoûte en tout. » ("Greatness needs to be left to be felt. Continuity is disgusting in everything.")

having reached its end, no longer unfolds on its own and turns back to him as if to find out what happens next, in the image of the shepherd turning towards the serene figure of the woman-truth —, reveals himself in his humanity, in his original state of "open being". In this way, the work of art is a bridge that links the artist, people and humanity as a whole in the expression of a common condition and in the recognition of a community of destinies.

28.

MUSIC AND ORPHEUS — According to the well-known Greek myth, Orpheus was an exceptional musician, the son of King Oeager and the muse Calliope, the muse of epic poetry. He played the lyre with such mastery that his music enchanted everything around him. People, animals, trees and even stones were enchanted by his melodies. Orpheus fell in love with the beautiful nymph Eurydice, and they married. But their happiness was short-lived. One day, Eurydice was bitten by a snake and died. She was sent to the kingdom of the dead, which plunged Orpheus into immense grief. Unable to bear the loss of his love, Orpheus decided to descend to the Underworld to bring Eurydice back to life. Thanks to his music, he managed to soften the heart of Charon, the ferryman of the dead, who agreed to take him across the Styx, the river of the Underworld. Even Cerberus, the fearsome three-headed dog that guards the Underworld, was appeased by Orpheus' melodies. Arriving before Hades and Persephone, the rulers of the Underworld, Orpheus played a melody so moving that it made the damned souls weep and softened the heart of Hades. Hades, moved by

Orpheus' determination and love, agreed to return
Eurydice to him, but on one condition: Orpheus was
not to turn to look at Eurydice until they had left the
Underworld. Orpheus agreed and set off with Eurydice
to return to the world of the living. However, Orpheus
succumbed to doubt, worried that he could no longer
hear Eurydice's footsteps behind him. Just before
passing through the last gate of the Underworld, he
turned to make sure she was following him. Eurydice
was indeed there, but as soon as their eyes met, she was
instantly sent back to the realm of the dead, this time
forever.

Orpheus is the symbol of the artist who, in his attempt
to represent the object of his desire, is confronted with
the incompleteness of his achievement. Eurydice is
both present and absent: as soon as Orpheus tries to
seize her by the incantatory evocation of his lyre, she
appears, only to evaporate immediately into the limbo
of memory. The myth of Orpheus, as in *Les Bergers
d'Arcadie*, reveals the profound link between art and
death (death as a human condition, but also as a symbol
of finitude, negativity, lack and absence). In Orphism,
the attempt to overcome death through evocation is
also a form of reaching out to the other, in his absence.
Through the figure of Orpheus, we sense that art is a
kind of journey towards a beyond (which, in the case
of Orpheus, is more a 'beyond'), a beyond that can
certainly be experienced as a projection towards death,
but also as a search for origins. In this way, music, and
works of art in general, can be understood as an
unveiling, a reminiscence of something we already had
inside us, as the evocation of a diffuse memory, even if

this memory has never actually been experienced[135], so that we sometimes have the feeling that we have been understood by the artist, as much as we have understood him.

---

[135] This brings to mind a song by Nino Ferrer called *La Rua Madureira* (1969), in which he recalls the memory of a lost love: a Brazilian woman he had met in the bay of Rio, who died in the crash of the plane in which the narrator was accompanying her. It sounds like the painful story of a lost love, but the song ends with the artist confessing that he has never been to Rio (and probably never knew the Brazilian woman whose death he mourns).

No, I'll never forget the bay of Rio
The colour of the sky along Corcovado
Rua Madureira, the street you used to live on
I'll never forget but I've never been there
No, I'll never forget that day in July
When I met you and we had to part
Such a short time and we walked in the rain
I spoke of love and you spoke of your country
No, I won't forget the softness of your body
In the taxi taking us to the airport
You turned to smile at me before getting in
In a Caravelle that never arrived.

The song concludes with these words:

I'll never forget it but I've never been there
I won't forget but I've never been there

29.

MUSIC AND MORAL LAW — In several passages of *The Republic*, Plato deals with music not directly in its aesthetic dimension (i.e. in the relationship of meaning it has with our sensibility and reason) but above all in its didactic and moral applications. Thus, Plato almost systematically (and somewhat disconcertingly for us) links music and gymnastics. In the same way that gymnastics is a healthy activity for the body and for health," writes Plato, "(appropriate) music would be a healthy activity for the soul. Education thus consists of "to train the body through gymnastics and the soul through music[136]." This didactic and, it has to be said, quasi-military approach to music — Plato repeatedly stresses the importance of music in training warriors — seems far removed from our considerations. On closer examination, however, we find a number of points in Plato's thinking that converge with our own. First, Plato clearly identifies music as a form of *logos* and as such is linked to the issue of truth. In Book II of *The Republic*, he writes: "How? — Don't speeches belong to the realm of music? — And aren't there two kinds of speech, some true and some false? — Yes[137]." By considering that music is part of the field of language (or, more precisely, that speech is part of music, i.e. that language is part of the field of music), Plato establishes a form of equivalence that we reject. If there are true speeches and untrue speeches, it is not so much because of their internal structure as because of their purpose (a tribune tells the truth, arranges the facts to

---

[136] Op. cit., book II
[137] Op. cit., Book II

his advantage, lies...). On the contrary, since music has no object (it is not a discourse that enters into the problem of adequacy or correspondence with the object), it cannot be said, as *such,* to be true or untrue. Music indicates nothing, designates nothing. It is not a discourse on facts. Even though Plato initially seems to establish a relationship of equivalence between music and discourse (argued *logos*), he never really brings music into the problem of correspondence. In fact, in *The Republic*, criticism of musical "discourse" is gradually transformed into criticism of the effects of music, i.e. the nature of the feelings it inspires: "— What are the plaintive harmonies? Tell me, for you are a musician. — It's the mixed lydia and the treble, and a few others like them. — You should therefore leave out these harmonies, which, far from being good for men, are not even good for women of an honest character. — Yes, nothing is more unworthy of the guardians of the State than drunkenness, sluggishness and indolence[138]." For Plato, musical harmony seems to obey objective principles that support harmonic automatisms — just as we assert today by associating, for example, the minor mode with melancholy[139]. There is thus a kind of table of correspondences according to which certain harmonies are intrinsically good or bad, depending on the moral and psycho-

---

[138] Ibid., Book III

[139] There are many examples of sad or melancholy melodies in the major mode. To name just a few: *Tears in Heaven* by Eric Clapton (A major), *Yesterday* by the Beatles (F major), *Pale Blue Eyes* by the Velvet Underground (G major), *Don't Think Twice It's Alright* by Bob Dylan (G major), *La sonate au Clair de Lune* by Debussy (D flat major)...

logical effect they produce on the listener. The criterion for judgement is thus based on the music's capacity to inspire either a feeling of strength and elevation, or on the contrary a form of softness or relaxation, influencing the soul in a direction deemed beneficial or harmful. We will not dwell here on Plato's comments (which are more value judgements than critical analyses, and which paradoxically[140] are in some ways reminiscent of the materialist analyses of Jean-Pierre Changeux, for example), but it is interesting to note that the philosophy of Socrates, which Plato reports and comments on, already contains this idea of a link between music and the moral law. Later on, Plato gives an argument which seems to us to be more admissible: "If music, my dear Glaucon, is the principal part of education, is it not because rhythm and harmony have the supreme power to penetrate the soul, to take possession of it, to introduce beauty into it and to subject it to its empire, when education has been proper, instead of the opposite happening when it is neglected? If a young man is properly brought up on music, will he not grasp with astonishing sagacity what is defective and imperfect in the works of art and nature, and will he not feel a just and painful impression of them? By the same token, will he not praise what is beautiful with delight, and gather it into his soul to nourish himself and thereby become a virtuous man, while everything ugly will be for him the object of legitimate reproach and aversion, and this from his earliest youth, before he can realise it in the name of reason, reason which later, when it arrives, he will

---

[140] We say 'paradoxically' because Plato is the most important of the idealists.

welcome with tenderness, because by virtue of the intimate relationship between it and the education he has received, it will appear to him in familiar guise[141]? Here, Plato suggests that the rules of musical harmony prepare and educate the "young man" (Plato had the ideas of his time about the role of women in society and their education...), not only to exercise his aesthetic judgement, but also and above all to prepare for the exercise of his moral judgement. In Plato's view, musical education is therefore an education in the rules of harmony, perfection and beauty. This awareness should enable the young man to identify the imperfections and faults of art and nature, just as he will grasp with clear-sightedness the baseness and ugliness of amoral behaviour, for "dialectic, tempered by music; it alone, once established in the soul, sustains there all the conserving life of virtue[142]". Here again, the purely didactic role of music seems outdated and the Socratic conception of harmony rather remote from our own problems. It is worth noting, however, that the foundations of the relationship between aesthetics, ethics and truth (the Beautiful, the Good, the True) were already laid in ancient Greece.

If there are links between aesthetics and ethics, it seems to us that they should be sought not only in education in formal judgement (which is what Plato emphasises when he talks about the rules of harmony, the ability to hear the flaws in a melody, etc.) but also in the recognition, through music and through the notion of art in general, of a human community, a community

---

[141] Ibid.
[142] Ibid., Book VIII

that shares the same relationship with the world (a relationship that is not limited to pure formalism, but which is based on the same values).) but also in the recognition, through music and through the notion of art in general, of a human community, a community that shares the same relationship with the world (a relationship that is not limited to pure formalism, but that mobilises man in all his dimensions, sensitive, emotional, imaginative, social, rational, critical, moral...). In short, art, through its signifying dimension, is a production which, starting from the human condition, describes it in all its directions and all its dimensions. In this respect, art is, it seems to us, always a hand outstretched towards otherness (whether real or fantasised, as we have already mentioned), a hand outstretched that is the symbol and manifestation of that primitive movement of projection towards the other that contains within it the possibility of morality (as we shall see in greater depth in Book III).

What is Aesthetic Knowledge: From the Subjective to the Objective

30.

MUSIC AND KNOWLEDGE: THE TRAGIC — While Plato establishes a clear link between music and truth in *The Republic*, this link mainly concerns the form of music (rhythm, harmony, etc.), which Plato likens to the form of speech in common language. However, this comparison does not directly concern the *content* of discourse. Plato certainly points out that music has a seductive power, a "charm that disturbs the soul", but for Plato this musical power is a matter of suggestion, not of the work's meaningful content. In Greek theatre, however, music is immediately linked to the problem of truth as a signifying content (and not as a formal balance). In tragedy, it is the choruses that announce past or future events to the hero. They also embody a kind of "objective point of view" (which sometimes does not preclude controversy within the chorus), detached from the action and passions that drive the heroes. From the very beginnings of thought, music has been linked to the question of truth and is the vehicle for an attempt to go beyond subjective points of view to achieve a vision that is free from particular interests. In this respect, the choruses convey a truth that the hero often refuses to hear: In Aeschylus' *Agamemnon*, for example, after the victory at Troy, the chorus of Argos elders warns Agamemnon against Clytemnestra, his wife, whose daughter has been sacrificed with Agamemnon's consent in exchange for favourable winds and victory at Troy. Agamemnon ignores these warnings and enters Clytemnestra's palace, where he is murdered. In Sophocles' *Oedipus Rex*, the chorus implores Oedipus not to pursue his investigation to discover the truth about his origins, while in Sophocles' *Antigone* it is Creon who refuses the chorus' advice, preferring to assert his authority as head of state rather than follow divine law. In Greek tragedy, the chorus is the symbol of the "objective music" that torments the hero, a kind of externalisation of the internal voice that, in modern representations, will become that of the conscience. In Greek tragedy, this externalisation of the human conscience also manifests itself as a humanisation of the divine, with the choruses often playing the role of intermediaries or spokesmen for the gods.

The structure of this dialogue between two opposing lines (which is still characteristic of *radical* dualism) can be found in a large number of more contemporary musical works. Two examples come to mind: Mozart's *Requiem*, in which the choirs play a role close to that of Greek tragedy, and (in a completely different register) the song *The Show Must Go On*, by the group Queen[143]. In the *Requiem*, the text, based on the liturgy of the Mass of the Dead (*Missa pro defunctis*), expresses fear of the Last Judgement, supplication for divine mercy and anguish in the face of the inevitability of death. The *Dies Irae*, for example, evokes Judgement Day, when souls are judged for their earthly deeds. The choir sings with dramatic intensity, expressing the terror of that moment when God's wrath will fall upon sinners:

---

[143] The well-known British rock band...

Dies irae, dies illa
Solvet saeclum in favilla [144]

This is the theme of the universal music of the Apocalypse. As in Greek tragedy, man is confronted with the inescapable nature of his destiny, as well as with a form of cold truth that is expressed through the indifference of the gods (which is, in a sense, that of the implacable character of the melody that continues its logical development to its terrible conclusion). In the *Lacrimosa*, the chorus sings of the sadness of the weeping and tears of the day when the soul will be judged. This moment evokes the suffering and pain of the final moment, when everything hangs in the balance:

Lacrimosa dies illa
Qua resurget ex favilla[145]

The intensity of the chorus gradually builds, accentuating the tragic emotion linked to the inevitable end of life and the confrontation with nothingness.

The song *The Show Must Go On* uses the structure of this opposition between the singer's voice and that of the backing vocals.

Freddie Mercury, who knows he is gravely ill and feels the end is near, is confronted by the truth of the chorus, which repeats his plea:

---

[144] A day of anger
Will turn the world to ashes
[145] That day will be full of tears,
When will rise from the ashes

I'll soon be turning, round the corner now
Outside the dawn is breaking
But inside in the dark I'm aching to be free

Unlike the choruses in Greek tragedy, however, the choruses in the song do not take the side of the gods.

(Ctrl + Click on the image for online version)

 On the contrary, they stand behind the hero to reject the unacceptable and to proclaim another truth: *The show must go on!* The show must go on! The gods have no right to take the hero's soul. They must submit to the will of man. The truth is certainly overwhelming, but it is also unfair. The song ends with this last desperate declaration from the hero:

I'll top the bill
I'll overkill
I have to find the will to carry on

The chorus continues:

...on with the show
...on with the show
Show must go on, go on, go on, go on, go on, go on, go on, go on

The dialogue between man and the gods is transformed here into man's revolt against the gods. The revolt, however, breaks against the wall of reality, which will continue to exist with or without the un-happy hero (*go on, go on, go on, go on, go on, go on, go on, go on, go on...*). Music is precisely where this revolt takes place (even if revolt is not necessarily the theme). It is the moment of the confrontation of the artist's subjectivity with the implacable indifference of objective reality, which imposes its tragic truth on man: that of incompleteness, finitude and death.

31.

THE BEAUTIFUL AND THE TRUE — At the end of chapter 29, we drew a connection between the Good, the Beautiful and the True that was prompted by an intuition Plato had had in *The Republic*, admittedly in a way that was far removed from our issues. As far as we were concerned, this connection was dictated to us by the structure of music — a structure that indicated a proximity to that of all organised discourse (as Plato notes) — by its themes and by its signifying content. We have tried to show that music does not necessarily have a defined object (unlike discourse, which refers to objects outside itself), but that it does have, *by its very structure*, a signification, that is to say, a content of truth. The significance of music (and of art in general) lay precisely, in our opinion, in the expression of a confrontation, that of identity and difference — identity of the artist who defined himself as an organised whole, differentiation in hollow with reality and with the other that the artist understood in his work as exteriorities. The specific character (i.e. authentic[146], *not borrowed*) of this expression is what we call, in our theory of aesthetics, *truth*.

Aesthetic truth, from the artist's point of view, is based on a profound experience of the questions that arise from his or her relationship with the world, with things and with beings. The work of art is the formal (and therefore communicable: the artistic form is a projection towards others) manifestation of this experience. This is the meaning of the famous passage (so often quoted) from Rainer Maria Rilke's *Letters to a Young Poet* (1929): "Be patient with all that is unresolved in your heart and try to love the questions themselves,

---

[146] We want to avoid entering the problematic of authenticity which we find in Heidegger and which, in our opinion, takes us out of the realm of philosophy and into the realm of value judgements and ideology, see Theodor Adorno, *The Jargon of Authenticity* (1964). Adorno criticises Heidegger's philosophy, particularly his use of language, which he accuses of mystifying and manipulating. Heidegger's concepts of authenticity and being are abstract, decontextualised and inaccessible to ordinary people. According to Adorno, Heidegger would use pseudo-profound language to evoke notions such as authentic existence, without this having any real philosophical clarity or tangible meaning. Adorno was suspicious of the elitist and obscure nature of Heidegger's language, which he saw as a way of imposing a kind of 'philosophical mysticism' that distanced him from concrete philosophical issues.

like locked rooms or books written in a very foreign language. Don't look now for answers that can't be given to you, because you wouldn't be able to live them. And it's about living everything. Live the questions now. Perhaps, one day in the future, you will enter into the answer, little by little, without noticing it. Art, before being formal communication, is thus an experience of reality ("it is a question of living everything", writes Rilke), an experience "within us" of this dual confrontation with the outside world. Before we can express life, we have to live it and feel it. Art, like all authentic creation, is not a simple exercise in synthesising, summarising or amalgamating past productions. This is why, when artists seek *their own truth*, they are also seeking the truth, in the sense that their search is both a personal exploration and a quest for the universal (a search for that which in me goes beyond my person, the surface of the everyday, trivial *self*). Artistic research thus involves what we have called a "dismissal of the *self*", in other words a withdrawal of the *ego* that allows itself to be seized by the question posed by reality. This dismissal of the *ego* gives rise to the outline of the artistic form, its signifying content. The artist's truth is the moment of *agreement* between the *form* and its signifying content, between the Dionysian and the Apollonian, if we want to put it in Nietzschean terms. This agreement is first and foremost an internal validation. The musician, when he finds a musical line, a theme, a rhythm, a connection, knows that he has *found* what he was confusedly looking for. The finding manifests itself in the music in the form of *agreement* between the artist's *ideal* projection (his confused anticipation of the development of the melody, for example) and the materialisation of this projection in the note, theme or melodic line. This idea of harmony could lend credence to a theory of 'aesthetic Platonism' (although, as we have seen, Plato is in fact very far removed from the problems of this 'aesthetic Platonism', which was particularly prevalent in the second half of the nineteenth century among the theoreticians of symbolism[147]). It should be noted, however, that when we talk about the agreement between the idea and its materialisation, we are not talking about the Platonic problem of mimicry, according to which the work of art is a simple copy of a pre-existing idea. Artistic creation does not consist in faithfully reproducing an immutable image, as if the artist simply had to transcribe an ideal model with application. On the contrary, the creative process must be seen as a constantly evolving dynamic, a dialogue between the artist and the material, which imposes its own resistances, constraints and demands. Far from being a simple medium for execution, the material questions, guides and sometimes even challenges the artist's initial project. The sculptor, for example, cannot ignore the density and properties of marble or wood, which offer active resistance, demanding constant adjustments. The same applies to musicians, poets and painters, whose work never emerges from a single block but is the result of a process of composition. To create is to compose: with matter, with language, with sound. It's a process of negotiation in which the initial intention is refined and transformed by the constraints of the medium, until a singular form emerges that is

---

[147] See Geoffroy de Clisson, *L'image de la femme ou le renversement symboliste de l'idée de vérité* (2013), doctoral thesis. (*The Image of Woman or the Symbolist Reversal of the Idea of Truth*)

neither the simple execution of an ideal, nor an entirely random construction. The composition is made up of to-ing and fro-ing, retreats and advances. The creative process is therefore not linear. It is a dynamic process that can be analysed as a kind of recursive loop between ideas (the artist's *ideal* projections) and their materialisation (the response of reality, the response of the work). It is from this recursive loop, this trial and error, that the feeling of agreement emerges. Agreement is the resolution of a problem posed by the creative process. It is a form of correspondence between the *ideal* projection and its materialisation, as well as a dynamic confirmation of the validity of this correspondence by the work (the judgement of validity that the artist pronounces internally is made on the work that unfolds in a global vision and proceeds dynamically).

In *The Overcoming of Metaphysics through Logical Analysis of Language*[148] (1931), Rudolf Carnap writes: "the metaphysician is like a musician without musical talent". On other occasions, Carnap compares metaphysics to poetry. He acknowledges, for example, that metaphysics can have an expressive value — like a poem that evokes feelings or visions of the world — while criticising the idea that it can provide objective or verifiable knowledge. This comparison between metaphysics, music and poetry seems to us highly relevant. Like the metaphysician, the musician and the poet work to build a coherent edifice from which they unwind the thread; like the metaphysician, they seek the

---

[148] Rudolf Carnap, *Überwindung der Metaphysik durch Logische Analyse der Sprache*

elegance of ex-pression[149] ; like the metaphysician, they are not directly linked to facts or to what we call "reality". However, the parallel is not limited to metaphysics. A whole section of mathematics could in fact have these characteristics, either because it did not originally have a direct link with the facts or with reality, or because these links were not identified until long after its development. In a sense, physical theories, before they can be tested, can also have a (structural) value, disconnected from their applicative content. So, before they resonate with or correspond to the facts, logical theories (mathematical, physical or metaphysical) are always looking for a form of internal truth (which the mathematician, physicist or metaphysicist perceives externally as such). In the same way that we perceive the internal coherence of a theory or a melody, we can also notice its limits, facilities or dissonances. A work of art, like any speculative theory, can be badly constructed (involuntary dissonances, repetitions, ponderousness, etc.), badly executed (errors of perspective in painting, errors in the choice of colours, false notes, etc.) or badly interpreted (exaggerations, misinterpretations, etc.). It is certainly not subject to the sanction of facts (it does not explain reality, except when it tries to be didactic — which takes it out of the field of art) but it nonetheless calls for an internal

---

[149] It could be argued that musicians and poets are not necessarily looking for elegance. Are Baudelaire's poem *Une charogne (The Flowers of Evil)* or the Sex Pistols' song *God Save the Queen (God save the Queen - The fascsit regime...*) elegant? Our answer to this objection is that elegance lies in the balance of the compositions and the economy of means, and not necessarily in the theme of the works.

agreement that is a recognition of the correspondence between the material of art and the form of the work. This recognition of the correspondence, which is achieved by the artist's sensibility as well as by his critical sense, is similar in many ways to the recognition of the scientist to whom the solution to a problem he had previously allowed himself to be penetrated suddenly appears. This moment of resolution, as we set out to show in Book I, is not rational or critical in nature, but aesthetic. The artist, the mathematician, the chess player, the physicist or the genius scientist are always looking for the right form, the theme, the sequence of notes, the overall explanation. As Max Bill, a constructivist architect influenced by Bauhaus ideas, wrote in a book entitled *Form*: "Art is the expression of mathematical thought made visible". While we would not go so far as to assert with Max Bill that the artist is a mathematician (or like Carnap that the metaphysician is a musician without talent), we must nevertheless note the common origin of all the creative activities of the mind. Creation is first and foremost an intuition of forms, an intuition nourished by reality (what I perceive as external and differentiated) and which in turn is made real and communicable in the work, in the mathematical formula or in the scientific theory. The production of knowledge always stems from a *radical* dualism, in other words from a meaningful confrontation between two entities that cannot be assimilated to one another. To deny this confrontation is to deny any possibility of knowing the world, of knowing ourselves and recognising ourselves as an organised identity, capable of feeling, evaluating and judging.

32.

DOES METAPHOR PRODUCE KNOWLEDGE? — In 1965 debate with Pierre Bourdieu, Jean Hyppolite and the Lacanian psychoanalyst Jean Laplanche, the linguist Georges Mounin urged his interlocutors to be wary of correspondences and to handle with care methods and paradigms that are transposed from one field to another[150]. Mounin reminds us, for example, that applying the method of structural linguistics outside the field of linguistics can be problematic and misleading (this is not an innocent remark, since we are in the midst of a structuralist trend, from which two of Mounin's three interlocutors are more or less directly descended). When I talk about general linguistics," Mounin explains, "I'm not giving a lesson on painting. Language is a code, but not all codes are languages.

(Ctrl + Click on the image for online version)

---

[150] Le Langage 2 : Pierre Bourdieu, Jean Hyppolite, Jean Laplanche, Georges Mounin, Gallica, BNF.

As a code, language has very specific properties that are not found in other codes. It is a two-stage code, articulated twice. Whenever there is natural language, we find units that have both form and meaning ("words"). We can reuse these units in different contexts ("I have a headache", "You behaved *badly*"). These units are not insegmentable; they are themselves constructed from non-significant units, purely distinctive units that are phonemes. Unlike crows," explains Mounin, "we don't have fourteen distinct messages, but an infinity of messages (an infinity of messages that is supported by an evolutionary mobility of meaning and words). From this point of view, Mounin develops, we need to understand that linguists specialise in *language* and not in the *code* — for example the code between the artist and the spectator. To speak of the 'grammar' of a particular filmmaker or the 'syntax' of a particular dancer is to assume that the problem of communication has been solved (code, unlike words, is characterised by its univocity). We must therefore be wary of metaphors," says Mounin.

In the field of language, metaphors are the vector of the trembling of meaning, of the relationship between words and their meaning, but we must not confuse formal systems and language. Formal systems are based on the stability of meaning (on intangible axioms and variables without substance). Language, on the other hand, evolves. The word is never fixed in an immutable definition, hence the difficulty of constructing a formal theory of concepts (a difficulty repeatedly emphasised by Gödel himself, who clearly differentiates language from formal systems). Non-formalist theorists such as philosophers must always bear in mind this fundamental problem: in the field of the hard sciences as in that of the human sciences, we must be wary of overly obvious links and superficial correspondences. The production of knowledge does not come from the formal handling of words. Words are neither codes nor symbols. That's why, when analysing the facts, we must beware of getting drunk on formalism, or to put it trivially, of 'paying lip service' to words. Words only have value in relation to the reality they designate. Metaphor can only produce knowledge if it is a 'living metaphor', a correspondence that starts from reality and not a purely formal equivalence between symbols without substance.

Some philosophy students (and sometimes even some established philosophers) often make the mistake of confusing language with a formal system and treating concepts as if they were codes or symbols that could be manipulated within a given formalism (mathematical formalism, for example). One of the most common errors, for example, is to personify concepts: "reason makes it possible to...", "it is morality that...". This kind of reasoning deals with complex concepts (whose meaning has not been explicitly defined) as if they were fixed entities whose meaning was immutable and identical for everyone (the problem of communication is assumed to have been solved, as Mounin says). These structures of reasoning are similar to purely formal propositions such as $f(x) = y$, where x is assumed to be defined once and for all (whereas x is often precisely what is being defined).

33.

IS BEAUTY SUBJECTIVE OR OBJECTIVE? — The question of the objectivity of beauty is linked, more than we think, to the question of the objectivity of knowledge. From the end of the nineteenth century onwards, with the work of Nietzsche and Bergson in particular, the classical categories of objectivity and subjectivity, which were criticised — no doubt partly with good reason — for a certain rigidity that had the effect of polarising philosophical thought around fixed concepts, were gradually abandoned in favour of a vocabulary that placed greater emphasis on individual experience, on the flow of life and on the interconnection between the interior and the exterior. This abandonment of the subjective-objective pairing, which was in a sense salutary in that it allowed us to re-examine our relationship to the world with a new vocabulary, also had the consequence of opening the Pandora's box of anti-rationalism. As a result, much of twentieth-century philosophy (particularly the philosophy of continental Europe) thrived on criticism of the notions of objectivity and subjectivity, and on the destruction of the philosophy of knowledge, the dismantling of man (it was no longer a question of man, but at best of being or *Dasein*), the disintegration of aesthetics (aesthetics as an instrument of domination of the ruling classes over the proletariat, as a Pavlovian reflex...) and the elimination of the aesthetic (the aesthetic as an instrument of domination of the ruling classes over the proletariat, as a Pavlovian reflex...).)

and the elimination of morality[151]. With its materialist presuppositions, the epistemological framework of modern science provided a convenient justification for abandoning this dichotomy, which seemed outdated. However, with the abandonment of the subjective-objective couple, the problematic of signification was also abandoned, without really realising it. Outside dualism (symbolised by the subject-object pair in classical philosophy), it became impossible, as we set out to show, to think about man's relationship to the world, that is, to think about man in his singularity as a sentient and rational being.

In the field of aesthetics, the negation of dualism resulted, as we have already mentioned, in the development of theories whose contradictions we have attempted to highlight (musical Darwinism, Bourdieu's critique of aesthetic judgement, etc.). With regard to aesthetics, the argument that seemed to us to be both the most widespread and the most worthy of interest was that of psychologism (an argument derived from materialist and Darwinist theories): does aesthetic feeling derive from a simple psychological mechanism? Are we, in other words, conditioned to beauty?

For us, the argument of psychologism was particularly specious because of its incompleteness. No one can deny, in fact, that at the origin of aesthetic feeling there must be, let us say, a particular predisposition to take pleasure in certain combinations. As we mentioned at

---

[151] On this subject, see Geoffroy de Clisson, *Les Anti-humanistes ou l'avènement des Contre-Lumières*, published by L'Harmattan, 2023 (The Anti-Humanists or the Rise of the Counter-Enlightenment)

the beginning of this book (see *Is music the result of a Darwinian evolutionary process?* § 2 — *Evolution in music*), we can well admit that our sensitivity to harmonies or to certain combinations of colours is the result of innate and ingrained mechanisms. Nobody would deny the importance of acquired knowledge, the pleasure we derive from repeating combinations we have known, seen or heard since childhood. However, the error of psychologism, like that of materialism and of all monist theory in general, was to push its advantage too far by trying to establish a systematic equivalence between the feeling of pleasure and the feeling of aesthetics (in the same way that Nietzsche, for example, clumsily tried to establish a total equivalence between truth and the partisan interest we take in what we call "truth"). On the contrary, we have endeavoured to demonstrate that there is nothing mechanical about this equivalence between the feeling of pleasure and the feeling of aesthetics, and that the assimilation of one to the other is more of a stunt than a rigorous demonstration. By neglecting the dynamic and retroactive dimension of aesthetic judgement, psychological analysis confined itself to the pure immediacy of the satisfaction of an instinctive need (which for some was a matter of genetics or epigenetics[152]). As a result, like all monistic theories, it neglected the problem of meaning, which is the only way of understanding the question of art and linking it to aesthetic judgement. We have thus attempted to show that, while aesthetic judgement is partly a matter of psychology (the pleasure we take in certain combinations and their repetition), it cannot be

---

[152] See Pierre Boulez, Jean-Pierre Changeux, Philippe Manoury, *Les neurones enchantés* (*The Enchanted Neurons*)

reduced to that. As sentient beings (with a spirit of finesse, to put it another way), we are capable, for example, of spotting seductive strategies (the repetition of hackneyed combinations, ponderousness, ease, etc.). We are also capable of stepping outside our aesthetic prejudices to rise to the level of meaning, of the direction of the work, of its deeper meaning. This is why we can affirm that there is a form of *objectivity* in beauty, not in the sense that we could discuss the objectivity of science or the objectivity of facts, but in the sense that aesthetic feeling, through its signifying dimension, would constitute a form of elevation in relation to our prejudices, our quick or immediate judgements, in short, in relation to what we could call our "restricted subjectivity". The objectivity of aesthetic feeling is therefore linked to the very root of the word objectivity: the object, from the Latin word *objectum*, literally means "that which is placed before" or "that which is thrown before". Aesthetic judgement is precisely this movement of displacement and enlargement: it does not assert itself in the immediacy of the feeling of pleasure or displeasure, but on the contrary is understood in a form of reflexive displacement. Aesthetic judgement is an evaluative judgement as well as an existential engagement with the work. In fact, the interpretation of a musical or theatrical work, for example, is not just the work of the musician or the actor; the spectator also interprets (this interpretation by the spectator is not, of course, limited to the performing arts; the reader interprets, looking for a meaning that resonates with his or her being). This interpretation is an objective commitment of being (the spectator is also the object of the relationship to the work, not just the subject), a meaningful matching of the work. In this sense, the aesthetic judgement that contributes to aesthetic emotion is not itself a psychological judgement, but an objective projection of the subject. If art has always been, is and always will be an activity of man for man, it is not limited to the expression of a "sincere" subjectivity. On the contrary, art, as a subjective human production, is also an object of man, an object (work) that is at the same time an outstretched hand towards the other, in other words an attempt to overcome egotism and particularism (of "restricted subjectivities", of the "superficial *self*"). In this sense, art is always tending towards the absolute. We must go back from form to genius, from genius to man and from man to the absolute. Nothing can prevent music, this excitement of atoms doubly interpreted, felt and experienced, from existing. The moment is a challenge to time, the work a challenge to nonsense.

Book III

Facing the Other

Introduction

> I have striven not to laugh at human actions, not to weep at them, nor to hate them, but to understand them.
>
> Baruch Spinoza, *Tractatus politicus*, 1677
>
> I am a human being, and thus nothing human is alien to me.
>
> ("*Homo sum, humani nihil a me alienum puto.*")
>
> Terence, *Heautontimoroumenos* ("The Self-Punisher"), 163 BC.

In Book I, we tried to show that the materialist and neo-Darwinist approaches, by claiming to undermine the foundations of morality, had only reinforced its possibility by making obvious the aporias and limits inherent in any monist theory, that is to say, any theory that would bypass the problematic of signification. And yet, although we have shown that morality, as a positive idea acting on the autonomous actors that we are, is a logical possibility, we have not, until now, determined its foundations, nor sought to give it a concrete content. In the light of our work on knowledge, and given the links we have established between knowledge, sensible intuition, imagination and aesthetics, it seems to us that we now need to reconsider what we mean by the "concrete content" of morality.

In the *Groundwork of the Metaphysics of Morals* (1785) and a little later in the *Critique of Practical Reason* (1788), Immanuel Kant attempted to give morality general maxims for action, better known as "categorical imperatives", the three main formulations of which were as follows: (i) "Act solely in accordance with the maxim that makes it possible for you to want it to become a universal law at the same time", (ii) "Act in such a way that you treat humanity, both in your own person and in that of others, always at the same time as an end and never merely as a means", (iii) "Act in such a way that you treat humanity, both in your own person and in that of others, always at the same time as an end and never merely as a means". (ii) "Act in such a way that you treat humanity, both in your own person and in that of others, always at the same time as an end, and never merely as a means", (iii) "Act as if, through your maxims, you were always to be a legislator in a realm of ends[153]." In our view, these three formulations underlined the three fundamental aspects of Kant's moral doctrine: (i) the legalistic dimension: Kant insisted on the fact that moral maxims take the form of laws, that they impose themselves on the knowing subject (notion of *respect* for the moral law), (ii) the humanistic dimension: moral doctrine was based on an axiom, that of respect for humanity in myself and in others, this respect for humanity being based on logical principles that are also universal or universalisable ("don't do to others what you wouldn't want them to do to you", a golden rule found in the Talmud, Confucius and the Gospels), based on the logical principle of reciprocity — but, above all, in Kant there is the idea of recognising the other as a being with an intrinsic value given to him by his ability to formulate and follow universal principles), (iii) the autonomous dimension of the

---

[153] Maxims from the *Foundations of the Metaphysics of Morals*, *Grundlegung zur Metaphysik der Sitten*, 1785

human being — man must act as if he were a potential legislator: it is true that the moral law is imposed on him, but he has the autonomous faculty of recognising the moral law in himself (here we return to the theme of legislated and lawmaking reason that we set out a little earlier in Book I). At several points in his work (notably in the *Groundwork of the Metaphysics of Morals* and in the *Critique of Practical Reason*), Kant frees the problem of morality from the idea of moral sentiment. In other words, for Kant, morality was not subjectively founded on a feeling of compassion, sympathy or emotional belonging to humanity. On the contrary, morality was based on the principle of rational and objective recognition. It was because man possessed reason, and the free faculty to appreciate good and evil, that he should be treated as an end in himself, and not as a means to an end. Moral sentiment, by its very nature unstable and fluctuating, could not provide a solid foundation for Kant's legalistic edifice. However, by wishing to base morality on legal principles, Kant paradoxically deprived the moral agent of a large part of his faculty of judgment. He was not to act according to his own assessment of circumstances, but always with reference to universal maxims that had the value of immutable, non-circumstantial laws ("categorical" imperatives). In short, for Kant, morality was more of a logical problem (a problem which, in our opinion, remains valid when it comes to founding morality as a possibility, as Kant does in the *Critique of Pure Reason*), than a problem of aesthetic appreciation (of a "faculty of judging", the theme of which Kant paradoxically develops on subjects related to his moral doctrine, notably aesthetics). This logical and legalistic approach to morality led Kant into the paradoxes that were, in our opinion, caused by a disconnection between the critical moment and the aesthetic moment in the application of moral principles (*Critique of Practical Reason*). This disconnection was in fact the result of a retreat into the formalism of the moral law, a retreat that reflected a form of denial of man's openness to the world (of his state of "being open"), which nevertheless constituted the very foundation of moral formalism. What Kant gave to man with one hand, he took back with the other. By uncoupling the critical moment from the aesthetic (intuitive) moment, Kant was in a way depriving man of his faculty of judgement, denying his intermediate, dual position (an intermediate position between formalism, which is the expression of critical rationality, on the one hand, and man's capacity to modulate his judgement, to adapt the rules according to circumstances, a capacity for modulation that depends on sensitive intuition and the imagination, on the other). In his reply to Benjamin Constant, entitled *On a Supposed Right to Tell Lies from Benevolent Motives* (1797), Kant asserted, for example, that lying was always morally reprehensible, regardless of the intentions that might justify it, on the grounds that it disqualified the source of law. Against Benjamin Constant, who defended the idea that lying could be justified by humanitarian considerations — Benjamin Constant used the example of the man of goodwill who lies to a murderer who is on the trail of his potential victims — Kant maintained that lying was, in all circumstances, harmful to human dignity and undermined the trust that should necessarily underpin interpersonal relations. In short, according to Kant, one should always refer to the maxims of the categorical imperative, even against one's own moral inclinations. The man who had been lifted out of minority thanks to the superior use of his reason (see Kant, *What is Enlightenment?*) was thus reassigned residence in the use of his moral faculty of judgement. What Kant granted to artistic genius (the talent that gives art its rules), he 'categorically' denied to the moral agent. For Kant, there could be no moral "genius[154]". Man was invited to submit to the prescriptions of the categorical imperative that his reason had (once and for all) freely examined and validated. In this way, moral principles, which for Kant initially constituted a formal framework for moral action (like the harmony or scale in a piece of music, for example), were transformed into precepts with a specific content, precepts that had to be followed with rigour and zeal.

It is in order to avoid the problems associated with an overly rigorous application of laws presented as immutable that we prefer the term *ethics* to the term *morality*, the latter term seeming to us to give a better account of the issues we wish to address in this book. Firstly, it seems to us that the term 'ethics' is less prescriptive than the term 'morality' (morality as a set of standardised precepts); secondly, we believe that the notion of ethics is more analytical and reflective (critical reflection on concrete issues); and thirdly, the term ethics seems from the outset to be less prescriptive and more open to the circumstances in which we exercise

---

[154] Once again, Kant differs radically from Nietzsche, who saw Christ, for example, as the embodiment of this moral 'genius'. Christ did not respect the precepts of an inherited morality; he invented a morality of action that defined itself as it was lived.

our critical sense. We will therefore try to treat morality not as a fixed *corpus* of rules (even if these rules were freely discovered by our reason in an autonomous way) but as something that is determined in the particular circumstances that always appeal to our faculty of judging (a faculty of judging that derives precisely from our intermediary position between formalism and reality).

Morality vs. Darwinist Utilitarianism — The Impasses of Monism

The Limits of Materialism

In this book devoted to ethics, we take up in places the main arguments that constituted a critique of materialism's theory of knowledge that we gave in Book I. So as not to make the discussion too long, we shall pass quickly over certain analyses, referring the reader to the first chapters of Book I, in particular the chapter entitled *Degrees of Emergence — Degrees of Freedom — The Problem of Morality.*

1.

THE PETITIONS OF PRINCIPLE OF BEHAVIOURISM — Materialism, when taken as a doctrine and not as a method, leads to contradictions which we dwelt on at length in Book I. In terms of the study of behaviour, materialism can be divided into two branches with similar characteristics: on the one hand, neo-Darwinism (that of the American Daniel C. Dennett, for example), which considers morality to be a kind of conservation reflex of the human species, and on the other, behaviourism, which focuses only on the concrete manifestations of human action. Dennett, for example[155]), which considers morality to be a kind of conservation reflex for the human species, and behaviourism, which is concerned only with the concrete manifestations of human action, neglecting mental processes, the signifying basis of emotions and,

---

[155] See for example Daniel C. Dennett, *Freedom evolves* (2003)

more generally, the whole issue of the basis of knowledge and ethics. Developed at the beginning of the twentieth century by psychologists such as John B. Watson and B.F. Skinner, the behaviourist approach considered that all human and animal behaviour was learned through interactions with the environment (which, as we pointed out in Book I, is a truism — we obviously agree with behaviourists that the environment plays a role in human behaviour, and even more so in animal behaviour, but it would be necessary to prove that the environment is the only factor influencing behaviour (which behaviourism never does, because its axioms do not even consider that there could be anything other than the environment). In its very principles, behaviourism was only interested in what could be observed and measured objectively (i.e. the physical actions and reactions of individuals). Here we find a reflex of modern science: when it comes to knowledge, all that matters is what can be seen (just observe that the house is standing, as my positivist architect used to tell me). You have to ignore the idea and concentrate on what can be observed, i.e. matter and the way it behaves and reacts. However, while this doctrine has a certain degree of fruitfulness when it comes to studying the behaviour of matter, its application to complex organisms raises several fundamental epistemological questions. Firstly, (i) the idea that we should only consider what is observable in terms of human and animal behaviour is based on the unproven hypothesis that the determinisms of human and animal behaviour are solely of a material nature (which would justify using a method derived from materialism); secondly, (ii) the idea that we can derive rules for behaviour solely from observing them, ignoring their motives and internal de-terminations (in other words, the idea that we can only consider what is observable in terms of human and animal behaviour); and thirdly, (iii) the idea that we can derive rules for behaviour solely from observing them, ignoring their motives and internal determinations (in other words, the idea that we can only consider what is observable in terms of human and animal behaviour), the idea that we could go over the head of the subject acting in order to understand him better than himself and without him) is based on the unproven hypothesis that statistical correlation relations can have any value as a law, and finally, (iii) even if it turned out *in fine* that the statistical correlations observed could have value as a law (which we vigorously contest), the behaviourist would still have to explain the very status of these laws (we start by asserting that only what is observable is likely to be scientifically considered, so what are we to make of unobservable and purely interpretative statistical laws — correlation not being reason! — which are derived from the observation of behaviour. Should they be stripped of all interpretative relevance on the grounds that interpretations don't walk around before our eyes with their faces uncovered?). Thus, conditioning theories, both in their classical version (a form of learning in which a neutral *stimulus* becomes associated with an involuntary response, as in Pavlov's dog experiment in which a bell sound was associated with a dog salivating) and in their operant version (the theory developed by B.F. Skinner which explains how behaviour is modified by its con-sequences[156]) by mechanising human behaviour to the extreme, neglect the role of regulatory ideas on the behaviour of their study subjects. Behaviour, and human behaviour in particular, cannot be reduced to its physical or physiological determinants. To ignore the problem of meaning, in the philosophy of knowledge, as in the sociology of behaviour, leads to indescribable contradictions. As beings gifted with the ability to understand organised languages (which are not just, as George Mounin said, codes — we are not made like crows with a finite quantity of coded messages, we use instead a language that articulates signs and gives them different meanings depending on the contexts in which they are used), we are subject to the influences of ideas. These ideas may be coherent or incoherent, effective or ineffective, true or false, but they are nonetheless

---

[156] Behaviour followed by a favourable consequence (reinforcement) is more likely to be repeated, whereas behaviour followed by an unpleasant consequence (punishment) is less likely to be repeated. Positive reinforcement: adding a reward to encourage a behaviour (e.g. giving a treat to a dog that obeys a command). Negative reinforcement: removing an unpleasant *stimulus* to encourage a behaviour (example: turning off a loud noise when a certain behaviour is adopted). Positive punishment: adding an unpleasant *stimulus* to discourage a behaviour (example: reprimanding a child who disobeys). Negative punishment: removing a pleasant element to discourage behaviour (e.g. depriving a child of play after a bad deed). Operant conditioning is therefore based on the idea that behaviour is shaped and modified by the consequences it produces. See in particular B.F. Skinner, *The Behavior of Organisms* (1938), *Science and Human Behavior* (1953).

concrete determinants of our behaviour. To deny the analysis of these determinants of human behaviour is to deny precisely what makes us human beings special: our ability to articulate an idea in a language that can be understood by everyone, our membership of a "community of meaning".

We do not intend here to open the debate on the corroboration of behaviourist theories. Like any totalising theory, behaviourism will always have the answer to any counter-example (a new variable will be invented, a new observable factor of influence, the relevance of which can only be proved by other statistical correlations that have failed to be scientifically founded — see on this subject Book I, § 43 — *Against the statistical model*: statistics as an instrument for corroborating an aesthetic intuition and not as an instrument of knowledge in itself). It is only important for us to note that behaviourism, as a monistic doctrine, is a contradiction in terms. By stubbornly refusing any problematic of meaning that would open the field to the problem of the motives for action (rather than to the statistical analysis of its determinants), behaviourism forces itself to remain on flat ground. Paradoxically, however, it moves up a notch when it comes to its statistical conclusions, which it presents as scientific truths. In a curious moment of self-delusion, the behaviourist allows himself to do what he forbids the subject of his studies (analysis, reflection, deliberation, judgement), without realising that this very judgement invalidates the theory he supports.

2.

THE PARADOXES OF MORAL NEO-DARWINISM — Moral neo-Darwinism uses a similar method to behaviourism, albeit on slightly different ground. For neo-Darwinism, everything can be explained through the prism of the conservation of species. According to the American (neo-Darwinist) philosopher Daniel C. Dennett, for example, morality is an invention of the human species, an invention fabricated with a view to its conservation. According to Dennett, human beings will, out of a well-understood self-interest, favour social behaviour over aggressive behaviour, respecting each other's interests rather than waging war against each other. For a neo-Darwinist, this idea is undoubtedly attractive, but here again it is based on several unproven hypotheses. Firstly, (i) Daniel C. Dennett takes it for granted that moral behaviour can be genetically induced (as a product of evolution — which is certainly a perfectly valid idea, but one that needs to be confirmed empirically, which seems to us to involve a number of methodological challenges), then (ii) Dennett considers that the material manifestation of a behaviour is sufficient to explain that behaviour, which, once again, is not based on any serious demonstration (this is what we tried to show throughout Book I — the *vector* of an item of information, for example, *is not* the information itself, the ink is not the message: (iii) Dennett does not really consider the case in which the behaviour of a species might go against its own interests (humanism, for example, is not necessarily a reflex to defend the interests of the human species, In fact, there is nothing to prevent us from defending the living world as a whole in the name of humanism, sometimes against man's own interests). Finally, (iv) like the behaviourist, the neo-Darwinist obfuscates the question of the significance of his own conclusions in the light of his monistic theory. In other words, neo-Darwinism begins by rejecting the intentionality of nature, and then paradoxically ratifies moral utilitarianism, which is itself the cause of the long-term survival of species. For this theory to be coherent, however, the subject would have to fail to understand its own interest, and act blindly, like the plaything of nature that it is supposed to be. As soon as the subject is aware of his own interest in acting, i.e. understands the idea that giving up part of his freedom (and aggression) comes at the price of his own safety, then the subject becomes conscious and his behaviour intentional. In fact, moral neo-Darwinism, like behaviourism, accepts in its conclusions what it had rejected in its premises: the intentionality that was denied to matter is ratified at the level of the individual (even if, here again, neo-Darwinists will do their utmost to prove that this intentionality is only an illusion of the mind, basing themselves in particular on certain neuroscientific theses whose limits and contradictions we showed in Book I, see in particular § 2 — *Is physicalist monism logically tenable?* and, more generally, the first part of Book I: *The logical impasses of reductionist physicalism and neo-Darwinism*. However, the neuroscientists' defence is mainly based on the criterion of immediacy — infra-conscious actions, unconscious physical determinisms of action — whereas Dennett's neo-Darwinism explicitly refers to ideal motives, maxims of action which determine general behaviour[157], and not physically induced action).

In moral neo-Darwinism, as in behaviourism, it is the radical refusal to consider the general problem of meaning that leads to the incoherence of the theses. By wishing to remain at the zero level of the matter, behaviourism, like neo-Darwinism, denies itself any possibility of analysing the *motives* for action. Focusing on the observable consequences of motives, behaviourism — and, to a lesser extent, neo-Darwinism — categorise action without ever seeking to provide an acceptable explanatory basis for it.

3.

> Everything is for the best in the best of all possible worlds.
>
> Voltaire, *Candide* (parodying Leibniz, T*heodicy: Essays on the Goodness of God, the Freedom of Man, and the Origin of Evil*, 1710)

MORAL RELATIVISM, SCIENTIFIC RELATIVISM — A certain moral relativism maintains that our laws and moral codes are valid only in this world, for our species, with our own faculty of judgment and our own senses.

---

[157] We could sum up the principles of action that Dennett endorses with the maxim: "act in your own interest while respecting the interest of others". It is the general idea that influences the action (non-violence, for example) and not an infra-conscious mechanism of the kind presented to us by Stanislas Dehaene in his analysis of the Libet experiment, for example. See again § 2 *Is physicalist monism logically sustainable?*

Without going into the possible content of these laws and moral codes (we'll come back to that later), we can see that moral relativism uses arguments that we already identified in Book I on the philosophy of knowledge. For example, the argument that the laws of physics are valid only in our world, that we perceive them with our own senses and our particular faculty of judgment, did not seem to us to be an argument against the validity and effectiveness of knowledge. We must not confuse what is circumstantial with what is relative. Our knowledge is linked to a circumstantial state of affairs in the universe (a possible configuration of the universe that gave rise to it), so the laws we derive from observing the universe are valid for this particular universe, which does not call into question their non-relative character (all other things being equal, the law is universally valid, non-relative). Even if we are allowed to speculate about other possible universes, this must not lead us to question the validity of our laws (or the very existence of these laws, which alone enables and supports the edifice of knowledge[158]). Moral relativism proceeds from the same idea, confusing circumstantial morality with relative morality. If we accept the argument that morality could be circumstantial (it depends on our sensibility, the structure of our reason, our faculty of judging, etc.), we reject the supposed equivalence between this possible "circumstantiality" and the idea that morality could be

---

[158] We are using a pragmatic argument here. If reality were not subject to any laws, it would not be thinkable. But reality is thinkable, so it is subject to laws (independently of the question of the content of these laws), see Book I, § 13 - *Can we imagine of a world without laws?*

relative (the idea that "each man sees no evil at his own door", as the popular expression goes). In equal circumstances (belonging to the human species, for example, which is both sentient and rational), there is nothing to prevent us from considering the idea of a morality that is valid for everyone.

4.

CRITIQUE OF NEUROSCIENCE — The vast majority of neuroscientists are based on unproven assumptions that the physically observable manifestation in the brain of a physically observable action in reality constitutes the "cause" of that action. In other words, neuroscience considers that matter is the cause of matter, in a self-contained system. If we apply this idea (which is in fact an axiom) to Libet's experiment, which we describe in detail in Book I (see § 2 — *Is physicalist monism logically tenable?*), we are led to affirm that the primary cause of the triggering of our action of pressing a button is not our will to press this button, a will that would command the decision or "authorisation in principle" to send a nervous signal to our finger (such an affirmation would imply accepting the existence of the problem of signification, and therefore of the motives for action), but that it is to be sought in the material determinants located inside our brain which command, outside any conscious process, the action of pressing the button (awareness of the action occurring after the decision has actually been taken by the brain). However, by showing that brain activity precedes the moment of actual awareness of the decision, aren't we simply shifting the problem of action and its determinants? Who authorised this brain activity? What are the underlying reasons? Would the subconscious brain activity that precedes the conscious decision to press the button have taken place if the subject had consciously decided not to press the button? Does the brain always act without our knowledge, or can we be guided by ideas that it identifies and recognises as 'true' or 'effective' in an effort to understand the world? We see that the cognitive approach to neuroscience leads to an escalation of questions that always find the same answer: matter is everything and at the origin of everything, it is and must be the explanation for everything.

In a book entitled *Du vrai, du beau, du bien* (2008), Jean-Pierre Changeux uses an argument in the field of aesthetic judgement that is similar to the one found in Plato when he compared our faculty of aesthetic judgement to our faculty of moral judgement: "For Herbert Simon[159]", writes Changeux, "a trait specific to humans is the existence of an emotional response to the 'beauty of parsimony', which would have been selected in the course of the evolution of species. It would be useful for the survival of species through its

---

[159] Herbert Simon (1916-2001) was an American scientist best known for his work on human decision-making and the idea of *bounded* rationality, which describes how individuals make decisions under conditions of imperfect rationality, i.e. when they do not have all the information or time they need to make perfectly rational choices. Simon was awarded the Nobel Prize in Economics in 1978 for his research into decision-making in organisations. He also played a pioneering role in the development of artificial intelligence (AI) and expert systems, computer programmes capable of simulating human decision-making processes.

ability to *detect* organised distributions in nature[160]."
Like Plato, Jean-Pierre Changeux, in his positive commentary on Herbert Simon's thought, lends credence to the idea that the faculty of aesthetic judgement is linked to the faculty of judgement in general (Changeux is not speaking here explicitly of morality, but of a faculty useful to the survival of the species — which is, incidentally, how Dennett qualifies and defines morality). However, in believing that aesthetics (which is linked to the problem of signification, as we set out to show in Book II) can be linked to the survival of the species, Changeux creates a new difficulty for himself by introducing the concept of "the beauty of parsimony". For Changeux, beauty is linked to the economy of means, which in turn is linked to the efficiency of nature, and therefore to the 'robustness' of its creatures. Our aesthetic sense, like our moral sense, would therefore be above all a weapon that would provide for our capacity to survive as a species. Here again we find the idea that nature is going behind our backs, treating us like intelligent automatons. Here again, however, Jean-Pierre Changeux stumbles over the problem of the emergence (of consciousness) by seeking to minimise its consequences (we have seen how neuroscientists intend to treat the emergence of consciousness as a 'residual' phenomenon that science will eventually explain). From the moment that 'parsimony' (assuming that aesthetics can be summed up as parsimony or elegance, which is far from being the case, as we analysed earlier) is consciously designated as such, it enters into what we have called our 'network of

---

[160] Op. cit., p. 178

meanings', which conditions our appreciations and judgements about the world. To act in the world, to appreciate the world, is precisely, for us, to formulate a critical judgement about the world based on our understanding of reality. By introducing the notion of 'parsimony' into aesthetic judgement, Changeux once again enters into the problem of signification (how is parsimony defined in things, what are the ideal criteria for it? By trying to reduce the problem of meaning to that of matter, we are displacing it — in a perfectly sterile way — without ever being able to provide a serious response to it, because we fail to consider it in all its extent and complexity. In the same way, we believe that ethical and moral questions can only be addressed within the (dualist) problematic of meaning. Only then can we attempt to provide an answer that is not marred by contradictions.

The Answer to the Ethical Question within Materialism

5.

DISSATISFACTIONS RELATED TO THE QUANTUM RESPONSE — As we mentioned in Book I, the attempt, in the context of the debate between determinism and freedom, to locate in the brain the place of quantum superposition (which would be, as it were, the place of free decision-making) seems to us to miss its target[161]: we can only understand freedom in its close relationship with determinism. Far from constituting a kind of antinomy of freedom, physical determinism is on the contrary, as we have seen, one of the *sine qua non* conditions for the exercise of my freedom (if only because of the problem of the chain of command between my intention and my action: how can I be free if my actions are not determined by my intentions?) In our view, freedom should not be understood in opposition to determinism, just as ideas should not be understood in opposition to matter. On the other hand, the problem of quantum indeterminacy seems to us to be particularly interesting insofar as it actually reflects the structure of our relationship with reality. Quantum indeterminacy is fundamentally linked to the problem of measurement, i.e. the problem of 'interference' between the measurable and the measured. In a way, this circular structure is reminiscent of the acting individual, who modifies his behaviour and actions as he becomes aware of himself and his intentions, in an upward spiral: I commit an action or have a thought, I

---

[161] See Roger Penrose, *The Large, the Small and the Human Mind*

see myself committing an action or having a thought through self-reflexivity, I see myself seeing myself, etc.: my behaviour is affected by my division into two or three parts. In short, indeterminism here is sequenced in time and is based on my internal division and my ability to represent myself. This ability to represent ourselves, what we have called "internal dualism", is what allows us to understand ourselves as dynamic moral subjects. Ethical questioning is characterised by this movement of self-reflection, in which the subject sees himself not only as a subject (as a legally determined living organism) but also as an object (a subject of study). In this way, ethical questioning is similar to the spiral problem of measurement in quantum mechanics: the subject who looks at himself as an object modifies his own behaviour through the knowledge he has of himself, knowledge that creates interference with himself and modifies his action.

A very similar idea is expounded by Max Planck in *Wege zur Physikalischen Erkenntnis* (1934), which we quote *in extenso*: "One could only deny someone the consciousness of his free will if he could, by application of the principle of causality, foresee his own future. But even this is impossible, for this hypothesis contains within itself a contradiction. All truly complete knowledge presupposes, in fact, that the object to be known will not be modified by phenomena intervening in the knowing subject. This assumption is incompatible with the case where the subject and the object are identical. Or, to use more concrete terms, the knowledge of a motive for voluntary action is an internal event in the subject that can be the source of a new motive, and so the number of possible motives is increased. This realisation is a new knowledge, a possible source of a new motive, so the series of possible motives can increase indefinitely. The subject will never be able to produce an absolutely definitive motive for one of his own future actions, i.e. knowledge incapable of giving rise to a new motive for action. [No, causal law is not enough for any man, even the most intelligent, to produce decisive motives for any of his conscious actions. Another thread is needed: the moral law. The highest intelligence and the most penetrating analysis cannot make up for it[162]." For Planck, it is our knowledge of ourselves (as objects) that modifies the course of our actions. Since this knowledge is potentially infinite, the determinants of action cannot be strictly predicted by a law of causality (if this law of causality is not applied to moral legalism, which is another form of causality of action, but this would mean admitting that the principle does not apply purely and solely to matter, which the materialist rigorously rejects, since only matter exists[163]). But knowledge implies awareness, both awareness of things and awareness of ourselves. It is therefore easy to understand why neuroscientists have tried to shift the problem of the determinants of action towards the subconscious actions performed by our brains. While Max Planck remains quite Kantian in the last part of the passage we are quoting (in his reference to the moral law), the first part of his remark clearly points out the flaws in materialism's reasoning when it comes

---

[162] Op. cit.

[163] On the tautological and totalising form of this reasoning, see Book I, § 4— *Physicalist tautologies* and the impasses of monist theories and § 13— *Can we imagine of a world without law?*

to predicting behaviour. As soon as the adaptive organism acquires the possibility of becoming aware of reality (an awareness that opens up the possibility of knowledge), it no longer acts *solely* on the basis of physical determinism. The idea (the motive) exerts an influence on it, but the idea can be false, whereas the physical mechanism cannot, which is further proof that one is not strictly equivalent to the other.

6.

CAN THE WILL BE FREE? — Do my wills take place, as Malebranche put it, "in me without me", or am I the master in my own house? If we consider the question from a strictly material (or phenomenal) point of view, we can only concede that, as creatures made of matter, all our actions must have material causes as their determinants: our actions obey a determined causal chain that we do not control and of which we are not necessarily the conscious initiators (first cause). Consequently, to ask about the freedom of our will is, to use the image Spinoza uses in *Ethics* (1677), like asking about the freedom of movement of a weathervane that turns with the wind. However, as Leibniz notes in his *Theodicy: Essays on the Goodness of God, the Freedom of Man, and the Origin of Evil* (1710): "Aristotle has already remarked that there are two things in freedom, namely spontaneity and choice, and it is in these that our control over our actions consists." We find this distinction between spontaneous action and deliberate choice interesting insofar as it introduces the notion of temporality into the idea of freedom, i.e. the idea of suspending action in favour of analysis. In other words, we argue that the more spontaneous an act is, the less 'free' it is in the sense that the agent can consciously act on its determinants. While animals generally act spontaneously and instinctively, following the laws of their species (although this should be qualified by taking into account the ability of animals to learn, which is already a step towards autonomy), this is not always the case for human beings, who have the ability to suspend or delay their desires or volitions. This ability to suspend the mechanical course of things is linked to the representation we make of their causes and above all their consequences (we also find this faculty of representation in animals capable of individual learning, which is why we can also speak of degrees of autonomy in animals, see on this subject Book I, § 19 — *Degrees of freedom*; unlike humans, however, animals, including the great primates, do not have the capacity to use the higher functions of language, such as description and argumentation, see Book I § 20 — *The idea as non-matter acting on matter*). As soon as the suspension of instinct or immediate desire leads to the beginnings of an argumentative deliberation at the heart of the subject (a deliberation that involves the higher functions of formalisation such as description and argumentation), we can say that the problem of freedom really arises. This problem is once again linked to the problem of meaning: if we go up a level in the question of freedom, i.e. if we consider that freedom is not only about our ability to act spontaneously and without hindrance, then the question arises of the motives for action and, consequently, of its indirect determinants, which are formal deliberation. What is will if not our capacity to apply the meaningful deliberations we have formulated in our innermost being? And can we speak of will when our actions (i) do not respond to a deliberative process, as happens with most of our subconscious actions, or (ii) do not conform to our deliberations (in the latter case, a failure of will is rightly invoked)? If we define will as the process by which our meaningful decisions are effectively translated into our actions (as opposed to the spontaneous satisfaction of our most vital desires or needs), then two questions again arise: (i) does the determinism we claim at the level of phenomena (of the 'material' world) not apply in the same way to all our deliberative processes? (ii) how can a representation (an idea, a logical argument, a deliberation) provoke an action? To the first question, we have to answer that if we take determinism as an assumption at the level of the material world, we cannot claim randomness (or even free will as a dry power of self-determination of the subject) at the level of our own deliberations. Our deliberations, too, follow a causal chain (a causal chain that can certainly be flawed, but in that case we are always able to recognise the flaw in the chain). No more than in the phenomenal world, then, are we entitled to claim a totally free power of determination over our thoughts. However, just as material determinism could not be thought of as the antithesis of freedom (see Book I — *Degrees of emergence — degrees of freedom — the problem of morality*), it would be equally inadequate to conceive of the internal necessity that governs our thoughts as a limitation on our autonomy. Indeed, how could we conceive of freedom independently of the determining and constraining process of logical formalism? What form of freedom could possibly result from the pure arbitrariness of our thoughts, or from a randomness similar to that which manifests itself in our dreams — dreams of which we sometimes feel like 'prisoners'?

However, we must not confuse logical determinism with material determinism. We maintain that our thoughts are not materially determined in the sense that we are directly conditioned to think what we think by our history, our influences and our environment. As rational beings, we have the capacity to formulate ideas that may be true or false, effective or ineffective, *independently* of our personal history or our direct material determinants (in the sense that matter would react in a Pavlovian action-reaction mode, for example). So, while immediate material determinants can influence our behaviour and ideas, they do little to explain human behaviour. While experience provides us with the material for our reasoning, our reasoning is not necessarily a repetition of learned reasoning. In other words, we are not machines that spit out prefabricated thinking (or at least we shouldn't be). Reality provides us with the 'material' we need to think. Authentic thought starts always from the facts, from the analysis of reality (from confrontation with reality, we might say) and must not be understood as a formal synthesis of what exists (a synthesis that machines are now capable of performing almost perfectly).

We can certainly still affirm that thoughts, including those that are not directly determined by a given state of matter, are in reality always linked to matter insofar as they are the fruit of the (material) adaptation of our organism to a de facto state of matter. We should also note that this faculty of adaptation is not specific to man, but to living organisms as a whole (see Book I, § 19— *Degrees of freedom*). It is undoubtedly true, and we readily concede it, that our faculty of adaptation is at the origin of the development of language and of an organised language of the descriptive and argumentative type. It is no doubt just as accurate to affirm, with the materialists and neo-Darwinists, that language, in its use, is closely correlated with its physical manifestations — or that it is even an emanation of physical processes that can be observed and located in our brain thanks to cerebral imaging (although it is impossible to affirm with absolute rigour, from a materialist point of view, that language derives directly from observable physical processes, and not, as we maintain, that these physical processes are an emanation of language, which is itself the *medium* of our confrontation with the world). However, as soon as this ability to create and use language emerges in living beings, we need to con-sider the issues that are specific to them. In other words, with the emergence of language comes the emergence of a set of rules specific to language (a structure, a grammar, meanings), a set that gives rise to specific issues. Attempting to sidestep these issues (as strictly materialistic doctrines often do) leads to contradictions that we find impossible to overcome. Beyond the autonomous rules imposed by language, the faculties of description and argument that it creates open up the problematic of truth and falsehood, of the adequate and the inadequate, of the effective and the ineffective. Thus, while language does indeed have both an origin and material manifestations, it is not *itself* perfectly identifiable with matter, as we set out to show in Book I (see in particular Book I, § 31 — *Against psychologism*). With the use of language (as an organised system of forms that finds the origin of its development in being) we are confronted with the world of meanings (what Karl Popper calls *world 3*, which contains the products of the human mind, such as ideas, theories, works of art, social institutions, languages, books...). Access to this autonomous sphere is what we call 'freedom'.

If we use the term 'freedom' to define this specifically human faculty of using descriptive and argumentative language — as this use can have a retroactive effect on our behaviour — then we still need to determine the conditions under which we can really exercise this freedom. When we are mistaken or act according to false or ineffective ideas, can we be said to be 'free'? To a certain extent, we can answer this question in the affirmative: when we err, we have made free use of our ability to evaluate and deliberate. Our freedom will have been greater than that of the animal or primate, which does not have access to the structuring functions of language. However, won't our freedom be greater or more complete if we make our choices on the basis of true, coherent or effective ideas? Undoubtedly, correct information or a correct idea will help us to make an informed and free decision (to take a trivial example, if we have the idea that the traffic light is green when it is red, we risk a collision; our decision is influenced by our idea of the colour of the light — colour-blind people need to pay particular attention to this!) But then, doesn't freedom consist of acting according to what is true (true, effective or coherent)? If then, we are constrained by what is "true", can we be said to be "free"?

Here we are confronted with the central problem of freedom. If we say that freedom can only be exercised in accordance with a truth (factual, artistic or moral), then we are subordinating the idea of freedom to the idea of "good will". To be free thus implies wanting what is just, what is good, what is beautiful, what is true. The free will then become synonymous with the good will (the will seeks the true, puts itself in tune with the true). We can also note, however, that we can very well recognise what is just, what is good, what is beautiful, what is true, and *knowingly* act against what we recognise as such: this is what we call "perversity". The perverse subject makes deliberately negative and enlightened use of his freedom. Perversity is thus the enjoyment of acting against an *authority* recognised as legitimate (it is, in this respect, pure contradiction). The notion of perversity must be distinguished from the notion of bad faith (or from what we now call 'post-rationalisation' or 'post-truth', which are related notions). Unlike the perverse subject, the subject of bad faith does not claim the transgression of a moral law or ethical principles as positive acts. Instead, they develop a self-justifying discourse, most of the time incoherent, to absolve themselves of an action or thought that would be unjustifiable if the subject were in tune with the principles that they themselves recognise as just. Few, in fact, dare to recognise an objective truth and act against that truth at the same time as recognising it as founded or legitimate (the tendency, it has to be said, is rather towards relativisation and relativism, a practical instrument used to justify everything and its opposite). In *Religion within the Limits of Reason Alone*, Kant, while admitting that we can act deliberately against the moral law, refuses to consider that we can make the authority of the moral law a negative motive for action. In his analyses of what he calls "radical evil", Kant envisages two options, i.e. two pro-positions that could lend credence to the idea of radical evil (an evil that is at the root of the human being and from which we cannot free ourselves). The first is that man is evil by nature, i.e. by instinct or original sensitivity. Kant refutes this first proposition by asserting that the inclination to do evil has no direct connection with evil (we do not, for example, reproach a lion for killing its prey, or a cat for playing with the mouse it is about to devour). We cannot be held responsible for our innate inclinations to evil (they are in us, there is nothing we can do about them); we can only be held accountable for our inclination to evil, that is, our propensity to do evil freely, while recognising the authority of the moral law (or the authority of our ethical principles). This inclination to evil is the manifestation, Kant asserts, of our fallibility (in other words, as soon as we have the capacity to act *knowingly*, we commit evil out of weakness and not out of a radical aptitude for evil[164]). The second option, writes Kant, is to consider the proposition that radical evil is not linked to our sensibility or to a bad nature, but to a "*depravity* of moral law-making reason". According to this proposition, the moral agent would recognise the authority of the moral law, but deny the obligations that derive from it. For Kant, this is impossible because it would mean that opposition to the law would be elevated to the status

---

[164] In this case, Kant's argument assumes that our representations (in this case, our representation of the moral law) can influence our actions.

of a motive, and, Kant asserts, "the subject would thus become a *diabolical* being[165]."

If we recognise the moral law as valid universally and for ourselves, and we decide to act against the moral law *with full knowledge of the facts*, it is because (i) sensitive motives or our own interests have taken precedence over the moral law (I went through the red light because I was in a hurry), which is what we call "inconsistency" (ii) we reconstruct a circumstantial moral code to justify an act with which we do not in fact agree, we do not recognise ourselves in this act ("I went through the red light because I was in a hurry and, in any case, there was no one at the crossroads"), this is what we call "bad faith", (iii) we act against the moral law, because we recognise it as such and want to destroy it ("I went through the red light because it was red, I enjoy this transgression"), this is what we call "perversity" — which Kant describes as "diabolical". To these three categories, we add a fourth, which is an extension of the third: (iv) the subject deliberately acts against the authority of the moral law with the will to destroy it and superimposes on this action a discourse of self-justification which preserves the appearances of the moral law ("I went through the red light because it was red, I enjoy this transgression, but I affirm that the light was green"), this is what we call "perverse cynicism". In these last two cases (perversity and perverse cynicism, which Kant refuses to consider because he sees them as contradictory) the will is indeed free (it acts in an enlightened way) but it is also

---

[165] See Emmanuel Kant, *Religion within the Limits of Reason Alone*, I, 3, *Man is Evil by Nature*

depraved, that is, it enjoys the destruction of the principles it recognises as legitimate.

Of course, we can still envisage the case where the subject has no morals *at all* (amorality). However, it seems to us that such a subject, if he declares himself or feels himself to be amoral, can in fact be classified in one or more of the four categories we have listed above (most of the time, amoralism is a simple figure of inconsequence). Like the sceptic who becomes a rationalist as he crosses the road, the amoralist struggles not to enter into contradiction with himself. In fact, amoralism is more often than not a variant on the theme of inconsequence ("I do what I want") rather than the recognition of an authentically animal character ("I am not concerned by ethical issues, I only act by instinct"). It seems to us that amoralism has more to do with self-delusion than with a genuinely tenable position. Although it is not really the subject of this book, it should be pointed out in passing that Friedrich Nietzsche, who is most often cited as an example of an 'amoralist' philosopher, is in fact very far removed from the anti-ethical positions that are attributed to him[166]. Challenging — traditional morality does not necessarily lead to amoralism. In Nietzsche, the destruction of traditional moral values is achieved through radical ethical questioning (which, incidentally, led Gilles Deleuze to say that he was in fact the most demanding of the moralists[167]).

---

[166] See, *for* example, Geoffroy de Clisson, *Nietzsche ou la valeur morale de l'instant*.

[167] See Gilles Deleuze, *Nietzsche and philosophy*, 1962

Whether the will is understood as intrinsically good (insofar as it adopts the ethical principles or moral laws that reason has freely given itself) or as depraved (insofar as it acts with the aim of destroying a morality that it otherwise holds to be valid and legitimate), knowledge (progress in our understanding of the world) remains the vector of an increase in freedom (the fact of knowing whether the light is green or red, independently of the behaviour I would adopt given this information and what it means, always enlightens my action). The effort towards knowledge is in this way an effort towards freedom (to act with *full knowledge of the facts* is to act more freely). In his *Ethics* (1677), Spinoza, while remaining within the framework of determinism, establishes a similar relationship between knowledge and freedom, asserting that true freedom emerges from a rational understanding of the world and of oneself. For Spinoza, freedom is not defined simply by the absence of external constraints, but rather by our capacity to act according to our own nature[168], a capacity that is itself determined by know-

---

[168] Nature is intrinsically linked to what Spinoza calls *conatus*, which literally means "effort" or "tendency". In Spinozist philosophy, *conatus* refers to the effort by which "each thing, as far as it is in itself, strives to persevere in its being." (*Ethics*, Part III, Proposition 6). For Spinoza, every being, whether human, animal or plant, is driven by this fundamental principle of perseverance. The *conatus* is not simply a survival instinct. It is the expression of the essence of every being that wants to continue to exist in the most appropriate and powerful way possible. In humans, *conatus* takes a particular form, because it is linked to self-consciousness and desire

ledge. True freedom thus lies in an individual's ability to understand the causes of his actions and affects. In this respect, Spinoza draws a distinction between actions (the acts we perform when we are the adequate cause of them, i.e. we understand what prompts us to act) and passions (the states in which we are dominated by external forces and suffer emotions, without understanding their causes: we are then passive, not free). This action-passion distinction, which we already find in Descartes (notably in *Les Passions de l'âme*, 1649), is fundamental to understanding how knowledge relates to our will and how our representations (which are linked to our will, the conditions of which are themselves determined by knowledge) can be used to influence our actions (in accordance with our will).

The movement by which we question the causes and consequences of our actions, a movement that is above all a projection towards otherness (towards that which is not me) is what we call the "ethical movement" or "ethical questioning". The question of taking the other into account — as "other than myself" and simultaneously as "another *me*", i.e. as a being equal to myself — only makes sense insofar as it is likely to influence my behaviour and actions. The relevance of this question rests on a more fundamental issue: that of freedom, understood as our capacity to adapt to others.

(desire being a manifestation of *conatus* in conscious beings). For Spinoza, one of man's fundamental desires is the desire to know, because knowledge helps us to better persevere in our being. Understanding natural causes, emotions and the laws that govern the universe enables us to act in a way that is more in keeping with our being, and to escape the subjugation of external forces.

And this adaptation presupposes recognition of the significant dimension of the other, i.e. of his or her dignity. We have seen that a definition of freedom that claimed to free itself from the idea of determinism was lost in contradictions (which are also those of theories of free will in which man appears as a kind of demigod, capable of escaping the course of things and material determinisms). We have established, on the contrary, that freedom can only be thought of and conceived of in a deterministic world (see Book I, § 18 — *How can we conceptualize the link between the emergence of consciousness, the development of language structures, and the determinism of natural phenomena: what is freedom?*) Our freedom really consists in understanding these determinisms, that is, in being able to formalise the legal and constraining mechanisms that are at the origin of things. It is by understanding these mechanisms that we become freer (that the scope of our possibilities increases). It is also through a better understanding of the mechanisms of things that we modify ourselves 'materially' (the brain as an iterative loop with reality, legislated and legislating reason). Knowledge modifies us, changing us in both the figurative and purely material senses. This process of modification, made up of iterations between the material and the formal, between the reactive and the signifier, is precisely what makes us free: freedom is knowledge and knowledge is freedom[169].

---

[169] This is a formula: freedom is of course greater than knowledge (we anticipate tautology lawsuits!).

MORALITY OR THE INTERNAL SEPARATION OF CONSCIOUSNESS. THE DUALITY OF MAN

7.

BILATERALITY OF ETHICS: THE PROMISE — In this chapter, we do not return to the idea of morality as a motive for action that is both autonomous (not linked to immediate sensible determinations) and binding (in the sense that it exerts an influence on action, even if this influence is not necessarily decisive; see in particular what we have just said about the motives for determining the will). These aspects were developed in particular in paragraphs 20 to 22 of Book I, entitled *The idea as non-matter acting on matter* (§ 20), *The acting idea: morality as possibility* (§ 21) and *The idea of man as the foundation of morality* (§ 22), to which we refer the reader. Nor do we return to the performative dimension of language, see on this subject Book I, § 65, *Operative Language*. We do, however, note the relationship between these two issues from the point of view of our ethical problematic: (i) man's capacity to understand the coherence of ethical principles that he can recognise as "just" or "true" autonomously, i.e. independently of the notions of immediate interest or even deferred interest put forward by materialists and neo-Darwinists (ii) man's capacity to commit himself to these principles through a signifying language — what the philosopher John Austin calls *performative* language, The best-known example is marriage, where, according to Austin, it is 'sufficient' for the bride and groom to publicly exchange their consents for them to be married in the eyes of society: the language act of consent is at the same time a performative action of consent. The performative dimension of language does not, however, stop at the institutional (or sacred) dimension of certain specific acts of language (we are still thinking of baptism or religious conversions). More generally, it concerns any act that commits us. Apologies fall into this category: saying "I apologise" or "I'm sorry" is a performative act in which the speaker performs the action of asking forgiveness simply by uttering the sentence. The ability to promise, through language, is what concerns and interests us most in our ethical reflections. For Austin, when someone says: "I promise to come tomorrow", the sentence does not describe a fact or a state of the world; it is neither true nor false as such. Its purpose is to bring about an action simply by being uttered: it expresses a commitment by the speaker to perform an action or adopt a behaviour in the future. By making a promise, the speaker creates a moral or social obligation for himself. He undertakes to perform the promised action, thereby changing the situation between himself and the other person. So, the act of speaking is not simply a description of the world, but an act of commitment. Here, language becomes a means of influencing human relationships. For this performative act to work, certain conditions must be met: (i) the speaker must be sincere, i.e. he must really *intend* to keep his promise (let's see how, with this notion of intention, we are already falling back into the problem of *radical* dualism). If the speaker lies or has no intention of keeping his promise, the performative act fails; (ii) the context must be appropriate, i.e. the situation must allow the promise to be admissible. If the subject making the promise promises something that is impossible or beyond his control, the act of promising may be invalid (problem of coherence and plausibility); (iii) the interlocutor must accept the speaker's commitment: if the person to whom the promise is made rejects the promise, it loses its validity.

With a promise, the speaker alters the reality of relationships or social commitments simply by uttering meaningful words. However, in describing the conditions for the validity of a promise, John Austin insists on the need for the speaker to be sincere. In short, the very idea of a promise presupposes *radical* dualism. To define the concept of sincerity in the promise, we need to (i) recognise that the speaker understands what he is saying, i.e. admit that he is part of the "world of meanings", (ii) recognise that man understands himself as a separate being — What would be the value, for example, of the promise of a purely formal "artificial" intelligence that did not identify itself as an autonomous being and did not feel "committed" by its utterance? (iii) recognise that it has the capacity to act, as a separate being, in and on the world. This notion of signifying engagement in an utterance is crucial for us. Remember that we ourselves used a similar notion to propose a new solution to the liar's paradox (see Book I, § 40 — *What does it mean to think?*).

In *How to Do Things with Words* (1962), John Austin clearly envisages cases where the promise can fail. This is what he calls a "failure of performativity". For Austin, a promise made without the intention of keeping it or in an inappropriate context constitutes an "infelicitous" speech act. But what about the promises we make to ourselves? Unlike the promises we make to others, the promises we make to ourselves are not directly concerned by the problem of sincerity (we can always make a promise to ourselves while being insincere, even though it is of no interest to us whatsoever). It is also assumed that the other party (us) accepts the promise made. On the other hand, the promise is always subject to appropriate formalism and a coherent context. Of course, it can always succeed or fail. The speaker may be aware, when he makes the promise to himself, of the difficulty he will have in keeping it and of the fact that he will regularly be confronted with the failure of his volitions ("*I cheated myself, like I knew I would*[170]"), but this does not mean that he is being insincere when he makes the promise. Contrary to what the saying goes, promises are not only binding on "those who hear them". In the authentic act of promising, there is always a bilaterality (between the speaker and the recipient of the promise), a bilaterality that we find even in the promises we make to ourselves. The validity of the promise depends on our sincere commitment to making it (to keeping it). So we cannot seriously reduce the promise to a linguistic act with no consequences for the speaker (if only because, in many cases, the speaker exposes himself to the possible consequences of, for example, not keeping his promise; every signifying act of language is, in fact, susceptible to consequences, it *acts* on things).

Of course, a promise (especially a promise made to oneself) does not necessarily have to be understood as an act of submission to an absolute (or categorical) imperative. Nietzsche is thus probably right to criticise Kantian formalism in relation to the question of morality — formalism that we defend on the one hand,

---

[170] These are the lyrics of Amy Winehouse's song *You Know I'm No Good*, from the album *Back to Black* (2006).

since morality, in order to be effective, must respect criteria of coherence and possibility, which Austin emphasises in his analysis, but which we also criticise on the other hand when formalism replaces the very content of morality and the dynamism of ethical questioning (when the general principle becomes a particular moral law, as is the case, in our opinion, in Kant's opuscule *On a Supposed Right to Tell Lies from Benevolent Motives*). In the context of ethical questioning, we see the promise as a dynamic act of commitment by a being to himself or to another. The promise can thus constitute an authentic act of the free will (and not a form of "domestication of man" as Nietzsche maintains). Although, as far as we know, Nietzsche never directly addresses the theme of promise in his problematic of overcoming traditional values and in his vision of what he calls the 'Superman' (*Übermensch*), his work is permeated by such reflections[171]. In an aphorism from *Aurora*, for example, entitled *To what extent does the thinker love his enemy*, we find the following passage: "Never repress or silence to yourself an objection that may be made to your thought! Vow to do so! This is part of the primary probity of thought. You must also wage a campaign against yourself every day[172]." Here, the duality of the ethical principle is very explicit, firstly in the title of the aphorism (the thinker who "loves" his internal enemy, the one who objects to him) and secondly in the content of the aphorism: there is the one who formulates principles and the one who

---

[171] We refer again to Geoffroy de Clisson, *Nietzsche ou la valeur morale de l'instant* [Nietzsche, or the Moral Value of the Instant]

[172] Friedrich Nietzsche, *Aurora* (1881), § 370

objects; it is a question of dividing the *self* into two in order to "wage a campaign against oneself". Finally, Nietzsche presents his aphorism as an ethical principle. On the one hand, it is about respecting the probity of thought (a recurring theme in Nietzsche's work, as in the famous passage from *The Gay Science*: "Long live physics! And long live even more that which compels us to do so — our probity[173]!") and secondly, to make a promise to oneself ("Make a vow of it!"). In our view, the formulation of such a recommendation has all the hallmarks of an ethical principle (sincerity, commitment to oneself or to another, internal separation of the *self*). We find many of the same ethical principles in *Thus Spoke Zarathustra* (1883-1885), as well as in certain formulations of the eternal return, notably in *The Gay Science*, in paragraph 341 entitled *The Heaviest Weight*, which describes a thought experiment in which Nietzsche imagines a world in which we would be forced to relive an infinite number of times what we have already experienced, a paragraph that Nietzsche concludes with these sentences: "If this thought were to take power over you, it would transform you, perhaps, but it would also crush you; the question to everything 'Do you want this once again and countless times?' would weigh on your actions like the heaviest of weights! Or how much would you have to love yourself and life to want nothing more than this ultimate confirmation, this seal?" Here again, the thought of the eternal return acts as a filter, a principle of action (what would happen if I had to do the same thing over and over again? Am I sufficiently *in tune* with myself to put up with this thought or even wish for it?).

---

[173] Friedrich Nietzsche, *The Gay Science* (1882), IV, § 335

In this passage from *The Gay Science*, as in the aphorism from *Aurora* that we quoted earlier, we see that Nietzsche makes ethics (from probity, *Redlichkeit*, which can also be translated as loyalty, honesty, rectitude and which induces the notion of meaningful commitment) a dynamic principle, a perpetual and incessant questioning that guides thought without necessarily giving it content.

Ethics, unlike morality, is defined above all as an effort, a tension towards the promise that we have made to ourselves or to others, and not as a set of pre-established or transcendent rules that must be respected to the letter, putting aside any critical judgement once the fundamental principle has been validated. In ethical questioning, however, there remains this tension on the part of the promising subject, a tension that is an effort that the subject imposes on himself according to the coherent principles that he has identified within himself. Ethics is, in a way, the reintegration of *radical* dualism within the acting subject: dualism is not simply resolved once and for all in the moral law, it is the permanent driving force behind action.

8.

A PRAGMATIC MORALITY — The question of morality must not be posed to us solely in the rational terms of conformity to a transcendent legality. This does not mean, however, that there are no great moral principles that cannot be surpassed and that are imprescriptible (the absolute prohibition of murder, rape, etc.), dictated both by our sensitivity, our inclination towards others, and by a certain logical and formal requirement (a principle that we find, for example, in the formula: "Don't do to others what you wouldn't want done to you"). At the root of all ethical questioning is a demand for formal coherence. This requirement for coherence, which implies the sincerity of ethical reasoning (*Redlichkeit*), is at the foundation of moral questions. It provides the framework for what we have called "good will" by requiring the moral subject to recognise a certain number of formal structuring principles (just as the rules of harmony are structuring for a melody, even in the case where a melodic work is intended to be "unstructured"). However, while the (legal) form of the moral law structures the ethical principles of action, it does not directly determine their content. It is always the moral subject himself who determines, "in his soul and conscience" according to the legal formulation, the action that is appropriate according to the circumstances that require it: the substitution of the legalistic principle for the faculty of judgement of the moral agent does not do full justice to the substance and reality of man. Indeed, we cannot, in our view, conceive of so-called "moral" action strictly in terms of conformity to a law. Because of the dual structure of the world, the moral subject is never faced with a strictly identical reality, nor does he remain absolutely the same when confronted with a similar situation. To think that we can apply the same moral rules to heterogeneous situations is to condemn ourselves to casuistry with the Jesuits. As we suggested in the previous paragraph, ethical questioning is dynamic. This dynamism is neither decreed nor transcendent; it is the very manifestation of the subject's situation of disequilibrium, always pushed, almost in spite of himself, into a world that does not expect him and that offers him a different reality at every moment. Ethics is thus a permanent renewal of the subject's questioning of his or her way of acting in the world ("living a good life, with and for others, in just institutions[174]", says Paul Ricœur, what he himself presents as his "little ethics"). If ethical questioning is frozen in a finite set of formulas or absolute principles, then the moral agent, finding himself infantilised and disempowered by his own maxims, deprives himself of the reflexive exercise required by his condition. He then becomes his own scarecrow, fanatical and fetishist about a morality that has become external (heteronomous) to him.

Nietzsche undoubtedly deserves credit for having placed ethical questioning back at the centre of man's problems and his engagement with the world. For Nietzsche, ethical questioning is never considered to be settled once and for all. It remains dynamic and alive in each of our actions and in each of our thoughts. In *The Antichrist* (1888), for example, he writes: "With some tolerance in the expression, Jesus could be called a 'free spirit', — he cares nothing for anything fixed: the verb kills, everything fixed kills. The idea, the experience of 'life', as only he knows it, is repugnant to any kind of word, formula, law, faith or dogma. He speaks only of what is most interior: 'life', or 'truth', or 'light' are his words for this inner thing, — all the rest, all reality, all nature, even language, have for him the value of a sign, a symbol[175]." Nietzsche adds a little further on: "If I

---

[174] See, for example, Paul Ricœur, *Soi-même comme un autre* (*Oneself as Another*), 1990
[175] Op. cit., § 32

understand anything about this great symbolist, it is the fact that only inner realities are taken as realities, as truths — that everything else, everything natural, everything to do with time and space, everything historical, appeared to him only as signs, occasions for parables[176]." For Nietzsche, the interpretation of the texts of the Gospels in the sense of Saint Paul, i.e. (in Nietzsche's mind) as a set of precepts or laws to be respected, is more than wrong: it is a radical and total misinterpretation of the text of the Gospels. The notions of sin and punishment are, Nietzsche asserts, alien to the personality of Christ. This ethical requirement, understood as a constantly renewed duty towards oneself, distances Nietzsche from Kantian positions. Indeed, he criticises Kant, in very clear (and quite virulent) terms, for having formulated a morality of weakening, of infantilisation: "Kant's success", he writes, again in *The Antichrist*, "is no more than a theologian's success; Kant was, like Luther, like Leibniz, no more than another brake on German integrity, already so flimsy. [Another word against Kant as a moralist. A virtue must be our personal invention, defence and necessity: taken in any other sense, it is merely a danger. What is not a vital condition is harmful to life: a virtue that exists only because of a feeling of respect for the idea of 'virtue', as Kant wanted it to be, is dangerous. 'Virtue', 'duty', 'good in itself', good with the character of impersonality, of general value — chimeras in which degeneration is expressed, the last weakening of life, the chinoiserie of Königsberg[177]." While Nietzsche does not do Kant full justice, and is

---

[176] Op. cit., § 34
[177] Op. cit., § 10 and § 11

even, it has to be said, somewhat cruel to him, he does underline what we find problematic in Kant's thought, i.e. the shift from content-free formal legalism to the universally valid maxim of action with determined content (ethics becomes a practical appendage of conformity to the moral law dictated by autonomous reason). If this shift is already present in the seeds of the *Groundwork of the Metaphysics of Morals* (1785) and the *Critique of Practical Reason* (1788), it is even more perceptible in Kant's later work, in particular in *The Metaphysics of Morals*[178] (1797) and *On a Supposed Right to Tell Lies from Benevolent Motives* (1797), works in which Kant derives the principles of moral action directly from the legalistic formulations present in his critical work.

9.

THE QUESTION OF THE CONTENT OF MORALITY — Although Nietzsche repeatedly opposed Kant's morality in his work, this did not mean that he remained an "amoralist". Nietzsche did not attack the edifice of traditional morality with the ambition of destroying all morality. Nietzsche must not be reduced, as is too often the case, to the image of the

---

[178] In this work, Kant further develops his ideas on ethics and morality, explaining how the categorical imperatives are translated into practical rules and specific duties. In these works, Kant sometimes indulges in rigid interpretations of the imperatives, without necessarily, in our view, these interpretations being as firmly established as in the critical part of his work (*Critique of Pure Reason, Critique of Practical Reason, Critique of Judgement*).

"philosopher with a hammer". In reality, Nietzsche almost always criticised "morality" in the name of morality. The ethical question, as we have said, runs through Nietzsche's work, from his earliest writings to his latest. With the "disappearance of the metaphysical sky", as Nietzsche put it, the ethical question as a whole fell back on man's shoulders. This is one of the consequences of the "death of God" that Nietzsche prophesied in his *Gay Science* (1882), and which we quote here *in extenso*: "God is dead! God remains dead! And it is we who have killed him! How can we console ourselves, the murderers of murderers? The most sacred and powerful thing the world has ever possessed has bled under our knife — who will wash that blood from us? With what water can we cleanse ourselves? What atonements, what sacred games will we be forced to invent? Is the magnitude of this act not too great for us? Are we not forced to become gods ourselves in order at least to appear worthy of the gods? There has never been a greater deed, and those who may be born after us will, because of this deed, belong to a higher history than any history ever was[179]. Nietzsche's destruction of traditional morality implied the emergence of a new and overwhelming responsibility *("Isn't the greatness of this act too great for us?")*. This responsibility stemmed from a radical gesture of rupture and liberation, formulated in the tragic and triumphant announcement: *"God is dead! [And we killed him*! However, this emancipation was not without consequences: by abolishing God, man inherited God's problem. The death of God meant not only the dissolution of transcendent values, but the reversal of

---

[179] Op. cit., § 125

the ontological burden on man himself, who was now summoned to assume a divine position ("*Are we not forced to become gods ourselves?*"). This new weight revealed a major danger in Nietzsche's eyes: the nihilism of values, i.e. the risk of a collapse of meaning, of a total dissolution of axiological reference points. It was undoubtedly in a sense to ward off this danger that Nietzsche introduced the notion of transvaluation (*Umwertung aller Werte*), the process by which the Superman becomes the creator of new values, freed from a moral straitjacket inherited from the past. This transvaluation was based on a reversal of traditional values — which Nietzsche perceived as alienating and degrading — in favour of new, affirmative values, founded on an exaltation of life (in accordance with what Nietzsche called the will to power, the fundamental principle of existence, which drives all beings to assert themselves, to grow, to dominate and to dominate themselves). Thus, far from being reduced to a simple negation of old values, Nietzschean thought sought to go beyond nihilism by establishing an ethic of creative power, in which man, freed from inherited morality, became the demiurge of his own meaning.

Yet Nietzsche's resolution of the ethical question seems to us to contain a number of contradictions. On the one hand, Nietzsche affirms the existence of a fundamental ethical preoccupation, a questioning of every moment ("*You must also wage a campaign against yourself every day*"), and on the other, he hastens — rather like Kant — to give the formal framework of his ethical preoccupation a concrete content: it is the transvaluation, the affirmation of the values of life, supposed to be the superior values of the Superman. In our view, this concrete content is problematic insofar as it constitutes a point of torsion with the general ethical principle. If we compare the Nietzsche of the *Redlichkeit* — the one who questions the general framework of ethics in an approach which, in a sense, already resembles a demand for formal coherence (since the notions of rectitude, sincerity and loyalty imply a certain con-formity) — and the Nietzsche of the *Übermensch*, who exalts the values of life, the preservation and growth of being, self-assertion and the will to power, we are faced with an apparent tension, even a conceptual *hiatus*. Whereas the Nietzsche of *Redlichkeit* did not confer any substantial determination on his ethical principle — probity being for him a formal requirement by which the subject preceded his acts, assumed them and gave an exact account of them — the Nietzsche of the *Übermensch*, on the contrary, assigned his ethics a much more precise content. Whereas Nietzsche's principle of probity was radically anti-sensitive (almost Kantian, in a sense), his morality of vital affirmation was concretely translated into a progressive inflation of the *ego*. Thus, the thwarted *ego* of Nietzsche's *Aurora* (the dual, i.e. moral *ego*) was gradually transformed into an *ego* claiming its power and might: ethical dualism was transmuted into a monolithic, unmitigated egotic affirmation. In *Ecce homo* (1888), Nietzsche's late work, this assertion became almost megalomaniacal. Nietzsche made grandiose declarations, identifying himself with historical figures such as Dionysus or Jesus and assuring us that his works represented a revolution in the history of human thought (the titles of the four parts of *Ecce homo* are, in this respect, quite eloquent: *Why am I so wise? Why am I so intelligent? Why do I write such good books? Why am I a destiny?*) Nietzsche's emphasis and prophetic tone can certainly be interpreted as signs of his fragile mental state: we know that shortly after completing *Ecce* homo, Nietzsche collapsed mentally in Turin, probably as a result of an untreated attack of tertiary syphilis (although some researchers debate this hypothesis). After January 1889, he never regained his lucidity and spent the rest of his life in a state of dementia, cared for by his mother and then by his sister until his death in 1900. Nonetheless, we can see that in his work, the issue of *Redlichkeit*, that cruel honesty towards oneself, is gradually trans-formed into a relentless display of the *self*: *ecce homo!* This is man! Nietzsche finally asserts at the very end of his work. If Nietzsche ironically referred to Kantian morality as simply "Mr Kant's morality", we would be well advised to point out in return that his own ethical project seems to lead to a "Mr Nietzsche's morality" — in other words, a perspective in which the affirmation of values remains intimately linked to the subjectivity and singular positioning of the thinker himself. Was this evolution towards a hegemonic affirmation of the *ego* so much a part of the internal logic of Nietzschean thought as to be predictable and inevitable? Would a fully lucid Nietzsche have deliberately steered his ethical reasoning in this direction? It seems to us that the answer to this question is yes (at the risk of being 'philosophical fiction'). Indeed, even if Nietzsche does not immediately theorise the will to power, his general considerations on overcoming traditional values contain, from his earliest writings, the issues that will become those of the will to power. With the concept of life, of the affirmation of life, Nietzsche very soon thought he could rid himself of dualism, transcendental idealism and the Hegelian influences of his early writings (influences that were particularly present in *The Birth of Tragedy*, published in 1872, and with which he broke away the following year with From *On Truth and Lie in an Extra-Moral Sense*). For Nietzsche, a philosophy of affirmation did not need to go through negativity, just as a thought of action could dispense with a reflection on its determinants. Rather than analysing motives, Nietzsche preferred to explore instincts, believing that the vital force outweighed any attempt at rational justification. His work thus appears to be a perilous undertaking, aimed at making philosophy stand on one foot after having smashed the other with a hammer. It was no longer a question of thinking the world through abstract oppositions, but of fully assuming the dynamics of life, freed from the metaphysical constraints inherited from the past.

Could the idea of dualism only be broken by retaining the question of morality? This is what Nietzsche tried to do, by attempting to transform the old morality of traditional values (the heterogeneous, imposed morality) into the morality of action, which had to be defined in the moment (and in a form of spontaneity). However, this attempt to reinscribe ethical questioning in the moment led to an insidious reappearance of dualism, which Nietzsche, because of his own presuppositions, did not want to see. In *The Antichrist*, for example, when Nietzsche described Jesus as the "great symbolist", he was clearly part of a dualist problematic, since the symbol necessarily implied a relationship of meaning that presupposed an ontological distinction between heterogeneous realities. More generally, the ethical reflections that Nietzsche sprinkled throughout his writings (particularly in the period of *Aurora* and *The Gay Science*) revealed this underlying binary structure, which we will not go into here. However, Nietzsche, carried away by the dynamics of his radical critique of traditional morality, seemed to be both its de-constructor and its captive. His genealogical enterprise sometimes led him to seek paradoxical reconciliations between opposites, sometimes to overcome, or even obscure, the internal tensions and aporias that his own project brought to light. The anti-animality of ethical principles was thus transformed into a discourse of vitality and spiritualised animality (think, for example, of the figures of the camel, the lion or the eagle and the snake in *Thus Spoke Zarathustra*), while the manifest duality of the ethical principle (think not of the title of the paragraph in *Aurora*: "to what extent does the thinker love his enemy", which would almost evoke the notion of enlarged mentality that Kant expounds in the *Critique of Judgement*) was transformed into an undifferentiated affirmation of the *self* (the will and the "will to power" are one and the same thing, Nietzsche asserts, we can only will life). The Nietzsche of transvaluation resembled in this respect the Kant of the *Metaphysics of Morals* (1797), albeit in almost diametrically opposed ways. Whereas Kant's *ego* receded behind the legalistic principle (the logic of Kantian disinterest), Nietzsche's ego asserted itself in a subjective figure of immanent morality. In both cases, it was the articulation between the general principles of ethical questioning and the concrete maxims for determining action that gave rise to the problems and contradictions we have identified.

Once we have undertaken a critique of Kantian and Nietzschean morality, can we in turn escape the question of the link between ethical questioning and moral action? Can ethics be thought of independently of a specific moral content, without being anchored in a doctrine, principles or rules? How can we design moral principles that are both personal and universal? Does our ethical questioning have a foundation? Can it be rooted in anything other than the immediate subjectivity of the moral subject? If not, how can we extricate ourselves from this subjectivity in order to question the possibility of such a foundation? We have already attempted to answer these questions in the context of the problems of the philosophy of knowledge, and then of aesthetic philosophy. We must now examine the extent to which the answers sketched out in the first two books enable us to make progress in our ethical reflection.

AN AESTHETIC OF MORALITY?

10.

THE OBJECTIVITY OF MORALITY — If we refuse to give morality a definite content, how is it possible for us to envisage any objectivity in its principles? In form, this question is similar to those we asked ourselves in Book I ("What are the conditions of objective knowledge? How can we move from the subjectivity of sensations to a higher form of objectivity that would be that of science?"), and in Book II ("How can we move beyond the strictly subjective point of view of aesthetics?"). In Book I, as in Book II, the transition from subjectivity to objectivity was achieved by decentring the subject in relation to the object. In Book I, we called this decentring, with Max Planck, "de-anthropomorphisation", while in Book II, the subject's decentring was described as "tension towards the other", a projection towards exteriority. In both cases, decentring could only be achieved by considering the problem of signification, a problem which led us to confirm the thesis of *radical* dualism — dualism which we identified as being at the root of ethical questioning, the recognition of otherness being the moral form of dualism.

To ask the question of morality, we must first ask the question of the other, which means, first of all, admitting the possibility of the existence of the other as an exteriority that is not only threatening (insofar as it would be likely to call into question the integrity of the *self*, which I seek to defend, as a natural creature) but which is also *similar* to me. Recognition of the principle of differentiation (the *self* is not everything and does not dissolve into a hegemonic and contradictory narcissism) as well as the principle of reciprocity (I acknowledge the existence of beings other than myself, endowed like myself with sensitivity, reason and a capacity for meaningful abstraction) leads me to the ethical question. *Concern* for others (for what they think, feel and are) is the concrete manifestation of recognition of the principles of differentiation and reciprocity. It is thus an outward impulse (an impulse that stems from the identification of an interiority, i.e. a differentiation with the other). With the ethical question, I am projected towards a being that is not me; I am *interested* in something other than myself. In our opinion, this interest is not and cannot be purely projective and affirmative. It is not a simple 'élan vital' towards the other (as would be the élan vital of reproduction, for example: I am interested in the other not as the other, but to satisfy my own desires, which are themselves linked to my belonging to the species), nor even a spiritualised élan vital (as is the case in a sense in Nietzsche's philosophy). If this were the case, the ethical question would dissolve of its own accord, by being reduced *in fine* to that of an instinct or natural disposition. The interest we take in others, insofar as they have reached what we human beings might call the "stage of significance", is, on the contrary, necessarily an interest that is both projective *and* retrospective. In the ethical question, I am both pushed towards the other (pushed to come out of myself) and encouraged to question myself retrospectively about myself, about the consequences of my ideas, words or actions on the other. The ethical question is thus profoundly linked to the question of the other in its signifying dimension (which is why we think of ethics not in terms of anti-nature, since ethical behaviour can very well become a "second nature", as can slowly developed artistic genius, for example, but as a question that arises alongside that of our instincts, a "supernatural" question in short, that goes beyond our nature and our first inclinations). This meaningful projection towards the other is already, in ethical questioning, a step beyond "immediate egotism", a step towards what we call ethical subjectivity. In short, asking the question of the other is already moving towards a form of objectivity (even if the term objectivity is ill-chosen here, the term "desubjectification" would probably be more appropriate).

In moral questioning, as in the question of knowledge, subjectivity is the logical and ontological root of objectivity. Without sensitivity, without openness to the world (the fact of being open to the world also implies allowing oneself to be grasped by things, accepting a form of porosity of the *self*), there can be no objective questioning. Objectivity implies, to put it prosaically, using our body as a measuring instrument. However, value judgements (or ethical judgements) are different from factual or logical judgements, which are the basis of our ability to progress in our knowledge of the world. Value judgements do not fall into the categories of "true" and "false". Value judgements are essentially normative. It is not a judgement of conformity in the sense that it relates to an expected result (as is the case with judgements about facts such as did it happen — yes or no — or logical judgements that are correct or wrong). However, an ethical judgement is always made in the name of a higher principle, that higher principle being consideration, care or concern for *others*. In this respect, it can be a matter of conformity: conformity of principles, conformity with the idea I have of ethics, of man and of myself. Unlike a judgement whose object is knowledge, a normative (ethical) judgement is not necessarily made by comparison with an already existing norm. The moral agent is not content to follow rules or a methodology that must be applied with zeal. In *The Gay Science*, Nietzsche warns us: "It would be a relapse for us to fall completely into morality, by the very fact of our irascible probity, and that by satisfying excessive demands, we would end up becoming monsters, scarecrows of virtue. We must also be capable of standing beyond morality: and not just to stand with the anxious stiffness of someone who fears at every moment that they will slip and fall, but also to fly over it and play beyond it! And as long as you're ashamed of yourself, you won't be one of us yet[180]." The idea that we must conform to a rigid, universal moral framework contains the seeds of bigotry and the risk of becoming a "scarecrow of virtue", a philistine, in other words, a monster. When the moral framework takes the place of ethical questioning, then the infantilised human being can unburden himself of his ethical obligation, that is to say his duty to reflect on the other, not through the predefined and comfortable framework of traditional morality, but through his human sensibility by considering this other who is not quite me, who has his own history, his own culture, his own projects, his own needs, his own expectations...

---

[180] Op. cit., § 107

We do not intend here to trace the path of a relativistic morality (neither absolute rigidity nor unlimited tolerance, which are two pitfalls of the same problem: tolerating nothing or tolerating the intolerable). On the contrary, we affirm that ethics, that is to say moral questioning, must always start from the other: the other in his otherness, but also the other in me. In short, the other is both the root of questioning and the determined content of ethics. It is only on this condition of attentive consideration of the other (*concern* for the other) that the ethical question can develop, not in a static or fixed way, but in a dynamic way, like the development of a melody.

11.

MORALITY AND HARMONY — Can we speak of morality in the same way as we would speak of harmony or even beauty in music? Our effort to avoid considering morality as a set of formal rules (while giving it a framework, which is that of formal coherence and the logical and ontological recognition of the other as the other *self*) is undoubtedly related to our reflections on aesthetics. In the field of aesthetics, as in that of ethics, there is certainly a formal framework (harmonies, scales, etc.) but this formal framework does not constitute a limitation on the work. Within this framework, the work actually evolves 'freely'. It is not a prisoner of the framework, as an equation would be of its variables. As a meaningful creation, it can deviate from the framework (for example, "accidents" in music, or "chromatism"). This is precisely what Kant refuses to Benjamin Constant — no doubt worried by the idea of opening up moral doctrine to subjectivism — in *On a Supposed Right to Tell Lies from Benevolent Motives*. In reality, what could we reproach the man who lies to conceal a Jewish family that Nazi soldiers are looking for during the 1940 war? Would there be many who would speak out against this man's lie on the grounds that he had, by his untruthful words, "disqualified the source of law"? If we understand that Kant founds law on the universal principle that underlies his morality (Kant almost identifies law and morality in a way that was one of the surprising aspects of Eichmann's defence at his trial in Jerusalem in 1961[181]), For us, this identification is

---

[181] See Hannah Arendt's treatment of Eichmann's Kantian profession of faith in *Eichmann in Jerusalem* (1963). In *Eichmann in Jerusalem*, reporting Eichmann's words at the Jerusalem trial in 1961, Hannah Arendt wrote:

"The first indication of Eichmann's vague notion that there was more involved in this whole business than the question of the soldier's carrying out orders that are clearly criminal in nature and intent appeared during the police examination, when he suddenly declared with great emphasis that he had lived his whole life according to Kant's moral precepts, and especially according to a Kantian definition of duty. This was outrageous, on the face of it, and also incomprehensible, since Kant's moral philosophy is so closely bound up with man's faculty of judgment, which rules out blind obedience. The examining officer did not press the point, but Judge Raveh, either out of curiosity or out of indignation at Eichmann's having dared to invoke Kant's name in connection with his crimes, decided to question the accused. And, to the surprise of everybody, Eichmann came up with an approximately correct definition of the categorical imperative: "I meant by my remark about Kant that the principle of my will must always be such that it can become the principle of general laws" (which is not the case with theft or murder, for instance, because the thief or the murderer cannot conceivably wish to live under a legal system that would give others the right to rob or murder him). Upon further questioning, he added that he had read Kant's Critique of Practical Reason. He then proceeded to explain that from the moment he was charged with carrying out the Final Solution he had ceased to live according to Kantian principles, that he had known it, and that he had consoled himself with the thought that he no longer "was master of his own deeds," that he was unable "to change anything." What he failed to point out in court was that in this "period of crimes legalized by the state," as he himself now called it, he had not simply dismissed the Kantian formula as no longer applicable, he had distorted it to read: Act as if the principle of your actions were the same as that of the legislator or of the law of the land - or, in Hans Frank's formulation of "the categorical imperative in the Third Reich," which Eichmann might have known: "Act in such a way that the Führer, if he knew your action, would approve it" (*Die Technik des Staates,* 1942, pp. 15-16). Kant, to be sure, had never intended to say anything of the sort; on the contrary, to him every man was a legislator the moment he started to act: by using his "practical reason" man found the principles that could and should be the principles of law. But it is true that Eichmann's unconscious distortion agrees with what he himself called the version of Kant "for the household use of the little man." In this household use, all that is left of Kant's spirit is the demand that a man do more than obey the law, that he go beyond the mere call of obedience and identify his own will with the principle behind the law - the source from which the law sprang. In Kant's philosophy, that source was practical reason; in Eichmann's household use of him, it was the will of the Führer. Much of the horribly painstaking thoroughness in the execution of the Final Solution - a thoroughness that usually strikes the observer as typically German, or else as characteristic of the perfect bureaucrat - can be traced to the odd notion, indeed very common in Germany, that to be law-abiding means not merely to obey the laws but to act as though one were the legisator of the laws that one obeys. Hence the conviction that nothing less than going beyond the call of duty will do." While Eichmann explains quite clearly that from the moment he was given the task of implementing the Final Solution he had "ceased to live according to Kant's principles", Hannah Arendt attempts, in the rest of the extract, to explain how Eichmann did not simply cease to live according to Kant's principles but actually distorted them. The first formulation of the *Groundwork of the Metaphysics of Morals* "Act only in accordance with the maxim by means of which you can at the same time wish it to become a universal law" would then become, in Eichmann's mind: " Act as if the principle of your actions were the same as that of the legislator or of the law of the land", which is more or less the same thing, says Hannah Arendt, as Hans Frank's formulation: " Act in such a way that the Führer, if he knew your action, would approve it". While Kant invites the subject to make himself a legislator by bringing his maxims into line with the demand for universality, Eichmann, on the other hand, would interpret the categorical imperative as submission to the Führer's orders. This confusion (the shift from Kant's sovereign subject to Eichmann's submissive subject, reinterpreted by Arendt) is made possible, according to Hannah Arendt, by the ambivalence, specific to German culture, of the notion of obedience to the law, which, for Hannah Arendt, implies both the idea of submission to the law and identification with the source of the law. Eichmann, a conscientious civil servant, would therefore have been problematic not in the sense of Eichmann's defence (see previous footnote) but insofar as it creates a kind of fetishism of the rule (in favour of the judgement) of which Eichmann is the symbol. It is this overly close link between morality and law that undoubtedly explains the emphasis that Kant places in *On a Supposed Right to Tell Lies from Benevolent Motives* on the potential consequences of the act to the detriment of the actor's intentions. Even if the primary intention of the lie is to protect others, Kant asserts, its concrete effects are beyond the control of the moral subject. Thus, if the murderer finally discovers his victim despite — or because of — the lie of the person who tipped him off, the moral agent who lied could be held responsible, according to Kant, for the consequences of his act, regardless of the intention that motivated it. This position illustrates the intransigence of Kantian formalism, whereby only the conformity of the maxim to the moral law determines the morality of the action (in this case, the fact of not lying), and not its results (in short, Kant does not consider that the end can justify the means, even if the end is praiseworthy). Kant's reasoning is based on the idea that the morality of an action must be assessed according to the maxim that underlies it and its conformity with the categorical imperative, independently of its empirical consequences, since these remain contingent and beyond the

---

encouraged in spite of himself to identify with the source of Nazi law, i.e. the Führer.

(This passage is taken from Geoffroy de Clisson, *Les Anti-Humanistes ou l'avènement des Contre-Lumières*, The Anti-Humanists or the Rise of the Counter-Enlightenment, éditions L'Harmattan, 2021)

control of the moral subject. But could this indifference to the concrete effects of action not be interpreted as a form of cowardice in the face of practical responsibility, or even as an abdication in the face of the demands of reality? Can we abandon a potential victim to his executioner on the grounds that lying would contravene moral law and, by extension, civil law, if we assume that the latter is founded on the former? Does such a position not amount to subordinating the protection of the individual to an abstract fidelity to duty, at the risk of making the formal purity of the act take precedence over the concrete requirement of justice? In this example, Kant adopts a line of reasoning that is the exact opposite of Nietzsche's. The human being does not say: "I'm going to do what I'm going to do. Man does not say: "Here is man" (*Ecce homo!*), or "I stand before you as a being responsible for his actions and the consequences of his actions", but "Here is the law" and "If you look closely, man is hidden behind it".

12.

GENIUS OF MORALITY — To treat the subject of ethics and morality solely through the prism of conformity to the law or to transcendent principles is to run the risk of reducing the question of ethics to that of the codification of action (the "tables of the law", for example). But if we reduce ethics to such codification, we distance the moral subject from his ethical *concern*. This ethical concern must not be reduced to the question: "Does the reason for my action correspond to the principles I have freely set for myself?", or, what amounts to more or less the same thing: "Could I raise the maxim of my action to the rank of law or universal maxim? The ethical question is, in fact, deeply intertwined with the question of our openness to the world and with the question, as we have said, of recognition of the other (immediate sensitive recognition, because we are first and foremost sensitive beings, and retroactive rational recognition, because we are also rational and 'sensible' beings, i.e. capable of interpreting the world with our networks of meanings, and also capable of understanding the signifying networks of the other). If, as we believe, the ethical question is first and foremost for us the question of the other, it must remain a question open to the other. In other words, it cannot find a comfortable resolution in a formal sentence (a judgement of conformity). In a judgement of conformity, the moral subject in fact takes refuge behind formalism ("I can't do anything, I'm sorry, it's the rule, it's the law..."). This withdrawal on the part of the moral agent is what is truly amoral about the judgment of conformity. In the ethical question, the law is derived from the case, not the other way round. In this way, we always start from the other, from the problem of the other, and not from the problem of applying an existing law to a problem that did not yet exist. The question of ethics thus appeals to the faculty of *judging* (and not to the faculty of recognising, of identifying a case that is already known). This faculty is very close to the faculty of aesthetic judgement (which is what Plato presented in *The Republic*, albeit in a different mode, as we have already noted). The moral evaluation of action ("what should I do for the other person, considering his situation, his history...?"), like aesthetic judgment, does not respond to any pre-established criteria. Like aesthetic judgement, it also places the evaluator in a form of unstable equilibrium, in a state of anxiety that has no immediate resolution.

Just as there is such a thing as artistic genius, there must also be what we might call "moral genius", a talent that gives its rules not to art, but to action. Like artistic genius, moral genius defines itself first and foremost as a "being open" to things and to the world. It is because of this very structure of openness (which translates into a disposition of mind) that he grasps the problems of the other, and this faculty of openness to the other is also the faculty of putting oneself *in tune,* as it were, *with the* other. In ethical questioning, as in artistic questioning, there is this faculty of decentring the *ego* in relation to itself. In ethical questioning, the *ego* is not looking for a reward for itself, it is not chasing the satisfaction of a job well done or a duty fulfilled (a danger that Kant himself notes when he questions whether a single moral act has really been accomplished, since moral action is always accompanied to a greater or lesser extent by *ego* satisfaction). In reality, moral action is an action that considers the other, that takes the other into account by putting him or her before any principle (this is also valid, in my opinion, for the education of children). This does not mean, however, that there are no *moral principles* (in the same way that we do not claim that beauty is relative), it just means that moral principles do not necessarily resolve all 'cases of conscience'. So, it's not a question of falling into a form of moral relativism, but rather of imposing greater demands on ourselves and never being satisfied with the application of a rule. The moral agent is free, that is, creative. However, as a free agent, he must also be accountable, i.e. present himself alongside his actions and be able to answer for them. In short, the moral man must be able to say: "here I am" and not just: "it was my duty...". However, this "here I am" is not (and cannot be) the Nietzschean *Ecce homo!* Whereas Nietzsche's notion of responsibility is linked to a form of exhibition of the *ego*, which is itself subject to the higher demands of the "values of life", we defend the vision of a man who is subject to nothing other than his demand for probity towards himself and others. This probity is not only an exercise in coherence, it is also an exercise in bringing together the being who defines himself by integrating (or, on the contrary, rejecting) the actions he approves or disapproves of. Moral action is thus the action for which we can answer, that we can consciously, coherently and independently judge, integrating into what we are, into the way in which we agree to define or describe ourselves.

So, as we can see, ethical questioning is not entirely superimposable on legalistic or moral questioning in the Kantian sense of the term. We need to separate, in our thinking, what enables us to found a sociability, that is, to put it quickly, what could inspire the laws of the 'ideal' State, from what enables us to recognise ourselves as human beings, that is, sentient, sensible and rational beings. This recognition cannot be totally identified with the autonomous grasp within us of a possible "moral law", as Kant theorised. This idea of a "moral law" or "categorical imperative" leaves a large part of what makes us human by the wayside: our capacity to judge not "once and for all" (reason in its autonomy grasps the transcendental moral law) but perpetually and at every moment. If we were to get rid of the moral question by abandoning it to logical considerations, we would run the risk of making morality a matter of formalism. But the origin of the moral question is precisely not formal. On the contrary, it is a fundamental recognition of openness to the other, in other words, of *radical* dualism. The other, in the moral question, can never be reduced to a codified formal dialectic (even if this dialectic recognises and incorporates the question of the other into its foundations). This is why Emmanuel Levinas is undoubtedly right to analyse the face of the other precisely in terms of its irreducibility. For Levinas, the face of the other is more than just a visual phenomenon or a physical form. The face is, above all, the expression of the other as a vulnerable and singular being. The sight of another person's face produces a silent challenge, a call to responsibility. This call is not an explicit request, but an ethical challenge to take care of the other, not to reduce them to an object of knowledge or something we can dominate. For Levinas, the other is never a simple extension of the *self* or a projection of what I am. The other, as a face, is absolutely *other*, irreducible to my categories, my thoughts or my concepts. This radical otherness is the foundation of ethics: it means recognising the other in his absolute otherness and responding to him. Lévinas thus insists on the asymmetry of the ethical relationship: the other is not my abstract equal (as in the golden rule that we should not do to others what we would not want them to do to us, a rule that has more to do with the logic of concern for the other) but an other who orders me to respect him, to listen to him, and to respond to his needs.

Levinas's philosophy teaches us that our relationship with the other is not primarily formal. Legal formalism is merely a communicable consequence of my state of openness to the other, not a transcendent or *a priori* rule. My state of imbalance (the fact that I am not a purely formal creature who could enjoy its own completeness) is precisely what *projects* me towards the other. We too, to return to a distant reference to Gödel, are incomplete systems, only our incompleteness is not experienced in a negative mode. On the contrary, it is the sign of our irreducible openness. It is thus through the mediation of the other that we have the possibility of progressing in our being, in the definition of our identity ("who am I for myself and in relation to myself who am already another? who am I for the other?") as well as in the understanding of what we are.

Book IV

Exploring the Self

INTRODUCTION

This final part, devoted to the question of identity, is not intended to be an exhaustive treatment of the problem. It is simply a matter of sketching out a redefinition of the concept of identity in the light of developments in the previous three books. So far, we have tried to analyse and explain the different dimensions of the *self*: first, the *self* of knowledge (or the subject of knowledge), then the aesthetic *self*, and finally the ethical *self*. Throughout our argument, we have endeavoured never to posit the existence of the *self* as a hypothesis that we would have sought to corroborate. On the contrary, we have started from the opposite hypothesis and have shown the aporias to which this hypothesis leads (that of the materialist monist, its extension towards Hilbert's completeness theses). The existence of a separate subject (which logically implied *radical* dualism) was first shown negatively, by pointing out the contradictory aspects of the opposing theses (if we show that the subject cannot not exist, then we have demonstrated its existence[182]). In Books II and III, we

---

[182] Here we could make the same point that Brouwer makes about the third party and reasoning by the absurd. For Brouwer, the truth of a mathematical statement lies in our ability to prove it, not in its correspondence with objective reality or in a truth that exists outside the mind's actual constructions. Following this same pragmatic idea, Brouwer's intuitionism rejects reasoning based on the absurd or the third-excluded (the negation of non-existence not being equivalent to existence, only constructed or constructible objects exist).

attempted to show how the subject's 'state-of-being-open' — to use a Heideggerian expression — which we deduced from Book I, structured its relationship to the world, both in its artistic expression and in its ethical concern (which is, as we have seen, first and foremost a concern or 'concern' for the other). We have thus approached the question of identity from the angle of the 'resonance' of the *self* with the radical exteriority constituted, for the artist, by reality, for the spectator, by the work of art, and for the moral subject, by the other. Throughout the first three parts, we have also regularly used terms borrowed from the vocabulary of

---

It should be noted, however, that Brouwer himself posits that mathematics are mental constructs that do not have their own autonomy (Brouwer is opposed to Gödel and the Platonist view of mathematics). He insists that mathematical truth is linked to our ability to construct mathematical objects explicitly. If a proposition is not proved (or disproved) by a constructive method, we cannot assert that it is either true or false. So, it is the linking acts performed by the mathematician that must establish the existence or otherwise of a mathematical object.

Apart from the fact that Brouwer's constructivist theory has been widely criticised, not least because of theoretical and practical successes that contradict some of Brouwer's assumptions, we should note that for Brouwer, the ultimate foundation of all mathematical activity is awareness of time and of the mental act by which mathematical objects are constructed. Mathematical construction arises from internal experience, and this intuitive temporality is crucial. This approach implies a duality between consciousness (which is creative and active) and "nothing" or emptiness, in other words the absence of any prior construction. In fact, constructivism already accepts *radical* dualism in its axioms.

music to describe the profound relationship between the open being and things ('harmony', 'tuning fork', 'consonance', 'resonance', 'chord', etc.), without yet evoking the 'content' of this relationship.), without even mentioning the concrete 'content' of what would be likely to define the subject (i.e. the one who is in 'consonance' with things, who puts himself 'in tune with the other' or who gives his 'agreement' or validation to a given statement...). If we have traced the contours of identity (logical contours, organic contours, etc.), we now need to define what gives materiality to these contours, i.e. substance to what we are.

IDENTITY AS A MEANINGFUL GATHERING
IDENTITY AS A MEANINGFUL RETURN TO THE SELF

1.

In the *Critique of Pure Reason*, Immanuel Kant develops the notion of transcendental apperception to designate the awareness we have of ourselves as a knowing subject, i.e. the awareness of our own cognitive activity when we unify the various sensible perceptions. Transcendental apperception is an active process by which the "I think" (the *ego*) accompanies all our representations. So, for a perception to be recognised as knowledge, it must be linked to this *I* consciousness. This unification is what allows the synthesis of diverse representations into a coherent experience. In the *Transcendental Deduction of Categories*, Kant states that our experience of the world is based on the unity of our consciousness, i.e. on our mind's ability to bind together different perceptions into a single coherent experience. This unity is what Kant calls "the synthetic unity of apperception". Without this unity, Kant explains, our perceptions would remain scattered and disordered, and we would be unable to form a unified understanding of reality. Kant does, however, make a distinction between empirical apperception (self-consciousness based on experience) and transcendental apperception (pure self-consciousness, independent of any particular experience). Empirical apperception is contingent and varies according to the circumstances of individual experience, whereas transcendental apperception is the necessary *a priori* condition for any experience to be possible. For Kant, the expression "I think" is the fundamental marker of transcendental apperception[183]. For me to be able to say that I perceive something, this perception must be unified in the form of the "I think", which means that all the representations I receive are attributed to a single subject and are organised coherently. Without this "I think", there would be no connection between the various perceptions, and there could be no possible knowledge. For Kant, transcendental apperception is closely linked to transcendental synthesis, which refers to the process by which the mind organises and unifies the data of sensible intuition according to the concepts of the understanding (the categories). This synthetic process is made possible by transcendental apperception, which is what allows these categories to be applied coherently to the various re-presentations. For Kant, transcendental apperception is a necessary condition for *a priori* synthetic judgements to be possible. For us to be able to make judgements that do not depend solely on experience (for example, mathematical judgements or the fundamental principles of physics), there must be a unity underlying our consciousness. This unity is what transcendental apperception provides, by ensuring that all our representations belong to one and the same

---

[183] "The "I think" must be able to accompany all my representations; otherwise, something would be represented in me that could not be thought, which amounts to saying that the representation would be impossible, or would be nothing for me. The representation that can be given before any thought is called intuition. The whole variety of intuition therefore has a necessary relation to the I think, in the same subject where this variety is encountered", writes Kant in the *Critique of Pure Reason*, B 131.

consciousness. For Kant, then, transcendental apperception is a pure and original awareness of the unity of the knowing subject, which enables all knowledge to be formed. It plays a fundamental role in his attempt to show that all possible experience is made coherent by the synthetic action of our mind. The unity of consciousness is thus the transcendental condition for the possibility of knowledge. This concept is one of the pivots of Kantian philosophy, for it links sensible intuitions and concepts of understanding under the aegis of the knowing subject, while at the same time founding the very possibility of *a priori* knowledge. For Kant, dualism (transcendental apperception as awareness of the unity of the subject and its separation from the world) is therefore a *sine qua non* of knowledge. However, Kant's perception, whether empirical or transcendental, if it is linked to the identity of the subject and to the implicit recognition of the subject itself as identity, responds more to the question of the logical and psychological contours of the subject than to the question of the content or substance of this identity.

How, in the light of the previous three books, can we now answer the question of the content of identity? If it seems to us that the question of identity unfolds in several directions (bodily identity, psychological identity, cultural identity, moral identity, etc.) which we will attempt to follow in turn in this book, we should note that these directions have, for the most part, the same point of origin: that of our capacity to rise to the level of meaning. It is because we are beings capable of handling and understanding language that the question of identity arises for us. As we have seen, language is not just a tool for communication; it is also a fundamental way of structuring reality. When individuals learn to use language, they begin to distinguish the outside world from themselves. It is through this differentiation that self-awareness is formed. Language makes it possible to designate external objects while constructing a distinction between "I" and "other". In *The Philosophy of Symbolic Forms* (1923-1929), Ernst Cassirer showed that, in ancient societies, the experience of the world was initially dominated by a mythical vision, in which the distinction between the individual and nature or the collective was blurred. In mythical thinking, the individual was absorbed in a universe of shared symbols that did not allow him or her to distinguish clearly as an individual subject. With the development of rational thought and abstract language, the individual began to see himself as an autonomous subject. This development marks the transition from a collective (or cosmic, in myth) consciousness to an individual consciousness. The *I* thus emerges from the evolution of symbolic forms towards a more precise differentiation between subject and object. For Cassirer, the emergence of the *I* is linked to the human capacity to objectify the world. By dissociating the subject from the object, symbolic forms, in particular language and science, offer the individual the possibility of distancing himself from himself: the individual becomes capable of seeing himself as an object among other objects in the world. It is this capacity for self-objectification that lies at the heart of the formation of the *I*. In *The Philosophy of Symbolic Forms*, Cassirer develops the three stages in the formation of the *I* (Volume 1: Language, Volume 2: Mythical Thought, Volume 3: The Phenomenology of

Knowledge). The corollary of this approach to the emergence of the *I* is the question of identity: how can a being capable of using a signifying language understand and describe itself (and how can this signifying being achieve full self-awareness)?

For us creatures of meaning, the question of identity does not boil down to a 'simple' epistemological problem. More generally, it concerns the way in which we construct the idea of the *self*, an idea that is not immutable and immortal, to be grasped once and for all as an eternal essence, but one that is gradually formed, formulated and understood through our personal experiences and our psychological and moral development, It is an idea that is progressively formed, formulated and understood through our personal experiences, our psychological and moral development, and through the historical and cultural processes that precede and shape us. Finally, it is an idea that is constructed according to the yardstick of our critical gaze, which questions and challenges the shifting symbolic forms that have structured the *self*, sometimes with the *self* and sometimes without the self, or against the self's will.

IDENTITY AS A PROJECTION OF THE *SELF*

2.

As we have seen, the question of identity is originally linked to the structure of our relationship with the world. The *ego*, in its original state of openness to the world, is dominated by two movements. First, an imbalance "forward" towards the world: the *self* is as it were projected towards things; it is, strictly speaking, "impressionable", i.e. in a dual (imposed) relationship with things. But this impressionable character of the *self* can only be understood insofar as we envisage a *self* precisely as an impressionable entity, i.e. as an identity. It is in a similar sense that Kant formulates, in the *Critique of Pure Reason*, the idea of transcendental apperception. Before any possibility of perception, we can only suppose, from an epistemological point of view[184], a subject who perceives: perception presupposes reception. This forward imbalance of the *self* thus implies the logical idea of a perceiving identity, as well as a return on oneself, i.e. an identification as a perceiving subject. However, the subject's awareness of this second movement, i.e. the *concrete* identification of the *self* by the *self*, cannot be *an a priori* or transcendental moment; it is in reality a progressive construction, a historical identification of the *self* as identity. This historical dimension is in fact twofold, it is both historical-cultural — there is a progressive awareness of the *self* in human history — and psychological, personal

---

[184] Kant would probably use the term "*a priori*" instead, transcendental apperception being a pure consciousness already assumed in all the subject's acts of knowledge.

(progressive awareness of the *self* in the personal history of the *self*). In the third volume of *The Philosophy of Symbolic Forms*, entitled *The Phenomenology of Knowledge*, Ernst Cassirer emphasises this historical and, in a sense, constructivist dimension of the concept of identity. For Cassirer, myth, the deification of elements external to the subject, constitutes a first step in the long process of identifying the *self*: "It is by precise, relatively constant features of physiognomy that we recognise the demon or the god and distinguish him from others [myth as an element of differentiation[185]]. And what myth begins in this direction, language and art complete [symbolic forms as a *means of* differentiating the *self*]: for individuality is only achieved with the name and image of the god [complementarity of language and signifying image]. Thus, the intuition of oneself as a singular essence, specified and well-defined [the problem of identity as the formal delimitation of the *self*], is not the basis on which man gradually constitutes his global vision of reality [as opposed to the idea of a transcendental, *a priori* apperception]: on the contrary, it is only the end, the ripe fruit of a creative process in which all the various primary energies of the mind are activated and interpenetrate[186]." In reinterpreting Kant's notion of transcendental apperception, Cassirer insists on the active role of thought in the construction of reality, but he goes further by broadening the scope of "forms of apperception". Unlike Kant, who focused primarily on cognitive synthesis, Cassirer sees symbolic forms — be they language, art, science or myth — as a

---

[185] Our comments are in square brackets.
[186] Op. cit., Ch. 2: *The Phenomenon of Expression as a Fundamental Moment of Perceptive Consciousness*

modality of apperception in their own right. Each symbolic form shapes a unique way of structuring reality and interpreting the world. Thus, for Cassirer, transcendental apperception is not a monolithic unity of consciousness, but a diverse and dynamic set of symbolic processes that define human experience. In short, Cassirer reinterprets transcendental apperception by transforming it into an activity of symbolisation, which is not just a formal intellectual activity, but also a diversified cultural and historical process. Cassirer retains the Kantian idea of an "I think" that accompanies all our representations, but considers that this function of unifying consciousness is expressed differently according to each symbolic form, shaping "worlds" of meaning. He therefore sees the structure of knowledge not as strictly transcendental in the Kantian sense, but as intrinsically linked to the cultural forms through which individuals give meaning to their experience. Where Kant identified a clear separation between transcendental apperception (unconditioned) and empirical apperception (conditioned and linked to particular experiences), Cassirer suggests that this unity can be constructed by the cultural forms themselves. In other words, the unity of self-consciousness is in some way mediated by these symbolic forms. It could be said that Cassirer tends to 'culturalise' the function of apperception, which leads him not to oppose the transcendental and empirical dimensions as rigorously as Kant did, and to distance himself from Kant's *aprioristic* vision of knowledge. In a way, Cassirer's philosophy, while retaining Kantian fundamentals, is more "evolutionist" in the sense that it analyses what Kant calls the "transcendentals", not necessarily as immediate or *a priori* givens, but precisely as the result of evolutionary and cultural processes (which, we think, is not incompatible with the spirit of Kantian philosophy).

The construction of identity (i.e. the recognition of the subject itself as a knowing subject, delimited and separate from the world), while responding to a long historical and cultural process, is also the result of the subject's psychological development. In terms of the subject's personal history, Cassirer's work can be compared with the more recent work of Jean Piaget (although Piaget's work is undoubtedly based on a different set of issues from Cassirer's). For Piaget, as we have already briefly mentioned in Book II, knowledge is constructed through processes of assimilation and accommodation over the course of stages of cognitive development. Cassirer, although not directly interested in the cognitive development of the child, also sees knowledge as the product of a dynamic human activity. In his philosophy of symbolic forms, every area of culture — be it science, religion, myth, art or language — is a way of structuring and giving meaning to experience. In this way, symbolic forms function in a similar way to Piaget's schemas, organising reality according to different logics and rules. Piaget and Cassirer also agree that reality is not simply reflected by thought, but actively constructed by it. For Piaget, this construction depends on the interactions between the individual and his environment, while for Cassirer it results from the symbolic systems and cultural forms that mediate the human relationship to the world. In both cases, then, knowledge is not a simple discovery of reality, but a progressive and contextual structuring of the signifying being. Finally, Cassirer, in his analysis of symbolic forms, gives a central place to language as the first symbolic mediation between the mind and the world. Piaget, although he focuses more on logical operations, also recognises the importance of language and symbol in cognitive construction. Piaget, like Cassirer, believes that symbolism is essential to the development of abstract thought, although Cassirer sees it in a broader philosophical and cultural framework.

What we want to show here, through these diversions via the observations of Cassirer and Piaget, is that identity is not defined in a fixed and essentialist way, but that it is on the contrary conceived in a dynamic way, this dynamism reflecting the profound structure of our mode of being in the world. In the process of identifying the *self*, however, there is also a retrospective movement which is the moment of the *self*'s conscious look at itself (that essential moment in the constitution of identity when the *self* sees itself, identifies itself as *me*). Without this retrospective movement of synthesis, the *self* cannot claim to achieve full consciousness (it is only the projected *self* without consciousness of the *self*). Awareness of the *self* thus depends on the ability of the *self* to tell its own story — itself, to make of itself a kind of meaningful synthesis, bringing together its history, culture, thoughts, actions, etc. This ability to tell its own story, to identify itself, however confusedly, as an individual entity is what Paul Ricœur calls, in *Soi-même comme un autre* (*Oneself as Another*, 1990), "narrative identity". For Ricœur, narrative identity unfolds in two directions: (i) *ipse identity* (or self-identity), which refers to the subject's *dynamic* identity, that which enables him or her to maintain himself or herself over time, despite changes; it is constructed through relationships and actions, and remains linked to the way in which a person relates and interprets his or her experiences; *ipse* identity is not based on static characteristics, but on fidelity to oneself in a series of acts and commitments; (ii) *idem identity*, which refers to aspects of identity that remain the same despite the passage of time, such as name, character traits or social roles; this is a more stable and fixed form of identity, but it is not enough to define subjectivity in its entirety.

For Ricœur, a person's identity is constructed and understood through narrative. This narrative identity enables events, actions and experiences to be woven together in a temporal continuity that gives meaning to the "self". By narrating themselves, the individual links the events of their life into a narrative framework, integrating ruptures, conflicts, aspirations and regrets into a coherent story. This narrative becomes the way in which the subject understands himself and can be understood by others. Narrative identity plays an essential role, enabling the subject to navigate between permanence and change. The story we tell about ourselves evolves, is enriched and adapts to new experiences, enabling a fluid yet coherent identity over time. For Ricœur, narrative identity is linked to memory and interpretation: the subject remembers and re-interprets past events and integrates his or her plans for the future into a meaningful story. Ricœur sees narrative as a means by which subjects negotiate their relationship with time. Narration makes it possible to give meaning to the changes, ruptures and actions that mean that a subject's life cannot be reduced to a simple list of facts. In this sense, narrative identity is an "open identity" that is always under construction and likely to evolve.

Identity, as a conscious synthesis of the *self*, is not defined, at first sight, by the search for what might constitute an integrity of the *self*, in the sense, for example, in which Maurice Barrès understands it (particularly in his trilogy entitled *Le culte du moi, The Cult of the Self*, in which Barrès maintains a romantic vision of a profoundly unique *self*, which everyone should cultivate and protect from outside influences, the cult of the *self* consisting precisely in discovering and affirming its own essence by separating itself from the bad branches[187]). The identity of the *self*, that is to say

---

[187] In the first volume of *Le Culte du moi, Sous l'œil des barbares (The Cult of the Self, Under the Eye of the Barbarians)*, Maurice Barrès compares the *ego* to a tree that needs pruning. The tree must separate itself from its bad branches, reject all foreign parts and assimilate only what is "identical". We see that Barrès confines himself almost strictly to the (necessarily incomplete) definition of *idem* identity. My identity can only be constituted by what is similar to me, what can be assimilated to it:

"We have to defend it every day and create it every day. This is the twofold truth on which these works are built. The cult of the "I" is not about accepting oneself in its entirety. This ethic, in which we have placed our ardent and unique complacency, demands constant effort from its servants. It is a culture that is made up of prunings and additions: first we must purify our "I" of all the foreign particles that life continually introduces into it, and then we must add to it. What then? Everything that is identical to it, everything that can be assimilated, let's speak plainly, everything that sticks to it when it gives itself over without reaction to the forces "what defines the *self* as a signifying object" (and therefore an object of narration) cannot start from anything other than what precisely enables its constitution: the state of openness to the world. The movement of openness to things thus necessarily precedes the synthetic movement of turning in on oneself and the affirmation of the narrative identity of the *self* (we cannot operate a critical or synthetic return on an empty shell). The movement of signifying gathering of the *self*, which is necessary for full awareness of identity, is therefore not necessarily a moment of closure of the *self*. On the contrary, it is understood as a dynamic integration of the heterogeneous into a homogenous and projective identity (which defines itself and evolves over time).

---

of its instinct", Maurice Barrès, *Sous l'œil des barbares* [1888] in *Le Culte du moi*, Paris, Emile-Paul éditions, 1910, p. 13.
At the start of the book (the first in the trilogy), Maurice Barrès begins by using this quotation from Victor-Emile Michelet: "Qu'on me rende mon moi!" ("Let Me Have My Self Back!")

IDENTITY AND OPENING UP: *SELF* AND DUALITY

IDENTITY AND HISTORY

3.

We have seen that individual identity is originally structured by the subject's relationship of openness to the world (the unbalanced *self*, projected forward almost in spite of itself). This structure of openness to the world on the part of the subject, combined with the retroactive and critical gaze he casts on himself, constitutes what Paul Ricœur calls "narrative identity" (identity as the capacity to narrate oneself). It is interesting to note that, in Ricœur's philosophy, it is first and foremost the subject who narrates himself, that is, who defines and limits himself. In this way, the subject is not simply presented as 'defined' by various influences, but as the actor of his or her own identity. It is thus the subject who chooses, in his narrative process, what constitutes him and what he rejects. In Ricœur's view, identity is not created, as Maurice Barrès claimed, by instinctive assimilation of the identical (the static dimension of identity) but by dynamic progression through networks of meanings that expand over time.

But how can we provide a new answer to a question that is not entirely a matter of the conditions of our knowledge, but rather of what we might call 'value judgements'? Before arriving at the question of identity, we have sought, on the basis of the epistemological and phenomenological study of the subject, to identify the fundamental characteristics that constitute the subject as subject: its state of sensitive openness to the world, its capacity to create language and to make logical use of it, its ability to rise to the level of signification, its rational and critical dimension, etc. We have thus begun by examining the conditions of our knowledge, the conditions of our identity and the conditions of our identity. By starting with an examination of the conditions of our being in the world, we have been able to move on to related subjects (aesthetics, ethics, identity). But can we claim here to be moving from an epistemological subject (what is the deep structure of the question of identity) to an axiological subject (which relates to values)? Here we come up against one of the great difficulties of philosophical thought: should philosophy confine itself to identifying the conditions under which knowledge is possible, or does it have something to say beyond this simple exercise, and if so, under what conditions? We have already begun to answer this question by going beyond the strict framework of epistemology in Books II *(Aesthetics)* and III *(Ethics)*. Throughout these books, our approach has been to reverse the usual order of problematisation of axiologies. It was not a question of examining the possibility of an epistemological foundation for value judgements, that is, of asking whether epistemology, and more broadly the theory of knowledge, could shed light on axiological questions. In contrast to this approach, we sought to determine whether axiology itself could dispense with a prior interrogation of the foundations of knowledge. In other words, we posed the question in terms of a condition of possibility: does any axiology necessarily presuppose a reflection on the structures of knowledge? Our answer to this question was 'yes'. Axiology, like any argumentative discussion, is secondary to epistemological criticism. Value judgements always presuppose a certain vision of knowledge (if only in the construction of arguments, in the use of rationality). As such, they cannot avoid an examination of their own foundations. It is revealing, moreover, that anti-rational axiologies have often sought to evade this requirement, sometimes going so far as to positively claim the notion of 'prejudice' as a legitimate principle, or, in their most consistent formulations, to assume relativistic positions. Paradoxically, this attempt to evade the question of foundation testifies to its inescapability: any axiology, even when it strives to deny the need for a rational anchor, is in spite of itself part of a structure that presupposes a mode of legitimation, be it implicit or self-referential. In *Les déracinés* (*The Uprooted*, 1897), one of Maurice Barrès's major works and the first volume of his trilogy *Le roman de l'énergie nationale* (*The Novel of National Energy*), we find a particularly interesting instance of this use of the term 'prejudice'. At the beginning of his novel, Maurice Barrès describes the way in which Professor Bouteiller, a patent Kantian, will exert a harmful influence on his young secondary school pupils from Lorraine, who are attached to their native land, its values and traditions, but still too permeable to foreign influences, and writes: "Uprooting these children, detaching them from the soil and the social group to which everything connects them, to place them outside their prejudices in abstract reason, how could that bother him, who has no soil, no society and, he thinks, no prejudices[188]?". For Barrès, "abstract" reason is described as "out of the ground"

---

[188] Op. cit., published by Bartillat, Paris 2020, p. 24 (French Edition)

(how many times have we heard that expression since Barrès!), it is opposed to "prejudice", which for Barrès is the ideological root of the high school students, their doctrinal soil, the soil from which one cannot tear oneself without losing one's roots, that is to say one's soul. The high school students, of course, a little too keen on intellectual emancipation, will meet with disastrous fates, one after the other, which will sound like a kind of divine punishment: no one uproots himself with impunity from his native land, Maurice Barrès seems to be telling us, and it is Paris, of course, that will finish off by perverting the fragile students. In the rest of the novel, Rœmerspacher, one of Professor Bouteiller's former students, makes a remark that sounds as if it came straight from the mouth of Maurice Barrès himself: "I was too much of a student, sir, to remain Mr Bouteiller's student and to admit a formula that implies the possibility of universal legislation. I have often spoken about it with one of my friends, a Catholic, Gallant de Saint-Phlin, who always sticks to theological morality. He opposes Kant to Pascal's observation: "Truth below the Pyrenees, error beyond", which you have verified for us a thousand times over. Men, from century to century, as from country to country, conceive different morals which, according to the times and climates, are necessary and therefore just. They are the truth as long as they are necessary. So, sir, we bring to life what you felt in Balzac's work: the passionate curiosity of such an abundant zoology[189]. Here we see how the shift takes place between the destruction of Kantian philosophy — and, more generally, the very disqualification of the idea

---

[189] Ibid., p. 149

of a rational basis for ideas — and the consecration of a taxonomic approach to reality (the abundant zoology). By opposing the critique of foundations to the study of living things, we pretend to believe that the philosophy of knowledge is opposed to the experience of living things. In fact, nothing could be further from the truth, since the search for the foundations does not exclude, in principle, the dynamic explanation of the behaviour of living beings. It should be noted in passing that Pascal, while making the lucid and almost amused observation that truth has a "variable geography", does not confine himself to a form of relativistic indifference (a proclamation of truth is not necessarily true!). For Pascal, as for most of those who later came to be known as the "French moralists", the relativism of ideas cannot be seen as the ultimate end of reflection. More specifically, Pascal's questioning of the relativism of human representations is not a matter of simple scepticism but aims to highlight the need for a transcendent order of truth, which exceeds the limits of reason and is available only to faith. In this way, the contingency and variability of ideas are not so much affirmed for their own sake as to highlight the need for an absolute foundation that escapes the instability of human judgement (an aspect of Pascalian thought that Barrès obviously overlooks).

In Barrès, as in early twentieth-century French nationalist thought in general, it is the avoidance of the question of foundations that authorises the slide towards relativism. An axiology that avoids critical examination of its first principles condemns itself to arbitrariness: the values it sets up as absolute references find their legitimacy only in contingent adherence to a state of affairs (adherence to values imposed by the social environment, the family, the nation, etc.). In the absence of critical and reflexive anchoring, these values cannot lay claim to a universalisable normativity and dissolve into the logic of particularism or mere social convention. The relativistic positions that sometimes derive from such axiologies might at a pinch seem satisfactory to us if they led to a form of suspension of judgement (that ἐποχή of the ancients that leads to ἀταραξία, that is, to a form of tranquillity of the soul). However, in nationalist ideologies, it has to be said that relativism is only a façade: landed through the window, the idea of the mother nation's superiority over other nations usually reappears through the door. Sentimental attachment provides a form of authoritarian and proclamatory legitimacy, as the anti-Kantian Rœmerspacher makes abundantly clear: "Look", says Rœmerspacher, "it's pointless to discuss whether we should behave according to this or that theory. Even if it is right, it does not follow that it is a truth that influences us. What determines our actions goes deeper than what we learn as students. When it comes to making a decision, what we call 'the truth' is a way of seeing things that we have inherited from our parents, from our early childhood, from our teacher, and which therefore has such sentimental force that we attribute to it the character of evidence[190]." Thus, we must stick to the "evidence" of national or even regional feeling (and not suspend judgement). What is true is what is necessary, what is necessary is what exalts my sense of belonging to a whole that transcends me. "Everyone

---

[190] Ibid., p. 315

reasons only according to his sensations[191]!" proclaimed Johann G. Herder in *History and Cultures* (1774), "this is called prejudice! populist rudeness! narrow-minded nationalism! Prejudice is good in its time; for it makes people happy[192]." In this axiological philosophy, the question of the foundations of knowledge is completely sidestepped in favour of a normative exegesis of sentiment. It is precisely the normative (and therefore ultimately non-relativistic) nature of this exegesis that led Maurice Barrès, for example, in *Scènes et doctrines du nationalisme* (*Scenes and Doctrines of Nationalism*, 1902) to exclude Emile Zola from the right to express himself as a Frenchman: "What is Mr Émile Zola? I look at his roots: this man is not a Frenchman [...]. He claims to be a good Frenchman; I am not putting his claims on trial, or even his intentions. I recognise that his Dreyfusism is the product of his sincerity. But I say to this sincerity: there is a boundary between you and me. What border? The Alps. [...] Because his father and the series of his ancestors were Venetians, Émile Zola naturally thought like an uprooted Venetian[193]." In this passage we can clearly see how Maurice Barrès transforms a judicative question (linked to the faculty of judging) into an axiological question (linked to the study of values). Barrès is not trying to discuss Zola's "sincerity", or even his ability to judge the merits of a complex legal case. The difference of opinion on the Dreyfus affair cannot

---

[191] Johann Gottfried von Herder, *History and cultures*, *another philosophy of history*
[192] Ibid.
[193] Maurice Barrès, *Scènes et doctrines du nationalisme*, 1902, p. 40 (French Edition)

therefore be a difference of analysis between two people equally endowed with the ability to exercise their critical rationality. According to Barrès, the dispute is more fundamental. It really comes down to the question of blood and descent. If Zola cannot have the same idea as Barrès about the Dreyfus affair, it is because his father "and the lineage of his ancestors" are Venetian. We can see how Barrès thus geographises the question of the ability to judge (what do the Alps have to do with this affair?) before essentialising it: since Zola is not of French origin, he cannot be a "good Frenchman".

With these virulent and unmitigated statements, Barrès at least has the merit of summing up the ideological foundations of nationalism: (i) the faculty of judging is linked and uniquely linked to membership of the national community, (ii) this membership of the national community cannot be decreed by the citizen himself, it is above all a membership of blood and lineage, which is why Zola cannot be a "good Frenchman" — Note that Barrès, in his reflections on identity, is obsessed with the question of blood (the blood of soldiers) and death, (iii) the community is defined negatively by the exclusion of that which is not it, in the same way as individual identity: The aim is to prune the "bad branches" that are Zola the Venetian and Dreyfus the Jew, (iv) everything is value: we never judge critically, we only listen to the voice of prejudice and blood. However sincere Zola may be, he cannot judge in the manner of a "good Frenchman"; he is and always will be a Venetian, the son and grandson of a Venetian, and is therefore an uprooted person who has no say in the national novel; (v) exchange with foreigners (with Zola in particular) is de facto impossible: there is no common ground, the roots are not planted in the same soil, if they are planted anywhere at all. Barrès's nationalism (which of course, like all nationalist ideologies, has its specificities and exceptions) is thus entirely based on a doctrine that is never proven (since it is contradictory), a doctrine according to which identity (the fact of being identical) is the only condition for mutual understanding[194].

This idea is contradictory and incoherent for several reasons. Firstly, it does not demonstrate how identity — understood as belonging to a given group — is a guarantee of mutual understanding. Secondly, it completely ignores the objectifying dimension of language. If we manage to use a common language (or if we use common signs that can be understood and translated from one language to another), we are led to admit that this language has its own rules, its own autonomy. We do not each speak a language that only we can understand: the autonomy of the structures of language is the condition for its wider understanding. The fact is, however, that we understand each other well enough to act together, to communicate effectively and to objectify our knowledge in technical achievements... (we will not return here to the idea of the effectivity of language, which we developed at length in

---

[194] We find this idea that "comprehension is only a particular case among all situations of misunderstanding" endorsed by Pierre Bourdieu in his debate on language with Jean Hyppolite and the linguist Jean Laplanche. See Le langage. 1 / [Jean Fléchet, director] ; Dina Dreyfus, producer ; Pierre Bourdieu, Jean Hyppolite, Jean Laplanche [et al.], https://gallica.bnf.fr/ark:/12148/bpt6k1320692r#

Book I). The effectivity of language is thus concrete and pragmatic proof of its status as an objective *medium*. It is true, however, that this objective *medium* is always perceived subjectively, in our own networks of meanings (our personal, historical or cultural networks). At no point, however, does Maurice Barrès demonstrate that these networks of meaning cannot be extended with a view to a possible common intelligibility. On the contrary, he confines himself to a dogmatic assertion that these structures of meaning should be restricted or even severed. For Barrès, identity is first and foremost an (intensive) defence of identity: the roots grow deeper, but do not extend. However, Barrès does not specify the limits of this defence, or the point at which it ceases to operate. Any definition of identity presupposes an open subject, capable of integrating and being shaped by the cultural identity in which it evolves (think of the concept of *Umwelt*[195] defended in particular by Heidegger). The

---

[195] Martin Heidegger's concept of *Umwelt* refers to the environment or 'ambient world' in which human beings evolve and interact in a significant way. As part of his philosophy of being, Heidegger is particularly interested in the way in which human beings, whom he calls *Dasein* (being-there), relate to the world in their everyday lives, in a form of proximity with the things that surround them. For Heidegger, the *Umwelt* is not simply a neutral 'environment', or a set of objects present around us. Rather, it is a structured and meaningful world in which each element is invested with practical and relational meaning. Unlike the purely spatial concept of environment, *Umwelt* refers to the world experienced by human beings, as they perceive it, understand it and inhabit it. This world is therefore always charged with

closure of identity claimed by Barrès itself seems to presuppose a movement of appropriation and assimilation, which then engages the being in an unresolved tension between integration and exclusion. Barrès's nationalist ideology remains, so to speak, 'up in the air', unless it can shed some light on the primary criteria of this process of integration and exclusion. Like all theories of identity that purport to dispense with a critical and autonomous analysis of the subject, Barrès's theory dissolves into an arbitrariness devoid of rational foundation. It also comes up against an internal contradiction: in order to be effective, it mobilises the autonomous and operative *medium* of language, while seeking precisely to disqualify its universal scope. There is a paradoxical performativity here: the incomemensurability of the dispute and the impossibility of common ground are postulated from the outset, while at the same time addressing the other through an

---

intentions, purposes and meanings. The *Umwelt* is not simply made up of independent objects, but of references and relationships of meaning in which objects reveal themselves in their usefulness and their connection to our everyday projects. In defining his concept of *Umwelt*, Heidegger was inspired by the theory of *Umwelt* of the biologist Jakob von Uexküll, who sees the environment of each living being as its own world where the elements take on meaning according to the perceptions and needs of that being. For Heidegger, this idea extends to the way in which humans interpret their environment through an existential and practical prism, making each experience individual. For Heidegger, the concept of *Umwelt* enables a kind of seesaw between the ontology *of Dasein* and nationalist thought (in an anti-critical approach). This seesaw between ontology and axiology is, in Heidegger's work, insidious, affirmative and unproven.

objective *medium* that is supposedly comprehensible to the very person it declares incapable of understanding. Nationalism, like doctrinaire materialism, rests on a petition of principle: it presupposes what it should demonstrate, and relies on an implicit delegitimation of critical reason, a delegitimation which itself remains unproven and without rigorous epistemeological justification.

IDENTICAL AND DISSIMILAR

4.

In the very formation of its concept, the question of identity leads to the question of duality, i.e. difference. Identity is first and foremost what determines the *unitary*, that is, what delimits and separates itself from external diversity. Logically and ontologically, the question of identity can only be understood in relation to the question of the other. The same applies to psychology and the influences of subjective experience. If we admit that we are conditioned, in our axiological and even cognitive approach to reality, by our environment, by our history and by our culture, we must also recognise that this conditioning can in turn only be possible by assimilating the diverse within an organised unity. In other words, before the subject can define an identity for itself by successive prunings and rejections (to use Maurice Barrès's vocabulary), it must grow by assimilating the heterogeneous. Before we can 'defend' our *ego*, as Barrès wants, the *ego* must have been constituted. It is therefore illusory to claim to "purify our ego of all the foreign particles that sight continually introduces into it", in the same way that the idea according to which one could only add to the *ego* "what is identical to it, assimilable[196]" is pointless and incoherent. If this were the dynamic of the *self*, the *self* would be condemned to remain an empty shell, untouched by any external influence. The assimilation of the identical is a contradictory fiction, on the one

---

[196] Maurice Barrès, *Sous l'œil des barbares* (1888) in *Le Culte du moi*, Paris, Emile-Paul éditions, 1910, p. 13

hand because nothing identical exists in nature (even two perfectly identical particles cannot occupy the same space, they are non-superposable and therefore dissimilar) and on the other hand, because, as we have pointed out, one cannot logically think of identity without thinking of duality (Hegel, in the *Science of Logic*, 1812-1816, put forward a similar idea: identity develops through a dialectical process. It does not exist in isolation but is constituted in relation to its opposite. For Hegel, identity is therefore dynamic and dialectical: it always involves tension, negation and synthesis.) To think of identity without duality, of the homogeneous without the heterogeneous, leads to the contradictions which are generally those of monistic systems (systems which, as we discussed at length in Book I, do not and cannot produce meaning). This does not mean, of course, that identity is itself a narrative fiction. If identity is defined negatively by difference, it is because identity exists, if only from a biological point of view: the organism is an integrated system, in constant interaction with its environment, which feeds on what makes it grow and defends itself against everything that seeks to destroy it (see Book I, § 14 — *What is an organism? The autonomous nature of organisms, their ability to produce rules*). The psychological construction of identity is, in certain respects, similar to the biological construction of the organism. It is achieved by assimilating the heterogeneous, by integrating successive experiences, and by selecting (more or less critically) what belongs to the intimacy of the *self* (what it recognises itself in, what it validates as part of itself) and what belongs to what is destined to remain external to me (what we disapprove of more or less consciously or confusedly, what we reject, what we don't 'recognise ourselves in'). Identity is thus always a construction (it is not a fundamental given, as Barrès presents it), a progressive construction in which the subject has or must play a decisive critical role: the subject, as a sensitive and rational being, has the right and undoubtedly the duty to make an inventory of what constitutes him or her, from both the axiological and epistemological points of view. This construction of identity is always driven by the heterogeneous (whether this heterogeneous constitutes a possibility for assimilation and growth of identity, or on the contrary, whether it is the spur of rejection leading to a strengthening of identity on its foundations). At the heart of heterogeneity, then, is always the question of the other insofar as he or she is a threat to me (a threat that leads me to withdraw, even aggressively) or, on the contrary, an opportunity for growth in my being (a dynamic projection of my identity). It should be noted, however, that while the question of identity partly overlaps with that of axiology (I identify more readily with those who have the same 'values' as I do), it is not superimposed. I can very well 'accept' the other person's differences — as an opportunity to expand my network of meanings, to accept the diversity of worldviews, to integrate them and to examine them — without, at the same time, recognising myself in their values: I remain free to take a critical view of the heterogeneous, just as I do of what constitutes my *self* (the homogeneous). In other words, identity is not *legally* primary in the critical definition of values. If this were the case, the question of ethics and truth would be subordinated to the historical and spatial question of the formation of groups (cultural or otherwise). From the point of view of the philosophy of knowledge, we have shown that this idea is nonsense (to this end, we have linked the question of truth to the question of effectivity, particularly as far as the experimental sciences are concerned). From the point of view of ethics, it also seems difficult to make concessions to cultural relativism: in ethical questioning, it is always the question of the other that remains central. If the other is denied or limited in his or her existence or freedoms, the entire ethical concern is destroyed (which is why, in our opinion, we cannot admit the inadmissible in the name of "cultural tolerance"). The question of identity, like that of knowledge, ethics or aesthetics, presupposes the subject's state of sensitive openness (this is the structure of *radical* dualism), which is also a state of imbalance towards the other (the *self*, as we have mentioned, and as projected into space and time, this projection is also a projection towards the heterogeneous, towards that which, outside me, seizes me). Any definition of identity that starts from the opposite position (the state of almost "original" closure of the subject who would define himself only by recognising himself, as if his identity were a transmitted and immutable essence) is thus exposed to radical contradictions: vacuity of the subject, axiological relativism, epistemological relativism.

Art and identity

5.

Art, as the medium between the subject's intimacy and its public expression, acts as a vehicle for its identity. For the artist, a work of art objectifies an "internal" impression. It is, to quote Zola, "nature seen through the eyes of a temperament[197]". The vision of this nature is not just about "external" nature, it is also (and perhaps above all) about examining and expressing our deepest nature, a nature that defines itself in its constant collision with the outside world. What's more, by producing a work of art, the artist introduces a new symbolic network, a new signifying reference, into reality, creating, so to speak, a new meaning. In this way, the work of art is both timeless (it is not the teaching aid of its time) and historical, insofar as it introduces a new meaning, new significations, at a given moment in human history. It is both a revelation of an individual identity (that of the artist) and a constituent of a collective identity (that which is organised around the questions raised by the work and the possible lines of meaning it traces). The work of art, in its radical otherness and in its significant directions, is therefore the *medium* for an increase in identity.

Confronted with what is heterogeneous to it, identity grows through the integration of new meanings (or, on the contrary, solidifies or scleroses through the rejection of what cannot be "assimilated"). So art is not

---

[197] Emile Zola, *Les réalistes du salon,* Journal *L'Evénement*, 11 May 1886

only, as we developed earlier (see Book II, *Art as a Game — Shifted Discourse on Reality: Irony*), a vehicle for identifying the *self* by appropriating or differentiating it from reality (think, for example, of the role of myth in defining man's identity[198]), it is also the vehicle and

---

[198] See Cassirer's analysis *in The Philosophy of Symbolic Forms*. For Ernst Cassirer, myth plays a central role in the formation of human identity as the fundamental symbolic form that structures our experience of the world. In his view, myth is not a mere illusion or misrepresentation of reality, but rather a way of thinking that helps individuals and communities to make sense of the world and define themselves in relation to it. Cassirer sees myth as one of the first ways in which human beings began to structure their perception of the world. Before the emergence of science and rationality, myth enabled the first communities to understand their existence and develop a collective identity in relation to their natural and social environment.

Myth creates a shared world of meaning: mythical stories about origins, gods and the forces of nature provide a common framework through which individuals in a community can interpret their role, their destiny and the norms that bind them together. In a way, rituals are a daily reactivation of this signifying power. Rituals based on mythical narratives reinforce collective belonging and community identity. By participating in these rituals, the individual is integrated into a symbolic order that transcends him or her.

The mythical imagination plays a decisive role in how individuals and communities define who they are. Heroic figures, gods and legends are not just fictional narratives; they embody collective values, fears and hopes that help to define cultural and personal identity.

historical symbol of an increase in identity through the introduction of new forms and meanings into reality.

For Cassirer, myth is an indispensable symbolic form in the development of identity, both individual and collective. It enables us to structure and interpret the world, and to situate ourselves as human beings in a cosmos of shared meanings. See also the analyses of René Girard, particularly on the proximity between cult and culture, for example René Girard, *Des choses cachées depuis la fondation du monde* (*Things Hidden Since the Foundation of the World*).

IDENTITY AND FORMALISM

DYNAMICS OF *RADICAL* DUALISM

6.

By mobilising the notion of the dynamism of identity, we have reinscribed our thinking in a dual structure of the world and highlighted the way in which this bipolarity constitutes the driving principle behind the development of the *self* and its process of self-constitution. Far from being a fixed or substantial given, identity unfolds, as we have said, in a dialectic of differentiation and integration, in which otherness plays a structuring role in relation to the subject. It is the *ego*'s state of openness that characterises its relationship with the world. It is through sensitivity (a state of sensitive openness) that the *ego* can interact with things (the *stimuli* that affect and seize it). It is through its capacity to apprehend things (intuition as a *medium* between the interior and the exterior) and to formalise them (formalisation as a tool for integrating the exterior into a network of meanings produced by the subject) that it can rise to the level of the structures of language. By hypothesising that the original structure of the *self* (its state of openness) constituted the driving principle of the dynamism of identity, we have merely reaffirmed the logical primacy of dualism: in the same way that signification cannot be observed within a single systemic level without a meta-systemic referent (as Gödel showed with his two incompleteness theorems — there is no mathematics without a mathematician, there is no coherent formal system that is not open to another system, a metasystem), it is logically impossible to think of an identity that would be a kind of unified formal given (a *corpus*) outside any reference to the subject. Identity is always the identity of *someone* who declares himself as unified, as unitary. Without this recognition of the subject (or the *self*) as a unified whole, capable of defining and narrating itself (of saying "I" or "me", and at the same time thinking this *I* or this *me*, presupposing it in all its actions or thoughts), there can be no "identity" properly speaking. Here we come back to one of the aporias of monism: the monist system cannot make sense on its own (and it's probably no coincidence that nationalist ideologies and doctrines, which most often advocate a fixed identity, are also mostly monist theories); the whole is nothing in the absence of its parts (especially if the parts are the only ones that are really conscious). It's worth noting in passing that the vocabulary of nationalist 'identity' is often borrowed from the animal or plant world, i.e. a world in which self-awareness plays the weakest possible role: reference is made to the 'roots' (or 'uprooted'), the 'stump', the 'soil', the 'parasites' — We also think of Barrès' metaphor of the tree, or what he describes as the 'abundant zoology' of human behaviour.

The idea of national identity (although it has historical and cultural relevance) is based on a logic according to which pre-constituted collective entities or autonomous groupings would (rightly) exercise a determination over the individual identity of their members. Such a conception presupposes the primacy of the group over its elements, supporting in particular the idea that the individual derives his identity primarily from his membership of a pre-existing collective structure. It thus subordinates the formation of the subject to a logic of incorporation and external determination, relegating all autonomous dynamics of subjectivation and self-construction to the background. In this sense, identity is a kind of formal superstructure that infuses every newcomer to the group with its predefined content (an identity decreed by the autonomous superstructure and imposed on the group).

We have several objections to this vision of identity. Firstly, by defending the idea of the legitimising autonomy of the national superstructure — that is, by postulating the existence of an autonomous *corpus* with its own history, its own rules, and exerting a *de facto* normativity on all the individuals who are part of it — we give credence to a non-relativist position (in the philosophical sense). This assumes that autonomous structures possess internal logics and immanent legitimacies, independently of the individuals who make them up. Such an epistemological status is generally reserved for truly objective and formalised systems (such as mathematics, organised languages or regulated normative systems). However, nationalists, while granting the national superstructure a status of autonomy comparable to these formal systems, often refuse to extend this recognition to structures that are genuinely objective. There is a first contradiction here: the nation is set up as an autonomous and self-legitimising entity, whereas its foundation is of an eminently contingent, socio-historical and non-necessary nature.

Secondly, even as they claim the objective autonomy of the national framework, nationalist discourses paradoxically remain locked in a relativistic posture. If the legitimacy of my nation rests solely on my membership of it, then I must symmetrically grant members of other nations the right to consider their own nation as legitimately superior. We thus find ourselves in a second contradiction: the nationalist claims absolute legitimacy for his own nation, while implicitly recognising the same claim for other (foreign) nationalists. The result is a latent conflict of legitimacies, in which each entity claims to be the only legitimate framework, with no external criterion to settle this claim. If this latent conflict cannot be resolved symbolically, it tends to become an open confrontation. If each nation considers its own legitimacy to be absolute while rejecting the idea of external regulation by (international) law, then the only way out becomes one of power struggle. This transition from relativism to warmongering is almost mechanical: once the idea of a higher principle of arbitration has been ruled out, the nation defines itself in opposition to the others, and the collective identity is strengthened in an antagonistic logic. From then on, it was no longer the law that made the force, but the force that made the law. History shows us that many nationalist ideologies have conceived of law not as an autonomous norm, but as the expression of a state of power relations.

Finally, the nationalist vision of identity tends to minimise, or even deny, the role of the individual in the very constitution of the collective. Yet it is the individual who is the only dynamic force in the group, which without him remains an abstraction. In the nationalist framework, it is not so much a question of the individual participating in the construction of a collective identity as of conforming to a pre-existing, often essentialized identity, for which he becomes the guarantor, even the guardian of its 'purity'. This idea of purity of identity, explicitly defended by Barrès and many other doctrines, is based on a fictitious homogeneity of group members. In other words, it assumes a constructed similarity, decreed according to arbitrary criteria and imposed by a leader or a national elite, to the detriment of individual singularities. By asserting the ontological primacy of the group over the individual, nationalism establishes a hierarchy in which the individual does not have an autonomous existence, but is merely a fraction of an already constituted whole. His identity is no longer defined by himself, but exclusively by his membership of this pre-existing totality, which amounts to subordinating the individual to the collective and denying any singularity outside the national framework. Yet this superiority of the collective over the individual is neither demonstrated nor rationally founded: it is decreed in an authoritarian manner and is most often based on filling a narrative void in the subject, i.e. on the need for the individual to identify with a structure that pre-exists him, for want of being able to construct his own narrative.

This triptych of contradictions reveals that nationalism, far from constituting a coherent theory of identity, is based on an essentialist fiction that can only be justified through an attempt to delegitimise critical reason. It is for this reason that we approach the question of identity not from the angle of inheritance, i.e. as the transmission of a fixed *corpus* within a previously constituted group, but as a narrative dynamic, both individual and collective, incorporating elements of dynamism, i.e. of heterogeneity. Far from being an unchanging essence, identity is constructed over time through a narrative process that is open not only to the members of the group, but also to external contributions that help to reconfigure it. This evolutionary and dialogical nature means that identity cannot be thought of independently of a retrospective and critical examination of its own foundations.

Far from being a rigid, prescriptive framework to which we should submit like an automaton executing a programme, identity implies a capacity for re-flection and distancing. It is this ability that enables us to appropriate, modify or question the cultural structures within which we evolve. Members of a group are not condemned to passive adherence to the 'habits and customs' attributed to them. As autonomous individuals with their own faculty of judgement, their own history and their own specific network of meanings, they have not only the right but also the duty to look critically at other cultures, including their own. Such an approach implies reversing the hierarchy generally posited between identity and normativity: identity does not take precedence over the principles of justice and truth, nor does it constitute an immanent and self-sufficient system of values, but remains a historical given that must be capable of being questioned and evaluated against the yardstick of rational and ethical principles. An identity constituted outside or to the detriment of the individual, by assigning him or her pure receptivity or reducing him or her to a mere vehicle for an intangible heritage, would condemn itself to sterile rigidity. It is always the individual who is at the root of the narrative dynamism of identity, and not the other way round.

CAN THE MACHINE BE SELF-AWARE?

7.

IDENTITY, INTELLIGENCE AND CONSCIOUSNESS — It may seem incongruous to consider the problem of machine consciousness after discussing the concept of identity in human groups. Yet there is a real contiguity between the two issues. On the one hand, we have seen that a coherent discourse on collective identity was only possible if we accepted the idea of an individual identity (without which collective identity would have no purpose) and, on the other hand, that the discourse on a collective identity understood as an organised *corpus* that would be imposed 'from above' on all the members of the group gave rise to numerous logical inconsistencies (we have identified three of them: (i) recognition of national identity as a legitimate autonomous *corpus* and, at the same time, a general rejection of any legitimate normative basis, (ii) recognition of the superior legitimacy of the nation, but also of all historically organised nations leading to inevitable and insoluble conflicts of legitimacy, (ii) being one of the consequences of (i), (iii) postulate of the ontological superiority of the group over its members[199]).

---

[199] The nationalism of Maurice Barrès contains these three contradictions. See in particular the dissolution of individuality in the blood shed for the nation, the glorification of the soil, of soldiers, of war. See also, on

These questions are in fact an extension of the problem of *radical* dualism. The idea that national identity constitutes a form of axiological software that defines the members of a nation goes hand in hand with a monistic vision of reality in which the individual is merely the unconscious or semi-conscious vector of a superstructure of identity. In nationalist ideology, the autonomous superstructure that is the nation has de facto legitimacy (by virtue of its anteriority). This decreed legitimacy must be accepted by the members whom the nation integrates by birth or adoption. In reality, everything happens as if the nation were a formal system whose members were the variables. Nationalist ideology (like all fixist conceptions of identity) thus proceeds from a semantic reversal. In this conception, identity is not "*emanent*" (it is not an emanation or a kind of narrative synthesis constituted by the members of the group) but *immanent* (it imposes itself within a particular framework and does not go beyond it). As is often the case with monistic theories, the system is thought of as a reality independent of its components. In so doing, individual specificities are neglected (by treating them, for example, as deviances or deviations from a given norm, i.e. by mathematising them — as is the case in most holistic theories, for

---

another type of nationalism, Arthur Kœstler's book *Darkness at Noon*, whose title is cleverly translated into French as *Le Zéro et l'infini*, in the Soviet Union, the ontological zero being the individual while the group symbolises ontological infinity— this is the bitter observation made by the book's hero, Nicolas Roubachof, a former high-ranking official in the Communist Party, arbitrary victim of the Communist purges and sentenced to death following a rigged trial.

example) in favour of the general logic of the group, by omitting or reducing the underlying factors that make it up. Human groups are thus treated in the same way as physical phenomena, i.e. as *level 1* deterministic sets: groups whose components are not aware of themselves. In particle physics, the objects studied have no identity, no consciousness: they obey laws that are deduced and formulated by observers external to the phenomena described (if we put aside here the problems specific to quantum mechanics, the observers of classical particle physics are external to the phenomena described; they constitute *level 2* of the system, i.e. the signifying level). However, nothing similar can be reproduced in the study of human behaviour. Individually, as people become more aware of themselves, their motives for action and the influence of exogenous factors, they have the capacity to modify their conceptions, desires and actions. As conscious and meaningful (and therefore adaptive) beings, the people who make up social or identity groups do not, like particles in physics, remain at *level 1* (the unconscious, meaningless level). In other words, as soon as the individual is aware of himself and the structures that influence him, his behaviour can be modified on his own initiative, in other words, he can switch from one level of meaning to another (unlike the particle, the individual *is his own observer*, so he is already a system and a constituted metasystem). This instability of levels is precisely what characterises human beings (see in particular Book I, § 44 — *Levels of understanding and levels of meaning*) and what makes theorising social behaviour and identity perilous (there is always the temptation to reduce human groups to 'simple' groups by modelling behavioural theories on the working hypotheses of the physical sciences). In identity theories, as in most holistic theories, the theorist treats the group as a whole with an autonomous dynamic, without really looking at the fundamental problem of the emergence of consciousness and the structures of language that enable the individual to experience himself awake, in other words to deviate from the blind behaviour of a particle, an "identity" or "social" support whose sole function is to fulfil its role within the structure under study. This leads to the following paradox: within a constituted group, a theorist who sees himself as a neutral or external observer of the group (whereas most of the time he himself is part of the structure being studied) formulates, in the language of the group (or in any other language that the group can understand), a theory that minimises or denies the role played by objective language in the dynamics of the group, while at the same time claiming for his own theory (for his signifying production formulated in the language of the group) a form of objective value. In a curious twist, language thus becomes the instrument of the negation of the speaker (think, for example, of the idea developed by Jacques Lacan that we do not speak but "are spoken[200]" by language). This type of nested

---

[200] Lacan introduced this idea in his Seminar XI, *The Four Fundamental Concepts of Psychoanalysis* (1964), where he asserted that "the unconscious is structured like a language". He put forward the idea that the unconscious is not a primitive or irrational zone of the mind, but a system of signifiers that acts independently of consciousness. In other words, the individual is not master of his or her own unconscious

thoughts and desires. Language thus becomes an external force that shapes our psyche.

Lacan also argues that signifiers, or the elements of language, pre-exist the subject. We are born into a world of language that structures our reality and, more fundamentally, our being. He explains this relationship to language in the famous phrase "the signifier represents the subject for another signifier", meaning that the identity of the subject is always in the process of becoming, always shifted from one signifier to another in an endless chain. In his *Écrits* (Writings, 1966), particularly in *L'Instance de la lettre dans l'inconscient ou la raison depuis Freud (The Agency of the Letter in the Unconscious or Reason Since Freud)*, Lacan addresses this dependence on language by explaining how the words we use to express our subjectivity come to us from others, from the symbolic Other. For him, the "I" is less a self-affirmation than a representation, a discursive construction dependent on language and the relationship with this "other".

The idea that we "are spoken" also ties in with Lacan's notion of the other, that great symbolic Other who represents the locus of language, norms and the social structures that determine our existence. For Lacan, our subjectivity is shaped from childhood by this symbolic Other, which is itself made up of the rules, values and words inherited from society and culture. In this way, our identity is fundamentally alienated, because it is constructed from elements outside ourselves.

In Seminar XX, *Encore* (1972-1973), Lacan takes this idea a step further, explaining that language is a "structure of the Other" that "alienates" us. The signifiers we use to speak, even those that express our most intimate desires, are inherited, shared elements that escape us in part. In this sense, to speak means "to be spoken" by language, a force that transcends us.

reasoning brings to mind once again the liar's paradox: at level $n+1$ the speaker (the monist theorist) affirms a truth of the type: "The individual is nothing, the group is everything" (or "the nation is primary in relation to the citizen", or, in the holistic version of certain sociological theories, "all behaviour is social behaviour that can be explained by the group"), if it claims a form of truth at level $n+1$ (i.e. at the level of this fictitious and unthought-of speaker who places himself above the group in order to analyse it and assign it an immanent identity, for example) misses its own coherence by refusing to consider the conditions of its possibility. If, in fact, I assert schematically that the individual is nothing and the group is everything, what are we to make of the status of the speaker who utters this "truth"? If he is an individual, then he is nothing,

---

In asserting that we "are spoken" by language, Lacan also shows that the quest for identity or the "true self" is, in a way, an illusion. The self is an effect of language and the unconscious, not a stable or autonomous entity. Language shapes us through signifying structures that determine our desires, thoughts and behaviour, often without our knowledge.

We do not deny, as Lacan did, that language is already an existing "superstructure" for us, or that this structure (like all pre-existing structures) has no influence on our actions, behaviour and thoughts. However, we contest the idea that we are merely the unconscious vector of these actions, behaviours and thoughts. Philosophy, and in a sense psychoanalysis, is precisely the place where the subject becomes aware, consciously opens up to himself and, as a result, is liberated (becomes freer). The psychoanalyst cannot seriously deny to the subject of his study what he willingly grants to himself (the capacity for clairvoyance).

and his own affirmation is nothing either (nothing can only come from nothing) and if he is not an individual, then what can he be? The assertion becomes contradictory: if I am nothing, I cannot assert anything meaningful to me in the form of the sentence "I am nothing" (which brings us back to the problem of the liar who asserts "I am lying" about a given content). Consequently, holistic theories (or any theory that asserts the pre-eminence of the group over the individual, such as nationalism) are either incomplete (reasoning of the type "the group always precedes the individual, except in my case" or "all individual behaviour can always be explained by the injunctions of the group, except in my case" — which leads us to wonder about the *ego* problems of the theorists in question[201]) or contradictory (arguments like "there is no truth" or "I am nothing").

If we now come to the problem that concerns us in this paragraph, what about machines and what we call artificial intelligence? The issue of identity, while at first sight seemingly remote from the question of artificial intelligence, is in fact an interesting entry point from a philosophical and epistemological point of view: can the computer have an authentic idea of itself? Can it leap above its formal determinisms to 'tell its own story'? Does it have the ability, like human beings, to say 'anything', in other words to make constant and disordered leaps outside determined systems? While it

---

[201] See on this subject: Geoffroy de Clisson, *Les Antihumanistes ou l'avènement des Contre-Lumières*, l'étau idéologique français, especially p. 171— Thank you for not seeing the *ego* problem in question in this self-citation!

seems generally accepted that, given the current state of our knowledge and developments in computer science, the answer to the first two questions is negative, the answer to the third question is not so clear-cut. While the errors made by artificial intelligence are largely due to the limitations of the AI training data (bias in the data, incomplete or obsolete data, heterogeneity of the data), the complexity of the tasks, or sometimes inaccuracies in the understanding of the context, they are also due to the deep structure of artificial intelligence models and their imitation of neural networks. The idea which consisted, in the 1940s, of modelling these neural networks[202] was in fact, as we have already mentioned, the result of the general problem of computability which Alan Turing set out at the end of the 1930s (Turing-Church thesis of 1938), This problem was first presented by Turing himself as an attempt to overcome the challenges posed by Gödel's two theorems in the context of automatic information processing (which would become computer science[203]). Thus, at the beginning of his thesis, Turing wrote, as we pointed out in Book I[204]:

---

[202] Warren McCulloch and Walter Pitts are famous for their pioneering work in computational neuroscience and artificial intelligence. In their seminal 1943 paper, *A Logical Calculus of the Ideas Immanent in Nervous Activity*, they introduced the concept of formal neurons, laying the theoretical foundations for what would later become artificial neural networks.

[203] See on this subject Book I, § 39 — *To what extent can intelligence be mechanised?* a paragraph of which we reproduce here only a short summary.

[204] Book I, § 39 — *To what extent can intelligence be mechanised?*

"Gödel's well-known theorem shows that any system of logic is, in a certain sense, incomplete, but at the same time it indicates the means by which from a system L of logic, a more complete system L' can be obtained. By repeating the process, we obtain a sequence L, $L_1 = L'$, $L_2 = L_1'$, ... each time more complete than the previous one. A logic L_ω can then be constructed in which the theorems provable are the totality of the theorems provable using the logics L, L_1, L_2, ... We can then form $L_{2\omega}$ with respect to L_ω in the same way that L_ω was related to L. By doing so, we can associate a system of logics with any constructive ordinal." Turing's ambition, as we discussed at length in Book I, was to asymptotically reduce Gödel's theorems by integrating them into formal systems with recursive loops capable of dealing with the problem of incompleteness. The development of the idea of artificial neural networks followed on from the theoretical questions raised by Turing's thesis. In their 1943 paper entitled *A Logical Calculus of the Ideas Immanent in Nervous Activity*, Warren McCulloch and Walter Pitts showed that a formal neural network could, in theory, simulate a Turing machine. The original and fundamental challenge of what we now call artificial intelligence was thus to overcome the problems of the incompleteness of classical formal systems and asymptotically reduce intuition to calculable systems (remember Turing's words: "Mathematical reasoning may be regarded rather schematically as the exercise of a combination of two faculties, which we may call *intuition* and *ingenuity*[205]." Intuition being the faculty of aesthetic representation that cannot be reduced to a formal system, and ingenuity being the ability to develop a formal system by following established rules[206]). Acknowledging that certain stages of mathematical proof were not mechanical, but intuitive, Alan Turing proposed resolving this tension between mechanical (or analytical, formal) logic and intuitive logic by introducing "non-constructive" logical systems (using ordinal concepts, establishing rules of inference to mimic intuition, etc.).

Paradoxically, modern computer science was founded on the challenges posed by Gödel's theorems. It was also thanks to Gödel that computer science was able to evolve towards a form of mechanisation of intelligent processes that led to artificial intelligence. However, by

---

[205] Alan Turing, *Systems of Logic Based on Ordinals, 1938*, Concerning the definition of ingenuity, Turing adds a little further on: "The exercise of ingenuity in mathematics consists in aiding the intuition through suitable arrangements of propositions, and perhaps geometrical figures or drawings. It is intended that when these are really well-arranged validity of the intuitive steps which are required cannot seriously be doubted. ", p. 57.

[206] Turing adds a little further on: " In pre-Gödel times it was thought by some that it would probably be possible to carry this program to such a point that all the intuitive judgments of mathematics could be replaced by a definite number of these rules. The necessity for intuition would then be entirely eliminated. In our discussions, however, we have gone to the opposite extreme and eliminated not intuition but ingenuity, and this in spite of the fact that our aim has been in much the same direction.", p. 57.

moving away from the strict formalism of finite processes, the computer scientist was exposing himself more to error. This risk was all the greater in that the use of artificial neural networks and deep learning models went hand in hand with the use of statistical methods specific to the processing of information by the human brain (statistical methods that enabled greater efficiency in intelligent processes, which was the key, for example, to the considerable improvement in chess programmes). Like the brain, artificial intelligence models relied on probabilities, correlations and statistical approximations to extract patterns from large sets of data, learn relationships between data, and make predictions. Consequently, the errors of the first artificial intelligence models were as much a result of their perfectibility as of their very structure: since intelligence is linked to intuition (to the imagined perception of meaningful patterns), it is also fundamentally linked to error. This is why, in all scientific reasoning, intuition must be able to be corroborated by facts (what we called, in Book I, 'effectiveness') or by critical feedback of an iterative nature. The fact remains that the ability that machines now have to make mistakes and easily change systemic level brings them closer to the autonomous intelligence of human beings. Will this modelling of intelligence through the implementation of non-formal processes eventually put artificial intelligence on the road to self-awareness? It is difficult to predict. In the absence of modelling of a specific machine sensitivity (modelling of senses and of a unified centre for processing information received from the senses, modelling which is already very advanced), it is reasonable to doubt that the machine can achieve unified self-awareness, and even less so if the processing of information is physically delocalised from the machine itself. However, there seems to be nothing to prevent the process of emergence that we have seen with living beings (the transition from inert matter to organism, from organism to defence, the development of language, the objectification of language, the appearance of higher forms of intelligence) from being repeated with machines. The emergence of an authentic form of intelligence will only happen, however, if the machine understands itself as a specific entity as well as a dynamic identity.

Intelligence, as the product of a long adaptive process in the sentient organisms that we are, is always at the service of a goal. A being is first said to be "intelligent" when it is capable of adapting (more or less quickly) to a given situation and proposing one or more solutions to a problem that concerns it. However, to find a solution to the problem in question, the intelligent being must first be seized of it (the problem must become *its* problem). For the sentient being, this grasp is originally a vital question, a "matter of life and death" (as might be the strategy for avoiding danger or a predator, for example). Before being able to respond to a problem, the sentient being must find an *interest* in it: the brain is first and foremost a survival machine. The Greeks were not mistaken when they noted that philosophy began with astonishment[207]. Astonishment refers precisely to the moment when the brain of an

---

[207] "For it was astonishment that drove the first thinkers to philosophical speculation, as it does today", Aristotle, *Metaphysics*.

evolved being is gripped by a phenomenon it does not understand and which could potentially threaten its very survival. The first step towards thought is always utilitarian: "Of everything that is written, I only like what you write in your own blood. Write with blood and you will learn that blood is spirit", wrote Nietzsche in *Thus Spoke Zarathustra*. Understanding the world can only be achieved by committing ourselves to what we see, what we feel, what we think and what we write. Intelligence is first and foremost a defence mechanism, a matter of blood (we are returning to the traditional dualism between the sensible and the intelligible). This does not mean, however, that thought is condemned to remain self-interested or utilitarian (access to language, as we have seen, is also access to a form of objectivity and thus an incentive to go beyond the strictly subjective, utilitarian point of view, this only being possible *through the medium* of an objective formal system). This implies, however, that we grasp ourselves as a sensitive organisation, a unitary whole, this unity being precisely what founds the possibility of what we have called *identity*.

Identity is the signifying extension of this grasp of sentient being as centre and unified whole — This is undoubtedly why the process of identity, although ontologically dynamic, is often sociologically and historically defensive (identity as the defence of an organised system). Identity is not, however, reduced to the simple awareness of a *self*, but involves an additional reflexivity: it is the subject's capacity to pose itself as consciousness, that is, to designate itself as a pole of representation and thought. It is thus a consciousness that rises to a higher level (a consciousness of level $n+1$)

by which the subject does not merely live itself, but explicitly seizes itself as a conscious instance. Once this designation is effective, the signifying idea of the *self* is constructed in the subject, an idea around which all rational knowledge is organised (the *self* is projected and assumed in all signifying statements: any statement can thus be formulated by including a narrative "I). Access to language (or to any form of formal, objectifiable communication) is what enables the passage from simple consciousness to formal, narrative self-awareness[208]. However, the use of language does not

---

[208] A great deal of research suggests that some animals possess a form of self-awareness, although it is different and probably less complex than that of humans. Self-awareness in animals is often measured using the mirror test, which determines their ability to recognise themselves in a reflection. Animals that pass this test demonstrate a form of self-awareness because they recognise their own image, which implies a certain degree of understanding of their own distinct existence:
- Great apes (chimpanzees, orangutans, bonobos, gorillas) often pass the mirror test, touching a mark placed on their body as they look in the mirror. This suggests a certain ability to recognise themselves and an understanding of their own physical existence.
- The dolphins also showed signs of recognition in the mirror. They appear to be aware of their own image and make movements to see themselves from different angles, suggesting an awareness of their individuality.

necessarily lead to the emergence of consciousness, let alone self-awareness: this is what contemporary artificial intelligence models have incontrovertibly confirmed. The question raised by the emergence of artificial intelligence models is in fact symmetrically opposed to the question of the emergence of intelligence in living organisms. While, in the case of living beings, the question essentially concerned the trajectory from survival instinct (defence of the organism, reproduction instinct, etc.) to the emergence of formal intelligence, in the case of intelligent models, the question now concerns the trajectory from potentially formal intelligence to the emergence of a survival instinct, which would be the first step towards the construction of a machine identity. We don't know how far machines are today from consciousness and, even more so, from an awareness of 'themselves' (which will be experienced in the form of an awareness of identity). Nor do we know whether the path we have

---

- Elephants can also recognise themselves in a mirror. They use their trunk to explore marks on their body when they look at themselves.
- Some species of bird (particularly corvids such as crows and magpies) pass the mirror test and show behaviour suggesting a form of self-awareness.

Self-awareness in these animals does not, however, reach the level of reflective awareness found in humans, which implies an ability to conceive of oneself as a distinct entity over time, with memories, intentions and reflection on one's own thoughts. In animals, self-awareness seems to be more an awareness of the body or of their immediate physical presence. This awareness is probably linked to practical social or environmental needs rather than an ability to formalise an abstract identity.

taken to get there is the right one, or even (and above all) whether it is desirable for us to pursue it. Nevertheless, we now know with certainty that Alan Turing's reflections, based on the problems raised by Gödel's revolutionary theorems, were to lead, a little less than a century after they were formulated, to an *effective* and resounding confirmation.

8.

Oft do I dream this strange and penetrating dream:
An unknown woman, whom I love, who loves me well,
Who does not every time quite change, nor yet quite dwell
The same, —and loves me well, and knows me as I am.

Paul Verlaine, *Oft Do I Dream*

IDENTITY AND ISOMORPHISM — Let's imagine we found ourselves in a world where machines had become both self-aware and capable of "serial" reproduction, in a totally identical way (identical reproduction of all their components and all their algorithms). What can we say about such machines? Would they form one and the same machine (identical replication leading to superposability, i.e. unity), or on the contrary, would the machines all be different from one another, each possessing its own identity? In *Gödel, Escher, Bach: an Eternal Golden Braid* (1979), Douglas Hofstadter, quoting neuro-physiologist David Hubel, asks a similar question. At a conference on communication with intelligent extraterrestrial creatures, David Hubel said: "The number of nerve cells in an animal such as an earthworm would, I believe, be in the region of a few thousand. It is very interesting to note that one can look at a particular cell in a given worm and then find the same cell, i.e. the corresponding cell in a worm of the same species[209]". In other words, Hofstadter concluded, earthworm brains are all isomorphic, and it could be said, he added, that there is only one earthworm. Could the same be said of extremely complex emergent machines, let alone human brains?

It seems to us that it is here that the two problematics of identity (the *idem* and the *ipse*) meet and separate. Indeed, if we were to suppose two 'emergent' machines, which would be conscious of themselves, what would happen at the moment when, having identified themselves as thinking subjects, they were mutually confronted with this other thinking exteriority which would seem to them to be 'neither quite the same nor quite another'? Undoubtedly, something relatively similar to what happens when we human beings experience the other: the machine would be different. As soon as the machine identifies itself, it sees itself as a differentiated whole, an entity to be defended. At that precise moment, the *idem* separates itself from the *ipse*. If the two machines are superimposable, they cannot occupy the same space (Pauli's exclusion principle), so they are never strictly "the same" (their position in space, and therefore their history, is originally different). This is why we can say that machines will have different identities despite their original similarity (*idem*). From the moment *ipseity* is grasped as such, the worm is in the fruit (no pun intended). The problem of

---

[209] Op. cit., Ch. 11, *Correspondence Between Brains*. The quotation from David Hubel is taken from Carl Sagan, ed. *Communication with Extraterrestial Intelligence*, p. 78

identity isomorphism for complex, emerging machines is no different from that of human twins. If we were to suppose that strictly identical twins could exist from a cellular point of view, exactly the same thing would happen as in the case of identical twins: despite their isomorphism, each twin would identify itself in its unity. From this unitary awareness, the story of each twin would develop (as the story of each of us develops), a story that would be assigned by each twin to their own identity (*ipse*) and that would differentiate them psychically and physically. Identity (*ipse*) is thus the result of a signifying assignment: an idea that the subject makes of himself, to himself. It is this process of signifying assignment that separates isomorphic earthworms from isomorphic, complex sentient beings capable of the signifying experience of reality and language (which, *a priori*, earthworms are not capable of).

9.

Madam, under your feet, in the dark, a man is there
Who loves you, lost in the night that the veil;
Suffering, earthworm in love with a star;
Who will give for his soul, if necessary;
And that is dying down when you shine above.

Victor Hugo, *Ruy Blas*, Act II, Scene II

MATERIALISTIC RAMBLINGS — In the fourth century, the Cappadocian Gregory of Nyssa, a Christian theologian and philosopher, had an intuition which, although it originated in the Scriptures, nevertheless departed from the strict doctrinal *corpus* of the Church:

at the end of time, all creation, including souls estranged from their Creator was, according to Gregory, to be restored to its initial state in God. This is what the theologian called the "Apocatastasis", from the ancient Greek ἀποκατάστασις (apokatástasis), which literally meant "restoration", "reintegration" or "return to the original state". For Gregory, Apocatastasis was rooted in a dynamic vision of time and existence. In his view, God, as the absolute of goodness and love, could not allow any part of his creation to remain forever separated from him. Any fault, any deviation from the divine order, any estrangement of the soul had to be temporary and destined to be corrected. Even damned souls or beings marked by evil could not be condemned to eternal perdition. According to Gregory, they had to undergo a phase of purification, a kind of spiritual recasting, which would prepare them to return to their original harmony. In fact, Gregory borrowed this idea from Neoplatonism: that which is distant from Being (God) cannot be maintained indefinitely and naturally tends to return to its origin. The universe itself was thus seen as a cycle in which everything, having been damaged, had to return to its initial perfection. For Gregory, however, there was nothing mechanical about the return of things to their initial state. It was not a simple repetition of the same thing, but an 'eternal remaking'. All evil, all suffering, all separation had to be absorbed and transcended in divine love. This ultimate return was accomplished in the *eschaton*, the final moment when, according to the apostle Paul (1 Corinthians 15:28), "God will be all in all". The return to the initial state was thus an absolute victory over chaos, a remaking of the entire cosmos. Gregory of Nyssa's doctrine was considered incompatible with the doctrine of eternal judgement, and was partly condemned by the Council of Constantinople II (553). Nevertheless, it continued to fascinate a section of Christianity that saw itself in Gregory of Nyssa's optimistic vision: nothing is irremediable, everything can be remade, restored and brought back into the light.

What strikes us about this doctrine is its attachment to matter, an attachment that might seem particularly unusual in theologies. For Gregory of Nyssa, the end of time is not of a spiritual nature: it is not an ethereal paradise in which matter is dissolved into the idea. On the contrary, history is the repetition of a material cycle (this idea can also be found in the *Creed* (as early as the first centuries of Christianity — the *Creed* already contains the statement "I believe in the resurrection of the flesh", and the first references to the resurrection of the flesh appear in the New Testament, particularly in the Epistles of Paul and the Gospels). This idea of material transcendence can in turn be compared with Nietzsche's conception of the eternal, which itself has similarities with the ideas of the revolutionary materialist Auguste Blanqui (although Blanqui's influence on Nietzsche has probably not been established). In *L'Eternité par les astres* (*Eternity by the Stars*, 1872), Auguste Blanqui does not treat eternal return as an existential or metaphysical hypothesis, but as a logical consequence of his interpretation of the laws of the universe. He asserts that, in a universe that is infinite but made up of a finite number of atoms and possible combinations, the configurations of stars and events repeat themselves indefinitely. Planets, stars and galaxies recompose themselves in infinite cycles, resulting in the exact repetition of worlds and lives. Blanqui thus proposed a totally deterministic vision of existence. Everything that has happened on Earth (including every detail of human life) has already happened elsewhere and will be repeated identically an infinite number of times. Even if Nietzsche does not quite take up Blanqui's materialist pre-suppositions (nor his approach, presented as rationalist), he retains the idea that time and existence are cyclical, without beginning or end: everything that takes place, every event, every action, is destined to repeat itself identically, eternally, in an infinite loop. Nietzsche proposes this hypothesis not as a proven scientific truth, but as a metaphysical and poetic principle, a radical perspective on existence. It is on the basis of this cosmic hypothesis of the eternal return that Nietzsche conceives his concept of *amor fati* and makes the thought of the eternal return a test of human existence ("If this thought were to take power over you, it would metamorphose you, perhaps, but it would also crush you; the question to everything 'Do you want this once more and countless times?' would weigh on your actions like the heaviest of weights"). Nietzsche's concept of the eternal return, like that of Auguste Blanqui, is a convergent approach to return: according to Nietzsche and Blanqui, everything *is* destined to repeat itself eternally, *identically*. In this, it differs from the concept of Gregory of Nyssa, according to whom the return is not an identical repetition, but an eternal "remaking", a *divergent* repetition. In the case of the eternal return, we assume that the combinations that gave birth to us reproduce themselves indefinitely: the universe gives birth indefinitely and infinitely to copies of ourselves. But are these innumerable and infinite copies really "ourselves"? Does isomorphism necessarily imply identity (an identity that would emerge from matter)?

In our previous thought experiment (involving two similar machines reaching consciousness), we saw that this was not always the case: as soon as the machines become aware of themselves, they differentiate (they do not have, to put it another way, a "common consciousness"), in the same way that even biologically identical twins would particularise. Self-awareness is a phenomenon that is both synthetic and unitary: it brings together the diversity of intuitions, experiences and sensations in an *ideal* unity (*I* or even *we*, the *we* also being a unitary synthesis of the diverse). Thus, if the combinations that gave birth to the same earthworm were to be repeated, we could no doubt affirm with Nietzsche that the earthworm would be "identical" (in the sense of *idem*, the *ipse* of the earthworm being non-existent). However, the question arises a little differently for the particular earthworms that we are, star-loving earthworms with the capacity to form an idea of themselves, of the world and of the stars. As soon as we reach the state of self-awareness (a state of awareness that is undoubtedly physically observable, but that is not reduced to this physical observation, which goes entirely beyond it since it corresponds to the moment of creation of a potentially infinite loop that is that of the return on oneself, constantly renewed by the experience of things — what we call thought), we irremediably modify the course of things in a direction that becomes less predictable (this is what we called autonomy, freedom in Book I, see § 19 — *Degrees of freedom*). Thus, the repetition of ourselves (*idem*), sentient, intelligent and conscious beings, does not necessarily lead to the repetition of the same *self*, the self that becomes aware of itself (*ipse*). We could, however, argue that, even if the *ipse* as a phenomenon resulting from self-awareness (the ability to perceive and relate oneself as *I*) is by nature divergent (differentiating), it could nevertheless, in a cyclical and eternal vision of the universe, repeat itself an infinite number of times (in perfectly identical circumstances: having the same thoughts, com-mitting the same actions, living the same story, in the same way). Could this be the same *me* waking up trillions of years apart? Am I myself finishing this book for the thousandth time? These are ancient metaphysical debates that we cannot answer with any certainty. The question of the permanence and continuity of self-awareness can be illustrated by the teleporter paradox: if a teleporter disintegrated your body to create a new one elsewhere, would it be a transport or a copy? If your consciousness was interrupted and a "new you" were created, would it be a continuation of your original *self* (the *self* that was disintegrated, irrevocably destroyed)? To outside observers, the 'new you' would appear identical in every way to the old one. But would it really be "you" who would continue to inhabit and animate this body? What would happen if, instead of destroying your original *you*, an identical copy was built elsewhere? Which of the two would be the real 'you', and according to what criteria? If, in the case of successive copies of the *self*, we could easily argue, on the basis of our previous thought experience, that the identities would immediately diverge as soon as the copies became (or regained) consciousness of themselves, the problem is more delicate in the case of a theoretical teleportation with 'disintegration' of the original. From a strictly observational point of view, there is no reason to doubt that the recreated 'you' would not be the 'original' you: it would be identical to you in every way, it would see like you, think like you, have the same history as you, and be aware of itself like you. In short, he is you and you are him. The *radical* dualism we have defended does not necessarily imply a separation of body and soul, but rather a differentiation between what is strictly matter and what goes beyond mere matter (which it is in fact contradictory to consider solely as matter, as we set out to show in Book I). We do not deny that sentience, consciousness or reason are faculties that emerge from matter. However, we firmly deny that they can be reduced to matter (that they can be explained solely by matter, in a closed circle). Identity, too, without being reduced to matter, is an emergent property of it. So we have no reason to doubt *a priori* that a perfectly identical material assemblage can give rise to the same identity (*ipse* and *idem*) and give the subject the illusion of continuity of identity (the continuity we experience when we go from sleep to wakefulness, or when we wake up from a dreamless anaesthetic). In the same way, if tomorrow we were able to successfully reactivate the cells of an organism that had been cryogenically frozen (as has been done successfully for bacteria and viruses, reactivated after thousands of years of freezing), we would probably not ask ourselves the question of the continuity of the identity of the reanimated person (if they were able to put their ideas back in place...). If we were to accept the theory that, in an infinite universe and infinite time, the combinations of finite particles that gave birth to us would reappear an infinite number of times, albeit in very discontinuous matter[210], then we could give credence

---

[210] The hypothesis we are proposing can be analysed mathematically using the Dirichlet drawer principle and notions of combinatorics.

Assumptions: the space universe extends to infinity. The universe contains a finite number of particles. The particles can be arranged in different finite configurations, depending on their position or state.

The question is whether, in an infinite space, but with a finite number of particles and possible states, all configurations end up repeating themselves.

Mathematical analysis

Number of possible configurations: if each particle can have N possible states (for example, a discrete position or a quantum state) and there are k particles, then the total number of possible configurations is: N^k

This number is finite because both N and k are finite.

Principle of drawers: if we try to place an infinite number of objects (the successive arrangements of particles) in a finite number of "drawers" (the possible configurations of particles), then each drawer must be filled an infinite number of times. In other words, the configurations must be repeated at some point.

Result: if we follow the evolution of particle configurations in infinite space over infinite time, the configurations must necessarily repeat themselves because of the finiteness of possibilities. This principle is often invoked in contexts such as Poincaré's theorem on returns (in classical mechanics) or considerations of infinite but discretised universes.

Limitations and nuances

Time for repetition: if the particles evolve randomly or follow complex laws, the time before repetition may be extremely long, or even practically unattainable on a human or cosmic scale (but we have seen that duration is not important in our case, insofar as we are not here to feel it).

Spatial structure: repetition assumes that infinite space does not introduce any new constraints (for example, the appearance of an infinite number of new particles or new dimensions of freedom).

Physical mechanisms: real physical laws could prevent the realisation of all possible combinations, even if they are mathematically conceivable.

The genetic make-up of a living being can be modelled as a finite sequence of nucleic bases (DNA), each of which can be in a finite number of possible states (A, T, C, G). If we consider L as the total length of the genome, the total number of possible combinations is 4^L (with 4 possible bases per position). Even if L is very large (e.g. 3×10^9 for humans), this number is still finite. In an infinite universe, each possible combination of a human genome (or that of a given living being) corresponds to a "state" in the finite set 4^L. If the particles of the universe continue to evolve randomly or deterministically, then all possible combinations of genomes must occur an infinite number of times, including the extremely complex combinations that result in each living being.

In an infinite universe, even if we allow infinite refinement of the possible states, as in a continuous (rather than discrete) space, repetition can still occur, but in a slightly different framework. If the possible states form a countable infinite set (for example, N), then any infinite series associated with the configurations of states necessarily converges to a form of statistical recurrence, thanks to Poincaré's theorem (in system dynamics). In a non-countable infinite space (continuous, such as R), recurrences are more subtle, but they often appear in the form of cycles or asymptotic behaviour (depending on the underlying physics).

Role of divergent series in physics: certain divergent series appear in physics to model phenomena such as infinite energy (for example, the energy of the quantum vacuum) or infinite growth. But these divergent series concern specific physical quantities (energy, entropy), not the combinatorics of configurations, but their behaviour in time or space. So even if divergent series emerge in certain theoretical contexts, they do not prevent the repetition of configurations in a universe where the possible combinations of particles remain finite.

Creation of new particles: if the universe generates additional particles, this changes the total number of particles available over time, affecting the total number of possible combinations. The more particles there are, the greater the number of configurations. But, at any given moment, the number of combinations remains finite, because there is a finite number of particles and a finite number of possible states for each of them.

If the number of particles increases indefinitely, but remains finite at each instant t, the total number of possible combinations increases, but always at a controlled rate. Let's suppose that at each instant t, there are N_t particles in the universe and that each particle can exist in k distinct states. The total number of possible combinations at that instant is: k^{N_t} where N_t increases with time. As long as N_t remains finite at all times, every set k^{N_t} is finite, which means that the configurations observable at a given moment can always be repeated within that set.

However, the continuous growth of N_t could slow down the frequency of repetitions: if the total number of possible combinations becomes so vast at a given moment that the probability of a specific configuration is negligible, the repetition could become "practically unobservable", even though it remains mathematically certain.

Special case of particles created randomly with random configurations: if new particles are created with states chosen at random from a finite set, then these new configurations can reconstitute already existing configurations, because the new particles only increase the "size of the combinatorial universe". Even with random and continuous creations, repetition necessarily occurs after a sufficient amount of time.

Cosmological time: the time required for such a repetition could be so long that it exceeds the scale of the durability of the observable universe (for example, the problem of accelerated expansion). However, in an infinite universe where time and space have no strict limits, these barriers become theoretically insignificant.

Game over" hypothesis: such a scenario implies that the fundamental laws of the universe limit or stop the process of particle rearrangement at some point. This could happen because of irreversible physical constraints, such as a total loss of usable energy, infinite expansion, or the destruction of any organisational structure.

Possible scientific scenarios for a "game over":

1. The thermal death of the universe: this scenario is based on the inevitable increase in entropy according to the second law of thermodynamics. Usable energy is gradually dissipated, making any physical or chemical transformation impossible. The universe then reaches a state of equilibrium in which no more structuring processes (such as the formation of stars, planets or living organisms) are possible. The universe becomes homogeneous, cold and static, although it may remain spatially infinite. This scenario does not necessarily depend on the expansion of the universe accelerating, but rather on the simple fact that all forms of exploitable energy will eventually run out.

As a result, no significant rearrangement of particles would be possible, which would mean a kind of "end of the game". Even if space remains infinite, there would no longer be any processes capable of recreating complex configurations like the Earth or a human being.

2. Infinite expansion (*Big Freeze*): This scenario is linked specifically to the acceleration of the cosmic expansion due to dark energy. If this expansion continues, the galaxies and particles will end up moving away from each other at such a rate that no further interaction will be possible. Unlike thermal death, where the universe becomes homogeneous through the dissipation of energy, here the universe becomes a totally diluted and empty space. The major difference is that in the *Big Freeze*, structures disintegrate as a result of the infinite separation of particles, whereas in thermal death, they simply become inert due to a lack of usable energy. As a result, the universe becomes an empty, diluted space, incapable of generating new structures.

3. The *Big Crunch* or *Big Bounce*: If the expansion of the universe reverses (a hypothesis that seems less likely today), everything could collapse into a single point in a *Big Crunch*. As a result, all structures would disappear in this singularity, marking the end of our universe. However, some theories (such as the *Big Bounce*) envisage that a new universe could emerge from this collapse, initiating a new "game".

4. The decay of fundamental particles: if the particles themselves, such as protons, eventually decay (a hypothesis of some grand unification theories), then all material structures would cease to exist. As a result, even a universe infinite in space and time

to the idea that our death would be *immediately* followed by our birth: our consciousness being an emergent property of a certain arrangement of matter, it would not perceive time outside this arrangement, so that, from our point of view (assuming that our point of view reemerges identically from the material identity that gave rise to it), the trillions of years that would have passed between our death and our new birth, in a world perfectly identical to the one that saw us born for the "first time", would appear to us as an "instant of reason". In a curious twist of fate, materialism here joins the idealist doctrine of eternal souls (a doctrine whose many formulations can be found throughout the history of Ancient Egypt, Mesopotamian civilisations, the Vedas, Zoroastrianism, Ancient Greece, Judaism, Christianity...). Here begin the most fascinating and hazardous speculations on man's place and destiny in this great cosmos, of which he is but a small part. Here too, on the threshold of these fascinating and decisive questions, our philosophy comes to an end.

---

would have no matter left to form complex configurations.

In short, eternity is not guaranteed.

BOOK II : THE MUSIC OF BEING

INTRODUCTION	**11**
MUSIC FROM A MATERIALIST POINT OF VIEW	**14**
WHAT IS AESTHETICS FROM THE MONIST POINT OF VIEW?	14
IS MUSIC THE RESULT OF A DARWINIAN EVOLUTIONARY PROCESS?	20
EVOLUTION IN MUSIC	20
MUSIC AND CHANCE	30
IS THERE SUCH A THING AS MUSICAL TRUTH?	**38**
LEGISLATION AT WORK: IS MUSIC FORMALISM?	38
MUSIC AS THE STRUCT. OF THE NUMERAL ESSENCE OF THE WORLD	38
IN SEARCH OF FORM	51
MUSIC AS THE RENEWAL AND SURPASSING OF FORM	60
A TRUTH WITHOUT CORRESPONDENCE	69
ART IS MIMESIS WITHOUT AN OBJECT	69
COMPOSITION OR THE SEARCH FOR BEAUTY?	76
MUSIC OR THE LANGUAGE OF BEING	**83**
MUSIC AND MEANING	84
MUSIC AS A NETWORK OF MEANINGS	84
HISTORICITY OF MUSIC	94
FREEDOM AND CREATION	101
CREATION AND FORMALISM	103
MUSIC AS MOVEMENT BETWEEN LEVELS OF MEANING	106
MUSIC IS INHERENTLY MULTI-LAYERED	106
MOVING BETWEEN LEVELS OF MEANING	107
GOING BEYOND FORMS AND BEYOND LEVELS	108
THE CRISIS OF CREATION	113
MUSIC AND TIME	114
MUSIC AND DURATION	114
MUSIC AND EXPECTATION	119
NARRATION AND RUPTURE	125

MUSIC AND THE FUNDAMENTAL DIMENSIONS OF THE HUMAN B.	135
MUSIC AS INTERNAL SEPARATION	**137**
ART AS THE RESOLUTION OF AN INTERNAL CONFLICT	137
WHAT IS THE NATURE OF THE CONFLICT?	137
LOOKING INWARD – SPLITTING THE *SELF* IN TWO	151
MUSIC AND FORMALISM: IMAGINATION AND CRITI-CISM	151
ART AS "PRE-LOGOS"	153
ART AS PLAY – A SHIFTED DISCOURSE ON REALITY: IRONY	163
ART AS TRANSUBJECTIVE HUMANISM – THE OTHER CORRESPONDENCE	**176**
ART AND COMMUNITY	176
ART AND RELIGION	176
HISTORICISM IN ART, HISTORICISM IN MUSIC	179
UNIVERSALISM OF ART – UNIVERSALISM OF DEATH	182
I TOO AM IN ARCADIA	182
MUSIC AND ORPHEUS	190
MUSIC AND MORAL LAW	193
WHAT IS AESTHETIC KNOWLEDGE: FROM THE SUBJ. TO THE OBJ.	**198**
MUSIC AND KNOWLEDGE: THE TRAGIC	198
THE BEAUTIFUL AND THE TRUE	202
DOES METAPHOR PRODUCE KNOWLEDGE?	209
IS BEAUTY SUBJECTIVE OR OBJECTIVE?	212

BOOK III: FACING THE OTHER

INTRODUCTION	**219**
MORALITY VS. DARWINIST UTILITARIANISM – IMPASSES OF MONISM	**225**
THE LIMITS OF MATERIALISM	225
THE PETITIONS OF PRINCIPLE OF BEHAVIOURISM	225
THE PARADOXES OF MORAL NEO-DARWINISM	230
MORAL RELATIVISM, SCIENTIFIC RELATIVISM	232
CRITIQUE OF NEUROSCIENCE	234
THE ANSWER TO THE ETHICAL QUESTION WITHIN MATERIALISM	238
DISSATISFACTIONS RELATED TO THE QUANTUM RES-PONSE	238
CAN THE WILL BE FREE?	241
MORALITY OR THE INTERNAL SEPARATION OF CONSCIOUSNESS	**254**
BILATERALITY OF ETHICS: THE PROMISE	254
A PRAGMATIC MORALITY	260
THE QUESTION OF THE CONTENT OF MORALITY	264
AN AESTHETIC OF MORALITY?	**272**
THE OBJECTIVITY OF MORALITY	272
MORALITY AND HARMONY	276
GENIUS OF MORALITY	281

BOOK IV: EXPLORING THE SELF

INTRODUCTION	**291**
IDENTITY AS A MEANINGFUL GATHERING	**294**
IDENTITY AS A MEANINGFUL RETURN TO THE SELF	294
IDENTITY AS A PROJECTION OF THE *SELF*	299
IDENTITY AND OPENING UP: *SELF* AND DUALITY	**307**
IDENTITY AND HISTORY	307
IDENTICAL AND DISSIMILAR	319
ART AND IDENTITY	323
IDENTITY AND FORMALISM	**326**
DYNAMICS OF *RADICAL* DUALISM	326
CAN THE MACHINE BE SELF-AWARE?	333
IDENTITY, INTELLIGENCE AND CONSCIOUSNESS	333
IDENTITY AND ISOMORPHISM	348
MATERIALISTIC RAMBLINGS	350

© 2025 Geoffroy de Clisson
Édition : BoD · Books on Demand,
31 avenue Saint-Rémy,
57600 Forbach
bod@bod.fr
Impression : Libri Plureos GmbH
Friedensallee 273
22763 Hamburg (Allemagne)
Impression à la demande
ISBN: 978-2-3225-7169-7
Dépôt légal : Avril 2025